250+ BEST PRACTICES FOR

B2B
MARKETING
SUCCESS

250+ BEST PRACTICES FOR

B2B
MARKETING
SUCCESS

ALEXANDER KESLER

Skyhorse Publishing

Skyhorse Publishing books may be purchased in bulk at special discounts for sales promotion, corporate gifts, fund-raising, or educational purposes. Special editions can also be created to specifications. For details, contact the Special Sales Department, Skyhorse Publishing, 307 West 36th Street, 11th Floor, New York, NY 10018 or info@skyhorsepublishing.com.

Skyhorse® and Skyhorse Publishing® are registered trademarks of Skyhorse Publishing, Inc.®, a Delaware corporation.

Visit our website at www.skyhorsepublishing.com.

10 9 8 7 6 5 4 3 2 1

Library of Congress Cataloging-in-Publication Data is available on file.

Cover design by INFUSEmedia

Print ISBN: 978-1-5107-7402-5
Ebook ISBN: 978-1-5107-7444-5

Printed in the United States of America

CONTENTS

INTRODUCTION

Welcome to 250+ *Best Practices for B2B Marketing Success,* a step-by-step guide to becoming a leading marketing professional. I have worked in disciplines associated with B2B marketing for more than fifteen years, and I've seen what works and what doesn't. I've synthesized best practices that took me years to learn into an easy-to-understand (and easy-to-implement) guide. The information in this book is proven, ready to use, and contains steps that most marketers can apply right away.

This book serves as a resource for every level of B2B professional, from those taking their first steps into the B2B marketing world to the most experienced professionals. You will find my advice on everything from crafting basic content to measuring its effectiveness at the campaign's end.

To make the material as accessible as possible, I've divided this book into sections that correspond to stages in the journey that your customers make as they move closer to buying your product:

In the first section of the book, we'll look at how inbound and content marketing help you drive traffic, establish brand awareness, and generate vital leads.

In the second section, we'll examine how you can nurture leads with email marketing and automation software.

In part three, we'll look at paid acquisition strategies, and how they can provide extra bookings while still maintaining an excellent overall Return on Investment (ROI). We'll examine the use of both traditional techniques such as pay-per-click advertising, as well as newer tactics such as programmatic buying.

Part four of this book will explore Paid Lead Generation, and how outsourcing this portion can allow you to focus on producing great content and converting leads into clients.

Buyer's journey

In section five, we'll look at the strategies that can be used to increase customer retention and advocacy. The best advocate for your business is often your own loyal customers. We'll observe the use of public relations (PR) in a digital setting and how B2B marketers can collaborate with influencers.

The final section of this book will serve as a collection of any other useful tactics that fall outside the previously outlined sections. Some of these tactics include powerful elements of digital marketing, which could be useful tools that are specific to your business.

Above all, it is my hope that you'll find the strategies and practices in this book engaging and suitable for your business. I've aimed to keep everything short and to the point so that you can understand and incorporate these practices into your workflow right away.

Finally, let me note that I'm not just the author; I'm a practitioner. I'm a real person who works as a digital marketing leader in the industry, one who grapples with problems and challenges that might be similar to yours. I'm always happy to discuss any of the concepts presented in this book and to help you implement them into your own B2B marketing initiatives. Feel free to reach out to me directly at kesler@kesler.net.

Happy marketing!

—Alexander Kesler

PART ONE

INBOUND AND CONTENT MARKETING

For many companies in the B2B marketing space, inbound marketing has become the preferred method for attracting, retaining, and communicating with customers.

Traditional marketing and advertising techniques are rapidly becoming obsolete as audiences evolve. Business decision-makers now say that they prefer to get information about brands through a series of articles, rather than through conventional ads. The modern customer is more informed than ever, and the tried-and-true advertising messages simply don't work like they used to.

The mediums that customers use are now rapidly evolving and oversaturated with information. Useful and engaging content has proven to be one of the most effective ways to reach target audiences. Content marketing requires only a third of a traditional marketing budget and provides three times as many leads.

High-quality content is not only effective, but it is also one of the best ways to build trust in your company. Thoughtful content production demonstrates your dedication to truly helping people while also building a brand image of reliability and expertise.

Today, nearly all companies understand the importance of maintaining a strong social media presence, making it the organic content distribution channel most utilized by B2B marketers—95 percent of these professionals report leveraging these platforms. Recent studies show that the percentage of B2B businesses investing in social media and community building efforts increased vastly, from 39 percent in 2022 to 57 percent in the following year. In addition, 71 percent of B2B companies use social media publishing and analytics tools.

In this section, we'll explore how B2B companies can harness the power of high-quality content and understand the importance of deploying that content on social media.

CHAPTER 1

GETTING STARTED WITH INBOUND MARKETING

Instead of using traditional marketing tactics (that force advertising messages on audiences), inbound marketing focuses on creating value for prospective customers.

Whether you have already started an inbound marketing program or are just considering it now, these ten expert tips will help you get started.

MASTER YOUR INBOUND STRATEGY

Inbound marketing has the potential to deliver impressive performance; however, yielding desired outcomes from inbound marketing requires a well-formulated plan. If you haven't already crafted a plan, take a step back and think about the ways in which your website, blog, and social media accounts can harmonize together.

The first steps toward an effective inbound marketing strategy are:

1 | Defining your business goals.

2 | Thoroughly researching your industry and competition.

3 | Gaining a profound understanding of your customers.

Ultimately, Key Performance Indicators (KPIs) should focus on revenue generation, but you also need to decide precisely which metric you wish to grow. Is it the number of leads? The number of customers? Or just the revenue itself?

Once you've defined your KPIs, you'll be ready to move to the next level—researching your industry. It's useful to research how your competitors use inbound marketing or catch up on important industry statistics. From there, you'll be able to delve into how best to meet your customers' needs.

#2 FOCUS ON YOUR TARGET AUDIENCES WITH LASER PRECISION

Without a sharp eye for the needs of your target audience, it will be very difficult for any content marketing initiative to succeed. You'll need to consider demographics and top channels for communication. Then conduct detailed research of your potential customers' "pain points."

A great place to start this process is by creating semi-fictional buyer personas. These personas can represent groups of your target customers. Think about these personas as a way to identify their rationales for choosing to use (or not to use) your products or services.

While it's counterproductive to consider too many personas, it's also important to distinguish different groups within your target audience. In this way, you'll be able to connect with them on a more personal level.

Once you've designed these personas on the basis of real-life research, you'll need to map out the buyer's journey. This will help ensure that your messages are timed properly. Your messages will be most effective if they can target decision-makers who are actually ready to buy.

#3 ENHANCE YOUR LEAD NURTURING

Timing is crucial when communicating with leads. The aim of lead nurturing is to bring a potential customer to a point where they are purchase-ready. It's easy to overburden leads with poorly timed messages. This can make potential customers doubt whether they should have subscribed to your emails or unsubscribe altogether. Expertly timed lead nurturing will help you find the right balance.

If your sales cycle is a couple of months, aim to give people a nudge every other week. Use a careful choice of words adapted to the buyer's persona, and give your audience enticing incentives to stay active in your promotions.

Offering rewards is a great way to keep your audience active. For example, a free white paper or an exclusive trial of your services can keep your business in the minds of customers. These assets can feature your corporate branding and can help establish you as a helpful expert who keeps their best interests in mind. Just make sure that your giveaway is appropriate for how far along in the buyer's journey the lead is located.

 ## DEDICATE RESOURCES TO USEFUL AND TIMELY BLOGGING

Blogging is one of the most widespread channels for deploying targeted content and has proven to be an effective way to bring an audience directly into your online presence. Yet to stand out in today's climate of information overload, your blog has to be not only useful but interesting. It should offer innovative solutions to the real problems of your target audience and inspire them with original ideas.

It's important to remember that when it comes to content, quality beats quantity. Valuable, eye-catching information is what will motivate people to follow your company's blog. A well-crafted post can be shared thousands of times. In addition, your blog posts should aim to be consistent with your brand and with other posts. What will motivate people to share your posts? Remember, the posts must:

1 | Be useful   **2** | Be engaging   **3** | Solve problems

Additionally, no piece of effective content is truly complete without a call to action. This is something that gives your readers a clear path for what to do next. It doesn't necessarily need to be a "hard sell;" it can be something as simple as encouraging them to keep an eye on an issue or industry related to your work.

So how do you get inspired to start blogging? Inspiration for your content can be found everywhere, from FAQs to customer reviews to industry news. You can also refer to successful inbound marketing blogs to catch up on the latest trends and practices. Remember, nobody knows the story of your company better than you, and nobody else has your unique point of view.

 ## #5 DON'T FORGET ABOUT GUEST BLOGGING

Regularly producing rich content can be demanding, and sometimes the well just runs dry. When this happens, a great way to supplement your work is to invite guest bloggers to contribute to your owned media with original content.

Guest blogging is a great way to collaborate with industry authors, experts, and influencers. Along with fresh content, they will bring their audience to your company. How? When contributors publish a post on your blog, they are likely to promote it on their own channels as well. This means extra exposure for your website, and it also shows that the guest blogger approves of your brand.

 ## #6 USE THE POWER OF PREMIUM CONTENT

Want to create content that's even more impressive? Go premium. Premium content can take the form of white papers, ebooks, infographics, case studies, or how-to guides on topics that would interest your audience. Outsourcing these assets to a professional marketing company can boost your online presence, attract more people to your brand, and help to position you as an industry expert.

While blog posts can be quick and easy to produce, more comprehensive content can offer a long-lasting value that brings customers back again and again. Offering premium content is also a practical way to collect email contacts.

Content such as guides and white papers can be used as a "gated" way to get customers to subscribe to your content. This means that while they are offered for free, a visitor is required to provide their contact information in order to download them.

BUILD YOUR EMAIL LIST

Social media interactions, direct queries, and user comments are all useful for securing the contact information of potential customers to add to your email list. You can also add a subscription link to all your employees' email signatures. Or try promoting an offer, quiz, or prize on social media. No matter what methods you use, building an email list should always be a top priority. Try to see every interaction as an opportunity to collect contact details.

SHOWCASE CUSTOMER REVIEWS AND TESTIMONIALS

Attracting prospects to your platform is great, but only if they then find sufficient evidence that your company is credible and worth their time. One of the most effective ways to achieve this is to include customer reviews and testimonials on your company website, blog, social media networks, YouTube channel, and anywhere else you have presence.

Instead of merely churning out promises about your products or services, provide trustworthy accounts of what your prospects can expect when they choose your brand. When a customer not only sees a glowing case study but an endorsement from a business that is very similar to their own, they will be more inclined to choose you over your competition. Once you begin collecting the testimonials, you can organize them by region, industry, or any other demographic to help you better target your customer base.

#9 EMBRACE CREATIVE CAMPAIGNS

Many B2B marketers inaccurately believe that their target audiences will be "all business, all the time" and won't appreciate humor or unorthodox approaches. When you craft your inbound campaigns, don't forget that B2B decision-makers are people. While they need to make important financial decisions, they are also influenced by emotions like the rest of us. They react positively to things like humor and novelty. Your content should be educational, yes, but don't be afraid to surprise and delight your audience.

Not a natural at being funny and charming in a business context? That's okay. You can look around for inspiration. For example, B2C campaigns can be a great source of inspiration for your innovative B2B marketing efforts.

#10 DELIVER INTERACTIVE AND VISUAL MATERIALS

It's time to get visual. Graphics are processed more easily by our brains, so they increase the chances of getting more eyes on your brand. Studies consistently show that content with relevant images gets viewed more than 90 percent longer than words alone. People often prefer to check out an infographic or watch a video instead of investing time in a long read.

At a loss for how to begin using graphics? A great place to start is content repurposing. Turn your old white papers and guides into multimedia assets. These could be graphs, charts, interactive presentations, or witty and educational videos. Another advantage is that it's easier to share visual and interactive content over social media.

CHAPTER 2

EMPLOYING SOCIAL MEDIA MONITORING

Social media monitoring is the process by which companies track conversations across social media channels to measure the company's impact, visibility, brand image, and campaign success. Companies can also use it to find relevant conversations, form new partnerships, and assess the competition.

#11 UNDERSTAND CUSTOMER DISCOVERY

No social media strategy can be successful if you haven't properly defined your buyer personas. When you run an ad, you usually don't display it to just anyone. Instead, you narrow down your target audience based on their demographics.

The same rule applies to your social monitoring efforts. Do you know who your customers are? You may think you do, but companies often report that their products are used by an entirely different demographic than the one they had originally targeted. Either way, you cannot start listening to what people are saying if you don't know which people to listen to.

Even if you find you were wrong about your target audience in your initial research, social media monitoring is a great way to validate who your potential customers are. It all helps you become more targeted and confidently proceed with your marketing strategy.

CHOOSE THE RIGHT CHANNELS

In addition to knowing who your customers are, you also need to know where they are. While you should ideally aim to maintain a presence on all major social media channels, your efforts cannot be (and should not be) equally distributed across each one. For example, why should you devote equal time and money to two different social networks that provide results which vary greatly? The answer, of course, is that you shouldn't.

When it comes to B2B marketing, few disagree that LinkedIn is the place to be. If you are tight on time or budget, this is where I strongly recommend investing the bulk of your time. As a social platform aimed at professionals and networking, LinkedIn is where you can easily locate and join conversations relating to your industry. The platform also hosts groups for even the narrowest industry niches, enabling you to find prospects, enter conversations with them, and quickly establish yourself as a thought leader.

Once you have a target prospect, LinkedIn is also the easiest place to find any missing pieces related to that prospect. And although it's comparatively expensive, LinkedIn's advertising tool is also the most sophisticated and well-targeted.

Other contenders here are Twitter, Facebook, Instagram, and YouTube. Remember that your choice of which social media channels will always depend on the type of industry and the buyer personas you are targeting. So lead with LinkedIn, and follow up with others if you have the bandwidth.

 ## PRIORITIZE YOUR OBJECTIVES

If you were serious about networking at a big cocktail party, you wouldn't randomly go from one group of people to the next, attempting to aimlessly listen in and join their conversations. Instead, you would have a list of objectives that you would want to achieve by the end of the party. You would identify the people (and topics) you most wanted to interact with and go about pursuing them in the most effective way.

The same goes for social media listening. To narrow down your focus, you need to have clearly defined objectives. What is it that you want to achieve with social media monitoring? Is it to get feedback on your product or service? To help with lead generation? To analyze how the competition is doing? You can do all of these things, but you need to have a strategy in place.

#14 TRACK SPOT-ON KEYWORDS

Going back to the example of a cocktail party, you would most likely be engaged by conversations revolving around topics that interested you. The easiest way to find online conversations related to your field is by researching the keywords that are used most frequently in your industry.

This is related to knowing your buyer personas. What words do they actually use when communicating online? Do they say "bovine spongiform encephalopathy" or do they just call it "mad cow disease"? Do they use shorthand terms and abbreviations? All of this is important to know. You want to reach your audience in the terms they will actually use when communicating.

You can start by analyzing your blog and see which keywords brought visitors to your site based on each article category, and see if you can spot patterns. You can also use tools like Google Trends and Twitter's advanced search feature to look for a particular phrase's popularity over time. These tools can also show you what terms are currently trending in your area.

Don't only use the keywords that offer the highest yield, and don't be afraid to experiment and change the keywords as you go. In addition, don't forget to add your brand name, as well as the names of your competitors. Statistics show that almost a third of a company's mentions on Twitter do not include their own handle.

#15 IDENTIFY IMPORTANT INFLUENCERS

Once you start monitoring social media accounts, you will quickly discover that almost every time someone mentions you, there is an opportunity to spark up a conversation. When this happens, it's important to realize that all social media accounts are not created equal. And what is important is not always *what* people are saying, but rather *who* is saying it.

You will want to catch the attention of influential people in your industry—the more prominent, the better. Just a single retweet from a top Twitter influencer in your industry can do wonders for the reach of your campaigns and also boost your credibility. There are several social media tools that can provide comprehensive insight into the key players in your field.

How do you go about interacting with influencers once you've identified them? A good rule of thumb is to start slowly. Interact only when you have a genuine interest or connection to what they're saying. Make sure you have something more to contribute than just capturing their attention.

Think about what the influencer and their audience might find useful, novel, or unique. It's likely there are other people who are working to capture their attention at the same time, so influencers have to sift through many messages and will likely only pay attention to those who are bringing value to the conversation. Only approach them directly (via Direct Message, for example) if you feel that your relationship has progressed to the point where they would feel comfortable with you offering something directly.

Don't get discouraged too easily; building relationships takes time. It's useful to create a spreadsheet where you document the steps you've taken to interact with each of them. That's how you can make sure you are not wasting time on the same influencers without seeing any results. In addition, you can keep track of your relationships with influencers by creating a separate stream for influencers in your monitoring tool.

LOOK FOR PRODUCT FEEDBACK

Social media monitoring enables you to find product feedback in its most raw form. Unlike participating in focus groups or other types of feedback-generated research, people use social media to talk about your product and share their thoughts in a genuine way. Since no one is paying them or asking them to do it, this is the most "natural" scenario for receiving feedback. Accessing and learning from these thoughts is also the most budget-efficient way to approach customer feedback.

Create a real-time feed for keywords that feature all the products and services you want feedback on. If your company is new, don't expect a wave of branded conversation; it's okay if the feedback starts out slow. And as you gain traction, you will inevitably receive comments and complaints. Not all of them will necessarily be useful, but that's okay too. Sometimes people like to complain about things that are out of your control or completely unrelated to your company. We've all seen an Amazon review for a product that says nothing about the product itself, but rather about how Amazon handled shipments or refunds.

It would be useful to have a way to sort complaints into different categories. You will be able to see which comments are irrelevant and which seem to be centering on the same issue or feature. This is your cue to respond to these complaints or to make changes based on the feedback.

In this process, you also may discover new opportunities. For example, through feedback you might learn that a group of consumers is using your product or service in a way you hadn't initially considered. You can use that newfound data to develop your product or even incorporate this new use into your marketing.

 ## STAY AHEAD OF THE COMPETITION

Getting feedback about your products and managing your brand image is great, but you should never forget to track your competition's progress. Social media monitoring can be equally useful for this pur-pose as well.

Even if there is no sufficient feedback about your own company from users on social media, tracking your competition can serve as a generator of useful feedback. Are people talking about them, but not about you? Is there something about their product that users rave about that your product lacks? You can use this information to improve your own business.

Whatever tools you elect to use, remember that tracking your competition's progress can be a vital tool for tracking your own.

#18 MASTER LEAD GENERATION

The same feeds you use for keeping tabs on the competition and looking for product feedback can also be used to leverage lead generation.

A successful lead generation strategy can have many commonali-ties with a successful strategy for building relationships with influ-encers. Your goal shouldn't be to immediately push a product once someone mentions it. Instead, you and your team should browse through your monitoring feeds to find people expressing pain points. Once you know that a person is already looking for a solution, it is much easier to get them on board by offering a free trial, for example.

Add value by providing both external and internal resources, and be patient. If it helps, try and forget about your product itself for the moment, and instead focus on the person and their needs.

#19 USE ALL OPPORTUNITIES FOR STRIKING UP A CONVERSATION

Being on the lookout for specific keywords is absolutely necessary, and I hope I've made that clear. However, you shouldn't be so preoc-cupied with keywords alone that you forget to use other traditional ways of participating in online conversations.

For example, keep an eye out for Twitter chats that you can take part in, even if they're not directly linked to your industry. Twitter chats attract diverse crowds, so to find a chat opportunity, you can use Twitter's Advanced Search Feature or even ask your followers if they have a particular weekly chat they like to participate in. First-time participation in Twitter chats can be intimidating, but it's acceptable to simply sit back and watch others take the lead, at least initially. Before you join, make sure you understand any rules that may have been set for the chat, which are often listed ahead of time.

CHAPTER 3

FINDING STELLAR CONTENT IDEAS FOR YOUR B2B ASSET LIBRARY

Developing your content library is key in nurturing your brand's relationship with its target audience. Yet finding content ideas can be a daunting task for B2B marketers at any skill level. Thirty-five percent of content marketers struggle with generating new content ideas.

 ## #20 START WITH YOUR COMPANY'S EXISTING CONTENT

Explore what you have already created, and see if there are ways you can use or reuse it. Sometimes all it takes is a little edit to bring a piece of versatile content up to date.

You might be surprised to learn how many useful insights you can draw from existing assets. Case studies, reports, presentations, event briefs, project reports, and statistics are all great starting points for content that you can share with your audience. Dig into your company's archive to showcase your industry expertise. If you've compiled data from your own research, this can be priceless to your readers.

Once you've identified useful assets, you can either repurpose them into content marketing formats such as blog posts and white papers, or use them as inspiration to create new articles, infographics, and ebooks. Remember: testimonials on what current customers went through when selecting your products or services are going to be useful to future prospects.

Using this approach can save you time and resources and is often a cure for the writer's block that can accompany content creation. It will lift your spirits to know that you're not starting at zero because you likely have quite a few assets already in the bag.

#21 GET IDEAS FROM YOUR CURRENT TEAM'S KNOW-HOW

You can look for ideas for useful content from your own company's team members. Their expertise and fresh perspective can be used to create all kinds of information-rich content.

Make monthly rounds, ask about what everybody's working on, and get ideas from their wins. You can find out what your customers have been raving or complaining about, or write about projects they are currently working on. Once you have this employee input, you can use it to craft content assets such as do/don't blog posts, ebooks, how-to articles, infographics, and even videos.

Your customer service team should be at the top of your list for employees to speak with. They likely have a myriad of stories about customer experience with your products or services. These stories can then be adapted into engaging narratives for blog posts, solution guides, opportunity guides, product comparisons, strategy templates, and implementation plans.

#22 SHOWCASE YOUR COMPANY'S TALENTS AND INSIGHTS IN A CONTENT SERIES

There's one more method for repurposing amazing content from your company's experts. Work closely with your team members to understand their top talents, and then empower them to take part in your company's content creation. Personal insights from real people like your employees can be especially useful for creating effective content.

You can make consecutive video episodes that revolve around daily life in your company, or profile a number of team members as they're going about their daily routine helping customers. Another approach is to craft an interview series in which your experts share pieces of their knowledge in a way that would be useful to customers. The key here is to get creative and build trust with your team members to produce authentic content.

Other potential forms of content include webinars and podcasts or blog posts that build up significant know-how in a certain field of expertise. This will inspire your team members to participate. Also, there will be more of an incentive to participate if they have the personal reward of showcasing their talents. It could also help their careers long-term to be positioned as an expert.

#23 INTERVIEW INDUSTRY LEADERS FOR YOUR BLOG

Once you've exhausted all content ideas coming from within your company, look for external industry expertise. The first step is to identify prominent industry leaders and influencers in your field by researching your niche. Seasoned experts and active online bloggers are a great source of information that can be of high value to your customers. Their own audiences can offer a fresh influx of potential leads for your business. Exciting content ideas can arise from relationships with specialists, including guest blogging opportunities and content partnerships. As with your own team, find the right stimulus for experts to collaborate with you. Most of them will be flattered when asked to participate and see it as a win-win that also builds their own brand.

You can conduct interviews with experts and influencers to showcase their knowledge and provide useful information to your audience. This content is beneficial to the expert's influence but is hosted on your platform, which means more traffic to your website. You can also invite specialists to participate in your Twitter chats to create higher engagement and more excitement when connecting with your online audience.

GET IDEAS AND CONTENT FROM YOUR CURRENT CUSTOMERS

Current customers may want to illustrate their experiences with your products, or just ruminate on important industry topics. To facilitate this, you'll have to develop a good relationship with them by investing in continuous communication beyond the point of sale.

Testimonials are one of the most successful content formats. Your prospects are likely to find such assets useful, as they represent the trajectory of what your first-time buyers have experienced and give potential customers a sense of what they themselves can expect. They not only offer a narrative of the buying process but can also provide inspiration on where to focus your content.

You can ask your existing community questions of importance to your audience and then share this firsthand information online. Also, don't forget to make it easy for your customers to share their know-how, experience, and tips on your blog platform or social media channels. A monitored comment section is a great way to do this.

EXAMINE THE COMPETITION

There's nothing wrong with studying your competitors and adopting approaches that might work for you. As they are targeting similar audiences, you can get inspiration from their research findings on topics and content forms.

Begin by identifying the top-performing competitors in your field, especially the companies that are employing content marketing in the most interesting and innovative ways. Carefully study their online presence, review their websites, social media profiles, the language they use, and the topics they cover in their blog and social media content.

The purpose is not to copy their approach exactly, but to nurture your own content creation with fresh ideas. There are always different angles to the same story. Your competitors' content can also be a good source for industry news and important trends in your field. Plus, your company will have its own unique experience and interpretation of industry knowledge.

 ## SCOUT OUT INDUSTRY FORUMS FOR TRENDING TOPICS

Make a habit of regularly accessing industry community platforms such as Quora and Reddit. Follow topical social media feeds, news outlets, industry magazines, and newsletters. All these resources are available online for free. Tap into and use them for content inspiration.

You can follow existing conversations or start new discussions on these forums to spur meaningful exchanges. You can also use them to identify key influencers on these platforms and observe the topics they focus on.

Follow relevant people, like influencers and prospects, on social media, and note the topics they are discussing. What is important to them? How are their priorities like your own, or like those of your customers? What ideas do these discussions give you? Such sources can reliably provide you with a fresh take on topics for your content library.

 ## CREATE CONTENT PARTNERSHIP TOPICS

To come up with engaging and original content ideas, consider establishing partnerships for common creation. The marketing teams of your existing business partners might be open to such opportunities, or you might look for matching and complementing partnerships with other companies.

By identifying a common goal or goals, both teams can work on crafting a mutually beneficial content strategy. If the partner company possesses assets that fill in gaps in your team's skills, such as video production or graphic design, then you may be able to leverage these as part of the relationship. Your partner might also have compiled or researched valuable data that can be used in your field. Keep an eye out for anything unique or novel that your partner brings to the table.

Besides helping you to generate new ideas for content, such partnerships can also be useful for content distribution. Your channels and audience reach are often doubled since both partners will have existing distribution methods and followers. Just make sure your partner is as enthusiastic about getting the content out as you are!

 ## #28 MAKE SEQUELS TO YOUR BEST-PERFORMING CONTENT

When you see content connect with your audiences and get a positive reaction, a simple way to generate more effective content is simply to create a sequel to it. You can update statistics, revisit an interview, or do a "follow-up" report on a project or customer you may have already profiled.

To determine which content might merit sequels, simply analyze your existing content that proved successful. Dig into Google Analytics and learn which previous content brought organic traffic to your website. Focus on understanding the language, visuals, and timing that worked best so that you can imitate these factors in the next campaign that you create.

 ## #29 GO BEYOND THE LIMITS OF B2B MARKETING

When you feel you've exhausted the typical methods for creating content, I encourage you to explore methods beyond typical B2B marketing approaches. Who said that creativity and thinking outside the box don't have places in B2B? Not me! So get creative. Employ your imagination, break up patterns of content creation, and try something new. Your only risk is a small investment of time. And who knows? Trying something new might even generate some of your best content.

CHAPTER 4

CRAFTING POWERFUL TITLES FOR WHITE PAPERS

No matter how strong the content, an audience needs to decide if it's worth reading, and an effective headline can help with that. About 80 percent of people will read the headline of an asset, but only 20 percent will actually read the asset in its entirety. Crafting a headline that attracts and captures readers' attention is crucial: headlines have an effect on conversions as well as leads.

While there are many systematic ways to compose titles, three methodologies are most common:

- **The psychological approach** employs words and expressions that appeal to readers' desires or needs, their intelligence, and their curiosity.
- **The formulaic approach** presents a handy way of crafting headlines that follow a specific formula that is easily recognized by readers and carries a practical message and brings a sense of familiarity.
- **The scientific approach** to creating good titles analyzes which words capture and attract readers' attention based on data and statistics, and then employs those words in a targeted way.

Often these three approaches can overlap each other. For example, the formulaic approach can utilize psychological triggers, or it can make use of words that are successful at captivating readers. You may also find that these approaches can sometimes conflict with each other. Even so, the rules remain the same: test, analyze, draw conclusions, then try again.

Let's examine ten of the most popular and successful headline practices for white papers.

#30 CREATE SURPRISE

Surprise is an essential component of a headline that draws attention, and it works by creating a break in the norm. When readers expect something to read one way, you can surprise them by inserting words that break their expectations. Surprise can also create tension; it can establish that something is "at stake" when readers may have assumed nothing was at risk.

For example, consider a piece titled "Use These 10 Best Practices on Titles for White Papers—or Risk Failure." There's surprise, but also risk here, something your audience will want to avoid at all costs.

But when it comes to using surprise in a headline, you should also be cautious about venturing into "clickbait" territory. Recent studies suggest that audiences may interpret clickbait as a sign of low credibility and quality. If you become known as a shallow purveyor of clickbait, then audiences may not turn to you.

Good content delivers on the promise it has made, sustains interest, and offers value. Be surprising and compelling, but if your headline is going to promise something, your content had better deliver.

#31 ASK QUESTIONS

A title that strikes up a conversation by asking a question is a great way to attract readers' attention. There is a natural human reaction to try and answer a question when they see or hear it. And if they don't know the answer, a question urges audiences to continue reading until they discover it.

When formulating headlines as questions, again, be careful that you don't fall into the clickbait hole. The same caveats apply. Many writers have a negative view of titles that ask questions because they often come across as merely attention-seeking. For example, if you can answer any question headline with a "no," it's probably not particularly useful.

To avoid this pitfall, provide readers with a solution to your challenge. For instance: "Want to Know How to Craft the Best White Paper Headlines? Here Are Several Tried and Tested Approaches." Let your reader know that you won't only be raising issues and leaving them unresolved; you'll also be providing answers.

#32   ENGAGE CURIOSITY

One way to trigger readers' curiosity is by implying that you hold some valuable content that they may not already know.

For example, you could test people's knowledge directly: "So You Think You Know How to Create Great White Paper Titles? Let's Find Out if You Do!" This title appeals to the reader's ego by affirming what they already know while holding the potential to give them new information.

#33   GIVE IT A NEGATIVE TWIST

Being positive can work, but sometimes being negative can be even better. Titles utilizing the negative superlatives like "never" or "worst" performed 30 percent better than titles without superlatives. Those titles with positive superlatives had a 29 percent lower performance than neutral ones.

Similar results were also reported by Oribi in their definitive research on blog post titles in 2013. When using "without," "stop," and "no," content saw a drastic increase in CTR (click-through rate) and overall performance. These results might be explained by people's suspicion of overly positive things, which often can seem too good to be true.

Whether it's "10 Tips for Crafting White Paper Headlines You Can't Do Without" or "10 White Paper Title Tips That Will Kill It," make sure you try out a number of options. Remember: You want to be engaging and intriguing, and it's okay to "go negative."

TELL PEOPLE "HOW TO"

A "How to" headline promises that the content will provide structured steps readers can use in order to achieve something. It speaks to the audience's desire for usefulness, clarity, and even predictability. Human beings usually prefer clear directions that help us navigate the world and perform our job without the added effort of having to figure things out by ourselves.

In this connection, the "How to___" formula is always a good call whenever you have tips, advice, and guidance to offer that will be both practical and specific. "How to Create White Paper Titles Like a True Marketing Expert" is one such example.

Other examples include:

> "How to _____ for Beginners"
> "How to _____ in _____ Steps"
> "How to _____ without _____"
> (This makes use of a negative word, as well—and remember: that's a good thing.)

Furthermore, you don't necessarily have to begin with "How to" verbatim. Some variations can also work. Testing out different titles may show that, in certain instances, "The [Beginner's] Guide to ____," "An Introduction to ____," "The Secret of ____," and "X Ways to ____" may work better for your brand.

 MAKE A LIST

Much like "How to" titles, lists help us manage our expectations by creating a clear idea about what we will receive from a piece of content. People like lists; they're fast, informative, and package information in a quick and effective way.

The occasional "+" after a number may engage readers further, as offering "more than" a certain number of something can create a sense of limitlessness. Bigger numbers, as well as odd-numbered lists, have also been found to generate more attention than even-numbered ones.

The Ultimate Headline Formula also makes use of this approach and combines it with a number of other techniques. The formula goes like this: "Numbers + Adjective + Target Keyword + Rationale + Promise." Here's how you could reframe your title using this technique: "10 Best Practices for White Paper Titles That Increase Traffic."

Simple but powerful.

#36 ADDRESS YOUR READERS

Directly addressing your target readers (also called "audience referencing") is useful because it clearly specifies who an article or white paper is addressing. Audience referencing strikes up a conversation with your intended audience or buyer. Generally, people prefer to be named and identified, and addressing them can mean they will be more likely to respond. They also will understand that the article is more likely to be useful to them and to the demographics to which they belong.

Addressing readers can be done by using the second-person personal pronoun "you," or by addressing them by a title they identify with such as marketer, CEO, chef, blogger, banker, and so on.

For example, "10 Killer White Paper Headline Techniques for B2B Marketers" combines the technique of using a list, a fairly strong and even negative word ("killer"), and specifying that it is intended for professionals who operate in a B2B environment. Think of ways you can address your readers directly. The right words may depend on the nuts and bolts of your industry.

#37 MAKE YOUR TITLE SHINE

Another great technique to employ when crafting a headline is the SHINE formula, developed by Kissmetrics. It stands for Specificity, Helpfulness, Immediacy, Newsworthiness, and Entertainment value.

Although this formula doesn't require a particular set of words or a specific structure, it does offer a set of components that supply both the necessary information that readers look for in a title. SHINE can be combined with other formulas and techniques.

Here's an example of how you can revamp your title using the SHINE formula: "10+ (specificity) Great Practices for White Paper Titles (newsworthy) You Can Learn Now (immediacy) That Will Help You (helpfulness) Rock It (entertainment)."

#38 USE BRACKETS

The use of bracketed clarifications in titles (such as [Infographic], [Template], [Free ebook], or [Free Download]) has been found to significantly increase the CTR on articles, as well as page views and conversion rates. They specifically highlight the type of content readers can expect to get. Among these bracketed offerings, infographics and templates fare particularly well.

#39 USE "PHOTO," "WHO," "AMAZING," AND "NEED"

It has been found that the use of certain words like *photo* and *who* showed a consistent and significant increase in CTR.

By including "amazing" in your title, you are risking a decrease in CTR, but it may also lead to a notable increase in page views and conversion rates. Potential customers who are not turned off by that word tend to engage with your content and eventually convert at a higher rate.

Using the word *need* shows similar results with regards to CTR and page views because it comes across as pushy and urgent. Yet interestingly, it can also increase conversions.

Words such as *magic, trick, always,* and *best* have low and even negative indicators with regards to CTR, page views, and conversion rate. This is partly due to the effect that clickbait titles have had on viewers over recent years.

The interpretation of this data depends both on the context you are writing in, as well as on the other words in your titles. For example, don't feel the need to eliminate "you" and "how to" completely. And remember that when implemented correctly, a "How to" structure can yield tremendous results.

Keep in mind that the ideal headline is only part of a greater whole and is not the only indicator of success. It simply increases the likelihood of your content being noticed and engaged with. It may increase page views and conversions, but only if you deliver on what you promise.

CHAPTER 5
FIXING YOUR CONTENT MARKETING STRATEGY WHEN IT'S NOT WORKING

Many marketers have chosen to make content the centerpiece of their strategy. Yet, when it comes to results, not everyone is able to claim the same success.

 #40 **MAKE YOUR APPROACH FOCUSED AND STRUCTURED**

Content marketing can look deceptively simple. After all, you just need to create something and put it out there, right?

In fact, this couldn't be further from the truth.

In content marketing, the most effective approach is called the "Strategy—Execution—Analysis" Framework. It allows you to keep an eye on the big picture while keeping all aspects of your content marketing effort under control.

Strategy - Execution - Analysis framework

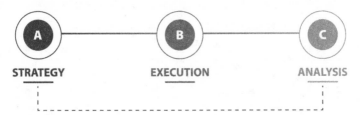

As the name suggests, the framework has three stages or phases:

1 | Strategy   **2** | Execution   **3** | Analysis

In the "Strategy" phase, you are setting your goals for content marketing and making choices about the best means to pursue them.

"Execution" is the stage in which you'll implement the plan you created in the Strategy phase. In this stage, it is important to keep an eye on the quality of the content you're producing and on implementing the specific tactics you chose in the planning stage to the greatest benefit.

In the "Analysis" part of the cycle, you need to spend time analyzing the performance of the content you created. Find out what works well, identify what makes sense but needs to be improved, and determine what should be slashed altogether. The Analysis stage allows you to go back to Step 1 of the framework and begin strategizing again, armed with more reliable (i.e., data-backed) information.

The most important issue when it comes to planning your strategy is actually creating one, and that step should include writing it down. Think through the most important aspects of your strategy, and then sit down to document your master plan. Whether you're working alone or as part of a team, a written strategy will help you keep yourself and your team accountable.

#41 DECIDE ON TOPICS AND KPIs TO TRACK

When engaging in content marketing, the impulse can be to produce as much content as possible, regardless of the topic. Though it might feel appealing, this approach is more likely to harm you in the long term.

Instead of simply hitting the ground running and churning out as much as you can, start by thinking about the target of your content marketing: what topics you need to cover to reach the people in your target audience, how you'll track success, and your KPIs.

Marketing personas are an invaluable tool and can help you to decide how best to reach your target audience. Use them to draw a picture of your target audience. Who's your customer? What are they influenced by? What does their buying cycle look like? How can you convert them from a visitor into a lead and ultimately into a customer? Take the time to stop and answer all of these questions.

Start formulating KPIs by deciding what your general aim is: to increase brand awareness, generate leads, or improve sales. Success would look different for each of these, so this will be your measurement for determining whether you're succeeding or not.

For example, you might be getting hundreds of thousands of page views on your blog posts, but if none of your visitors are leaving their email addresses, and your goal is to harvest leads, is your content strategy really working?

#42 SET YOUR TACTICS BASED ON YOUR STRATEGY

Content marketing comes in many forms: blogs, white papers, ebooks, podcasts, videos, infographics, etc.

Again, go back to your marketing personas and decide which are most likely to attract and convert your target visitor. Maybe your clientele is busy and doesn't have time to read lengthy blog posts. Maybe they live in a big city and have a long commute, which can be utilized for listening to podcasts. Whatever the case, the more targeted you can be, the more successful you'll be.

#43 CREATE A CONTENT CALENDAR IN LINE WITH YOUR BUDGET

Various opinions exist on what the optimal schedule for publishing and distributing content is, but you can look to your industry peers and to experts for a rule of thumb.

Content Marketing Tactics

Whitepapers · eBooks · Infographics · Webinars

Case Studies · Data Sheets · Checklists · Events

Guides · Branded Videos · Demo Videos · Trend Reports

Articles · Games · Competitions · Quizzes

Third-Party Reviews · Interactive Demos · Product Features · Trial Versions

Surveys · Interviews · Analyst Reports · Testimonials

As with any aspect of marketing, your schedule should be guided by your chosen field. If your goal is to increase brand awareness, you should aim to present yourself and your brand as many times as possible. This will require you to create more content, and at a lower level of detail. On the other hand, if you want to establish authority, you'd probably choose to produce less often, but create content which covers your chosen topics in more detail.

Your budget for content marketing is another constraint you'll have to take into account when deciding on your calendar.

Whether you're doing everything in-house (not recommended) or you hire someone to do it for you, content marketing is often an expensive exercise.

Producing and distributing content is probably the most cumbersome part of doing content marketing. It's time-consuming, and there's often a slim line between success and failure. Outsourcing content will save you hours and money in the long run. It will also allow you to focus on avoiding common pitfalls.

#44 STOP PRODUCING BAD CONTENT

"Create great content" is a catchphrase those of us in the marketing space have heard countless times. Unfortunately, we rarely hear what great content really is. The most obvious answer to this question would be, "It depends." Yet there are some common principles that will put almost any content producer on the right track:

- **Produce content that is helpful to your audience.** No matter what product or service you're offering, you'll want to help your customers address a "pain point" they have. When it comes to creating content, if it's not helping your audience, then why are you creating it?
- **Not a sales pitch!** While we're on the topic, make sure your content is not too self-centered. Remember, people come to your website to learn how to solve a problem. If you decide to mention your product/service, it should always be in relation to how it can help your audience. Never simply pitch for the sake of pitching.
- **Use the attention you already have.** Don't let the eyeballs you already have go to waste. Engage your current audience. Depending on your chosen medium, the first step could be as simple as having a "Please leave a comment" section on your website or blog. You could also urge your visitors to leave their emails to get updates from you (converting them into leads), or explore a topic in more detail (by downloading a white paper from your website).

- **Keep it simple and easy to understand.** Using unnecessarily complicated words and long sentences doesn't make you sound smart; it can alienate readers and lose their attention. Use all available tools to make your content as easily digestible and comprehensible as possible.

 ## #45 DON'T FORGET SEO

Ultimately, you're producing content for humans, but keep in mind that a large proportion of your audience will be made up of the SEO (search engine optimization) bots that crawl your site. Fortunately, search algorithms are becoming better at identifying and promoting the types of content that a human audience finds valuable.

Satisfy your SEO needs by optimizing all technical aspects of your website: performance speed, metadata, keyword targeting, page matching, and other critical elements. Don't forget that social media websites will also be impacted by SEO. How you implement page data determines how your information is displayed on those websites.

Remember to use text structure like headings and content length to your advantage. The majority of your visitors are still likely to come to your website as a result of a search, so perform keyword research and make sure to optimize the content you produce for the keywords you want to address. Know what your potential customers are looking for, and use keywords that will help ensure their search leads to you.

 ## #46 MASTER PROMOTING YOUR CONTENT

"Write it, and they will come" is the worst piece of advice you can follow in content marketing. Yes, you should focus on producing good content, but working on distributing it should be on par with the effort you put into creating it.

Successfully promoting your content is a question of finding the right mix of channels. There are many potentially successful approaches to take, but they vary in terms of effectiveness and cost, so I encourage you to experiment with a combination of them.

- **Content Syndication** is the process of republishing your content on other websites. This method is very valuable for building up your top-of-funnel audience. The main positive of this tactic is the opportunity it gives you to get your content in front of a new audience. The challenge with this approach is that the same content can appear in more than one location, but having duplicate content doesn't necessarily result in a negative impact.

- **Pay-per-click Advertising (PPC)** may feel like a counter-intuitive approach when you're considering content marketing, but it has great potential to guide and improve your related marketing efforts. PPC for content can be exceedingly useful on newer platforms such as the big social media networks. While traditional PPC is geared towards audiences who are already in the research and decision-making stage of the buyer's cycle, social advertising allows you to reach people who are looking for *both* information *and* distraction. This connects directly to the core purpose of content marketing. Social media sites allow granular targeting based on demographic factors. They make it easier to reach your target personas directly, without having to "burn" money on other people who are not the right fit for your offering. PPC gives you a wealth of data, which you can use to learn more about your potential customers and how to serve them better. One related approach you might want to consider is remarketing—targeting those who have already visited your website or interacted with you online. Not only will you be increasing your visibility with your targeted potential customers, but you'll also get to "follow" them around the web and learn more about their browsing habits and interests.

- **Social Media and Email** are direct and free (or very cheap) channels that shouldn't be overlooked or underestimated. Both can work with any chosen strategy. Delve into the details of each tactic and find out what works best for your content and your business.

#47 MEASURE THE RIGHT STATS

When it's time to measure your impact, look at the numbers that actually matter, even if the results aren't necessarily what you'd like. Measuring vanity stats is just as bad as not measuring at all. If you have a clearly set goal for your content marketing, put the bulk of your time and money into tactics that support reaching that goal, and assess your progress bravely and mercilessly.

Looking for the right stats can also help you use your time more wisely. For example, if you're selling a product that has a lengthy buying cycle which requires working with a warm lead for a long time, then ask yourself: "What's the purpose of running a blog with thousands of readers who are unlikely to convert to leads, but require my time and effort?"

#48 SPEND ENOUGH TIME TESTING

Every aspect of your content marketing strategy should be open to experimentation and potential improvement. Try different forms of content. You may find that certain approaches are just begging to be developed and tried.

Experiment with everything; test your titles, headings, and formatting to see when your visitors are most engaged. Experiment with day and time when publishing your content and track how that is reflected in the performance. Where is your audience, and when are they active?

#49 BE PATIENT WITH YOUR CONTENT EFFORTS

Patience is a virtue, so remember that content marketing is like a marathon, not a sprint. If you're not ready to be in it for the long run, it would be better if you didn't get into it at all. But if you're ready for a long-term investment, remarkable things can be accomplished.

At the same time, working via a long-term strategy does not mean you should sit back and relax. Stay enthusiastic! Use each cycle of the Strategy—Execution—Analysis framework to find ways to tweak and improve your strategy. Redistribute your efforts and your budget into the initiatives that give you better results.

PART TWO

AUTOMATION AND EMAIL MARKETING

Email is at the core of B2B marketing, and marketers frequently claim it to be the most effective channel for bringing in revenue. In my opinion, the importance of email marketing is definitely not overrated. Studies show that 68 percent of email recipients say recognizing the email sender's brand is the most important factor in deciding to open an email.

Why is email so effective in getting your message to the right audience? Because it allows for high levels of personalization and relevance. For example, using the very basic form of personalization—the recipient's first name or company name in the opening line of an email—can dramatically improve click-through rates. Marketing automation has gone mainstream, and companies of all sizes are taking advantage of the opportunities it presents.

The name *marketing automation* simply refers to the process of automating a number of recurring tasks. With its help, you can manage a high number of potential customers and identify those who are most likely to engage further, then apply various tactics to increase their likelihood to convert (note that the term *lead nurturing* is often used interchangeably with marketing automation).

CHAPTER 6
USING THE POWER OF MARKETING AUTOMATION

Believe it or not, automation actually humanizes marketing. This is because it allows marketers to segment audiences and initiate conversations with leads who are most likely to become customers. When people are segmented into like-groups, it feels more authentic because your approach is targeting them specifically. Yet many professionals still hesitate to try marketing automation because they fear (perhaps only from the name) that it requires a high degree of technical knowledge.

The rise of powerful new software applications has created a number of products that can make marketing automation simple and accessible, even for those who lack coding skills. However, despite software now doing much of the technical work, you'll still need to structure your strategic efforts in the most productive way.

Many digital marketers report experiencing difficulties when creating and implementing a robust, high-quality automation strategy. Creating a detailed plan is a must when engaging in lead nurturing. All the time spent in this stage of the process is an investment that will result in higher ROI from all your marketing efforts.

Here are ten foundational practices that assist marketers interested in automation to get started without missing any of the basics.

 #50 ENSURE ENOUGH TRAFFIC TO FEED THE AUTOMATION ENGINE

Marketing automation is an exercise in improving the performance of the middle of your funnel.

Lead nurturing campaigns can be costly. They require investment in both time management and in adopting a software solution. But before you start making these automation investments, you'll want to be sure there's enough traffic at the top of the funnel. Without enough engagement to feed the automation engine, it will be challenging to obtain any positive impact from your mid-funnel efforts. You also risk deriving the wrong conclusions about what works because of the skewed results that come from a limited group of people.

#51 GET MANAGEMENT AND INVESTMENT ON BOARD

It is crucial to get backing from management before you engage in marketing automation. Without support and attention from senior management, automation can all too frequently be treated as a "side activity" or as a secondary component. In actuality, it should be a primary tool.

Thus, various departments in your company will need to be involved and be familiar with the marketing automation program. Cooperation between marketing and sales teams, at a minimum, is crucial for the success of an automation campaign.

You'll also want to ensure that there is an organization-wide understanding of the basics and that at least one person on your team can become extremely familiar with it. One of the best approaches is to appoint an "automation champion," a person who is educated in both basics and more advanced techniques in automated marketing. This champion will be responsible for making decisions and pushing automation to the priority of company operations. They can also answer questions and concerns that less-acquainted employees might have.

In addition, your champion can be responsible for researching, building up the case, and ultimately making the decision on what software package will be used. Of course, different parts of the company will need to participate in this process as well. The selection of software will have an impact on other systems already in place.

GAIN SUPERIOR KNOWLEDGE OF YOUR CUSTOMER BASE

You can start segmenting your existing customer base by making sure you understand which groups of customers need to be targeted. For different products and services, there are always different types of clients, so you will need to tweak your marketing strategy to connect effectively.

The essence of marketing automation is the creation of a conversation with potential customers based on their true individual interests and needs. You do this by using personalization; identify groups (or segments) among your target audience, then find out as much about them as you can.

Marketing personas will rise or fall depending on the effectiveness of information derived from the segmentation research. By gaining knowledge of your customer base, you will create a fuller and more realistic picture of the person you've targeted through your marketing automation campaign.

Existing customers are a good starting point for creating marketing personas. You can complement the information you already have about them with customer interviews to get a more detailed picture.

Marketing personas are essentially fictional characters that portray target customers. Look at who the key decision-makers are and flesh personas out based on information relating to their job positions, their seniority at the target company, their demographic data, their goals, pains, values, and fears. Based on all this, you can then create an actionable portrait to guide your strategy as you influence and convert target customers. Keep in mind the stages of the buyer's journey:

1 | Awareness Stage **2** | Consideration Stage **3** | Decision Stage **4** | Purchase Stage

You need to know what the buying process looks like for your customers—what it feels like for them, what they are thinking about as they consider whether or not to move forward. Then you can consider what will be the best content to present to your customers at each stage of the automation process.

Marketing personas enable you to offer a high level of customization and relevance to your leads. This improves the chances of success of the campaign on several levels.

#53 USE CONVERSATIONAL MARKETING

Conversational marketing leverages targeted messaging and intelligent chatbots to engage with visitors while they're still on your website. This approach starkly contrasts with the standard practice of lead generation and communication, where people are required to fill out a capture form and wait days for a response.

Today, buyers expect to communicate with businesses the way they communicate in their personal lives—instantly and across multiple channels. This has created the need to move beyond email and implement a viable form of messaging. Communication through messaging is quick and fluid. It creates a more human buying experience and allows businesses to learn more about customers and their unique pain points.

Conversational marketing through chatbots makes your business available around the clock, giving you the ability to engage new leads instantly. The bots can ask the necessary questions and qualify those leads in real time. They will begin to better understand leads early in the process, enabling them to recommend the next steps for that particular person. Through intelligent routing, bots will pair the right leads with the right sales reps. The end result is a customer-first buyer experience that is more personalized and allows buyers to engage on their own terms.

#54 USE RELEVANT DATA AND HIGH DEGREE OF INTEGRATION

Before you start deploying automation techniques, you should take the additional step of auditing and updating your databases. You'll need to be careful and conservative with their data, removing obsolete entries and verifying that you have permission to send messages to each entry on your list.

This not only prevents issues with being labeled as "spam," but it can also improve key metrics such as conversion rate and ROI. Ultimately, this saves organizations time and money and can prevent wasted effort.

You can use information from external sources such as social media to improve your knowledge about a target customer or reveal signals that indicate when a potential customer is passing from one stage of the buyer's journey to the next.

Also, make sure to integrate existing solutions (customer relationship management, content management system, etc.) with your automation tools. This will ensure smooth cooperation between lead nurturing and sales teams.

#55 MAKE AUTOMATION CAMPAIGNS FEEL HUMAN AND PERSONAL

Note that you can combine demographic data with behavioral input (i.e., how leads interact with your brand across different channels) to further understand what content would be most relevant.

Personalization is another important point. Gathering segmented data about your audience gives you the power to customize many aspects of these campaigns, including messaging, tone, content, etc. All this creates a feeling of "human touch" for your audience. You will appear to be targeting them because you have a legitimate connection to their interests. This helps you start a relationship with those who are most likely to become clients.

#56 EXPLORE MORE THAN ONE CHANNEL

Too many marketers still think that automation is only relevant to email. In truth, today's advanced platforms give you the opportunity to engage and communicate with your audience across many channels. Email is just one of those many channels.

To take full advantage of the opportunities created by automation, use all the channels to engage with your audience, including email, but also social media and conversations occurring on customer websites, microsites, etc. Targeted emails are vital, but they're not the only route.

#57 KNOW WHAT INFORMATION YOU NEED AND HOW TO GET IT

You need to gather enough information on your leads to help them successfully complete the nurturing stage. One of the best techniques for this is "progressive information gathering." Instead of asking the customer to provide all the information you want in one go, you collect data gradually during each successive interaction. This creates less friction, lowering the frequency of customer abandonment (i.e., leaving the site without submitting information).

With all this gathered information at hand, you can prepare landing pages, forms, email copy, and other materials that help with data gathering. Remember to ask exploratory questions. Doing so will help you discern where each lead is currently within the buyer's journey. With this knowledge, you can then place leads into the most appropriate stage of your nurturing efforts.

#58 PREPARE AN INVENTORY OF HIGH-QUALITY CONTENT

Content is the currency of marketers when it comes to automation. Customer information is highly coveted, but making it usable still requires a stream of high-quality and relevant resources.

Make sure to package offered content to the target audience based on what you know about their background and their stage in the buyer's journey. A potential customer in the awareness stage is usually researching ways to fulfill identified needs. Provide them with educational resources such as e-books, white papers, and research findings. Someone in the decision stage is usually comparing available solutions. For them, feature tables, case studies, and comparison sheets.

 ## EMPLOY LEAD SCORING AND GRADING

Lead scoring is the bridge that connects marketing and sales. A lead scoring system enables you to quickly and accurately assess how prepared a lead is. To make this assessment, you assign points based on behavioral data. When a lead's score reaches the appropriate level, you can pass it on to the sales team.

Creating a robust scoring system can be challenging, but it pays off. It allows both marketing and sales to focus only on the leads with the highest potential. It eliminates unnecessary work and lets you focus on actions that are the most likely to drive business.

While lead scoring allows you to evaluate the readiness of each lead, lead grading can be used to segment leads into different bands. You can do this on the basis of how attractive each lead is to your business. When used together, lead scoring and grading give you effective tactics for quickly identifying leads who are A) the best fit to do business, and B) the highest level of readiness for the closing of a sale.

Sometimes leads are sent to sales prematurely. To prepare for this, you can create a lead recycling procedure to assign leads for "re-nurturing." You can also review the scoring framework to optimize the scoring mechanism to try to prevent future errors.

#60 CONTINUOUSLY ANALYZE AND IMPROVE

Throughout this process, you should keep collecting as much data as possible about the way prospects use your content. Add tracking to your website to measure the performance of various campaigns. Then analyze what works and what doesn't. It's also a best practice to test and experiment with every detail of campaigns, from headlines to calls to action.

There are many ways to determine whether a campaign has fulfilled its purpose. The metric you choose to measure success will depend on your marketing automation strategy goals. If the ultimate goal is to raise awareness, then the open rate and click-through rate (CTR) for the automation campaigns will be your most relevant metric. But if the goal is to produce new revenue flows, then the conversion rate will be your key indicator to examine.

CHAPTER 7

CREATING A WINNING EMAIL MARKETING STRATEGY

The average open rate for marketing emails across all industries is 21 percent. This means your email has a good chance of being opened and at least skimmed through by a significant portion of your audience.

Forty-one percent of B2B buyers say that content sent by email had influence over their buying decisions, and 40 percent say they consider leads generated through email as high-quality ones.

It's no surprise that 45 percent of marketers consider email to be the marketing channel most efficient at generating revenue. In that connection, here are ten useful practices to fine-tune your email creation and distribution processes.

#61   ALIGN EMAIL WITH YOUR OVERALL MARKETING STRATEGY

The first step to email marketing success is to ensure it is coordinated with your inbound strategy. Align your email goals with the goals of your company, and focus on resolving the pains of your buyer personas. Audiences will respond to messaging that is consistent with the brand they know and trust, and which addresses their needs specifically. You'd be surprised by how many B2B businesses overlook these fundamentals.

It's important to adapt your email messages to prospects at different stages of the buying cycle. Content should be targeted to avoid redundancy. The key is to maintain relevance and match the message to the prospect's expectations. Get to know your audience well, from their pain points and needs to the language they prefer to use.

Before you begin your first email campaign, ensure that your timing fits the rhythm your recipients are expecting. Sending an email too early or too late can immediately lead to an influx of unsubscribes.

#62 SEGMENT YOUR EMAIL LISTS

After getting to know your audience, you're ready for segmentation. Segmenting your contacts will improve open rates, decrease opt-outs and unsubscribes, and boost deliverability. How do you do this? It's simple: When you segment your email lists, you guarantee that the right message will reach the right person. This way, you avoid over-burdening your audience with emails that are irrelevant to them.

There are numerous criteria you can use for segmenting your email groups. The most common ones include location, age, gender, education, and job position. But there are many other factors you can also consider, such as the industry, organization type and size, and seniority level of the recipients.

You can segment on the basis of subscriber activity, such as past purchases, purchase cycle, and frequency of purchases. You can also try classifying prospects based on the styles and types of content they prefer. The better you know your targets, the more effective your messaging can be.

#63 FOCUS ON RELEVANT AND USEFUL FORMS OF CONTENT

This tip might seem like a no-brainer, but it can get lost within the myriad tasks that professional marketers have to handle. Sales-y buzzwords and long, dense paragraphs have no place in your marketing email; quick, compelling arguments backed up by data do.

Besides the wording and structure, the *type* of content you share will also determine whether your recipients find your emails valuable. Blog posts, ebooks, guides, and infographics are all available to you. Be ready to deploy the content most likely to connect with your audience. And while you're at it, don't forget that you can also offer your prospects a taste of your products or services through free trials and giveaways. Potential customers almost always find such offers relevant and useful. Your ability to do this will depend upon the industry you're in, but if possible, try offering email courses to your subscribers. This can be a great way to educate potential customers while boosting your brand credibility and positioning your employees as experts. The content you choose to share can also depend on your customer's stage in the buying cycle.

Using original content for email campaigns isn't the only option. There's always curated content, usually in the form of newsletters. Newsletters deliver a range of relevant and interesting information by linking readers to different websites or blogs. When working with a newsletter, you won't need to spend time creating as much content, yet you'll still have a way to communicate value to your prospects. As an expert, you will curate the best content for them—saving them time and bringing the most valuable industry news to the forefront of their attention.

 ## #64 CONSIDER THE BUYER'S JOURNEY

One of the primary functions of an email marketing campaign is to nurture leads. This means that to run the campaign effectively, you'll have to understand the intricacies of the B2B decision-making cycle. Sending the wrong message, or sending it at the wrong time can have detrimental effects on your relationships with potential customers.

To maximize your chances of success, tailor the content of your email message to the recipient's stage in the buying cycle. At every business, there are specific types of content appropriate for the awareness, consideration, and decision stages. Make sure you segment your audience and always deploy the right one.

The B2B sales cycle is rarely straightforward, but by offering your prospects the right type of information at the right time, you can help move them down the funnel with every message. Keep in mind that the purpose of your email campaign is to allow customers to make their own decisions. Post-purchase, customers will only be willing to continue the relationship with your brand if they are satisfied. So continue to send timely, useful information long after your customers have already purchased.

#65 DON'T SKIP COPY CREATIVITY

The importance of effective copywriting is often underestimated by B2B marketers. Largely, this is due to a common misconception that communication is most effective when it is serious and businesslike. Well, your campaigns won't be very successful without creativity and human connection. After all, B2B decision-makers are driven by emotions like the rest of us.

To offer your B2B prospects email messages that are as engaging as possible, I encourage you to make them sharp, short, and even witty. They can be business appropriate without being jargon, humorless, or overly formal. Psychological studies have found that messaging styles trigger different behaviors and reactions. You want a reaction that will make your recipient respond positively and move down the sales funnel. So personalization, clarity, and catchy headlines are what will help your copy achieve these goals.

Unleash your writing creativity, but don't forget to research keywords. Having an informal or unorthodox approach to copywriting can be great, but make sure to still include language that resonates with your recipients.

#66 WORK ON A BRILLIANT CALL TO ACTION

The call to action (CTA) is the sentence, phrase, or even single word that urges people to take the next step. While the CTA can't convert clients on its own, it holds the most power to make prospects click further down your sales funnel.

Selecting the right words for the CTA can be daunting, but there's plenty of research to guide you. You should promise value to the reader, create a sense of urgency, make the language highly personal, and cite statistics. Stay up to date on industry news so that your CTA is as pertinent as possible. You can also experiment with a subtle CTA that provokes thinking rather than commands an action. The right thoughts can also bring a prospect closer to a sale.

The CTA should also be aligned with the buying stage of the email's recipients. Sending an overly salesy message to people who are only just starting to get to know your brand can be counterproductive. At the same time, failing to provide nurtured leads with next steps can be a big missed opportunity.

 ## #67 DESIGN TEMPLATES AND LANDING PAGES WITH A TWIST

Once you've nailed the copy for your email campaigns, it's time to master design. The presentation of your email message design can be as important as the content itself. It's worth it to invest time and resources into creating appealing designs for your email templates.

You won't necessarily need strong visuals every time, but when you do, it's important to get them right. Good graphics help to improve readability and click-through rates. Try opting for a template in a recognizable, branded style, or using high-quality images to illustrate your points.

The design of your landing pages should follow the same theme as your email templates (and, if possible, your marketing materials). The purpose of your campaigns is to invite prospects to those very pages. That's where they will learn more about your products or services, or read further content assets. Your audience needs to have the sense that going from email to landing page is all part of the same journey. Every impression counts in your customer's decision-making process, so make sure your design creates a consistent and positive one.

#68 SETUP AUTHENTICATION AND DELIVERABILITY

If you're going to expend the effort and time it takes to craft effective emails, it goes without saying that you'll want to ensure they get delivered. To help make that happen, you'll want to set up authentication to avoid spam filters and facilitate your messages reaching your recipients' mailboxes.

The most common email authentication standards include Sender Policy Framework (SPF), DomainKeys Identified Mail (DKIM), and Domain-based Message Authentication Reporting and Conformance (DMARC). To comply with the rules, you'll probably want to involve your IT department in setting up your company profile. In doing so, you'll also be able to verify your company domain as a secure sender.

Consider ramping up your IP address's reputation gradually. Instead of sending an email to every contact in your database all at once, start by warming up your IP. This can be done in a time frame of two to six weeks to avoid spam monitors flagging your emails. Remember to regularly refresh your lists and make it easy for people to opt out, so that your messages don't go to the wrong people and aren't reported as spam. Roughly one out of every ten businesses, whether required by local data privacy laws or not, choose to set up double opt-in processes to ensure the highest level of engagement from your list.

#69 EXPLORE THE POWER OF MARKETING AUTOMATION

In the last chapter, we outlined the benefits of marketing automation campaigns. When applied to email marketing, automation can save significant time and resources, and allow you to measure your results more accurately. You can schedule campaigns seamlessly and get deeper insights into your target audiences.

Common features of email automation software include advanced email analytics, email previews, spam testing, and real-time alerts. Automation can also help you design and execute email campaigns tailored for different stages in the sales funnel. Marketing automation can provide lead scoring and grading, as well as ROI reports, so you get an in-depth picture of which leads are worth investment. Automation also allows you to manage cross-channel communication, which can otherwise be an overwhelming task. Remember to incorporate the power of marketing automation when building a winning strategy.

#70 TEST, OPTIMIZE, AND MEASURE SUCCESS

Practice makes perfect, and email marketing is no exception. When you're ready to deploy an email campaign, it's always a good idea to first test how your email will look with different email providers and on different devices. How will your message look on a phone? How about on a tablet computer? Make sure you optimize your emails for mobile and tablet devices, where a large part of your recipient list is likely to read the message. Also, test a text-only version of the email to catch HTML and CSS errors. Check the image-to-text ratio to ensure that filters will not see your email as spam.

Always take the time to A/B test different versions of your email in order to assess what approaches work best. Some variables that you can tweak include the subject line, call to action, layout, personalization, headline, and images.

You can learn a lot about your audience through this tweaking, and you can use your findings in future campaigns. This allows you to optimize your efforts as you go, paving the way for further testing and improvement, and potentially making each message more effective than the last.

You already know that your email marketing strategy needs to have clearly predetermined metrics to track success. The typical KPIs that email marketers use are click-through rate, conversions, bounce rate, list growth, and email forwarding. Use a combination of these that best suits the goals of your email campaigns, but always set it in advance and then measure rigorously.

CHAPTER 8

MASTERING YOUR B2B EMAIL DESIGNS

W hen it comes to ROI and lead generation, emails can be up to forty times more effective in customer procurement than social media.

However, successful results involve a considerable investment. If your email efforts are not consistent, your campaigns are likely to be ignored or deleted. That's why your email design needs to be flawless, correctly branded, and capture a reader's attention in just a few seconds.

Here are ten central B2B email design practices to help you make the most of your emails:

#71 ESTABLISH A THEME THAT CORRESPONDS TO THE CONTENT

A good email campaign begins with the design of the template and its theme. Perfecting the theme and template can pay off by yielding more responses, better branding, and deeper customer relationships. It can also lower bounce and unsubscribe rates.

As you craft a theme for your email campaign, you'll want to make sure it's linked to the content you are offering. This means you'll have to decide on a clear visual hierarchy within the email. For example, if you are sending out a newsletter and have a feature article that stands out more prominently among other items, that feature article could set the theme in terms of content as well as design. This makes clicking through the email more natural to users, which will help them quickly grasp what your email is about.

#72 PLAIN TEXT VS. HTML EMAIL

You'll have to choose between a plain text format or an HTML format for your email, depending on your ultimate intent. For example, newsletters and event invitations almost always look better with visuals, while follow-up and drip emails can be entirely textual while still being effective.

Both approaches have their advantages:

Plain Text:
- Universal readability
- Higher deliverability rates, because plain text emails are smaller in size
- Consistent rendering, since some email service providers (ESPs) will strip certain HTML elements as protection

HTML Format:
- Better CTR, because of the visual appeal
- Tracking codes that can help you track email open rates
- Improved message attractiveness and readability

If you choose HTML, it is always a good idea to include a plain text version as well for clients that can't download the email properly. In situations where ESPs block some of your HTML content, a few simple rules can be followed to ensure fewer problems. Make sure you don't design your email entirely with images, and don't use images when text will suffice. Also, if you are including buttons, use HTML/CSS-based buttons instead of images. Always include ALT text on all images from icons and logos. That way, even if some or all of the visual elements vanish, you'll ensure that your email will still make sense to users.

#73 BE CLEAR ABOUT THE PURPOSE OF THE EMAIL

You should always be clear about the purpose and function of every email you send out. The business goal should be at the heart of your design and content.

Emails are typically separated into two broad categories: marketing and operational (also known as transactional). The purpose of marketing emails is to promote products and services, inform about product updates, make announcements, or invite audiences to events.

Operational emails typically include notifications about a transaction or shipment, information about updates, confirmation of changes to a personal profile, or system status notices. Some emails can even contain a combination of these two categories.

Incorporating a recognizable brand name and message purpose have a positive effect on conversion optimization. Making the purpose of the email clear to users and helping them navigate it with a visual hierarchy increases the likelihood that they will engage with your brand in a useful way.

#74 CAREFULLY CRAFT THE SUBJECT LINE AND CONSIDER A "FROM" FIELD

The "from" field of your email is the first thing that potential customers will see when they receive your email. An email that comes from an unknown sender or from an email address starting with sales@ or info@ will often end up in the junk or spam folder.

Including the full name of the sender establishes trust and transparency and signals that your message is not coming from an anonymous source. This greatly increases the chances it will be opened. And over time, a consistent, personal sender can become a positive identifier, especially if you correspond with your business contacts on a daily basis.

If you are sending out a newsletter, report, blog email, or alert that people have subscribed to, you can feel free to use non-human email addresses. In these situations, audiences will be expecting an email from you and won't be concerned if it seems impersonal.

The subject line is just as important as the sender's email as it provides the recipient with a good idea of what your email is about. A typical recipient will decide within six seconds whether an email is worth opening or not. Although most people look to the sender to determine if an email is worth opening, the subject line is also an important factor. Thus, the sender's email address and the subject line need to work in unison to get the best possible result.

To connect with the recipient, subject lines need to be both snappy and relevant. They also have to be short, communicating their importance in as few words as possible (especially since they get cut short on mobile quite a lot). Including a relevant CTA within the subject line will also pique readers' interest. Studies have found that personalization can boost email open rates. Furthermore, including your company's name also improves email open rates.

 ## CREATE A COMPELLING PREVIEW PANE

The preview pane is another design element that can be used to improve your open rates. It consists of the first six lines of your email, which can be immediately seen by the recipient before it is even opened. If it contains nonessential information or features an image or logo that doesn't communicate the gist of the email, you risk losing readers. However, if it presents something compelling and relevant, your recipient will be more likely to open it and read the full email.

Test it and ensure the message looks good in the preview pane with both images on and off. Also, be sure to include compelling copy in that space, but without repeating the subject line. Create additional incentive to open the full email by adding viewable links for users to follow. Again, if you have an HTML version, make sure that all images have ALT text and include a call to action that can convert readers or trigger additional actions.

Be as clear as possible about the purpose of your message within the first six lines. Pretend that users can only see those six lines, and use that as a measure for which content to keep and which to remove.

#76 CHOOSE A DESIGN BASED ON THE TYPE OF EMAIL

These are the different types of email design and their recommended design elements:

- **Plain Text Email:** Does not require much design because it does not feature any images. Be sure that your email copy is conversational but to the point, and that it is properly personalized to make a good impression.
- **Newsletter:** To increase your newsletter's open rate, make your template entertaining and fun. Create a sound structure, make navigation easy, and provide quick and easy links to all the content you have included.
- **New Feature / Product / Service Email:** The design of this type of email needs to be very clean and simple, featuring only the most important details that users need to know. You can also provide instructional visuals to increase engagement.
- **Training and Events:** The most important information in this email should be clearly visible (such as schedule, times, and dates). Apart from the essentials, the template can also include a well-placed CTA that is relevant to the content of the email.
- **Event Follow-Up:** Once the event is over, you can follow up with an email rich in visuals, detailing the event. Photos or videos from the event can be a great asset in this kind

of message. Include easy-to-spot links and CTA, directing readers to other types of content and further engagement with your brand.

- **Holiday**: A holiday email is a convenient way to show off brand personality and culture, as well as build further rapport with your clients and subscribers. Include rich and fun visual material, but don't forget to make the plain text version just as compelling.

#77 ENSURE YOUR CTA IS CLEAR AND WELL-POSITIONED

The copy, position, and even the color of your CTA will determine whether readers notice and engage with it or not. A CTA positioned "above the fold" tends to work better, especially if a reader only views your email through their preview pane and does not scroll down. A CTA at the top of a message is crucial; however, you can also feature your CTA in a number of other locations throughout your email.

Your CTA should also stand out from images and other text. To further draw the attention of your readers, you can use vibrant colors. Yet, at the same time, you need to keep the CTA in line with the overall theme of your messaging template. Make it noticeable, but not out of place.

Your CTA should have a clear message about the action you want your readers to make. Use persuasive wording that incorporates a command such as "Sign up now," "Download this white paper," or "Subscribe to our list." Don't hesitate to tell your readers what to do in very clear terms.

Remember, if your readers do not follow your CTA, your email will be pointless, but if it is distinct enough, it will consistently increase click-through rate.

#78 DESIGN MOBILE FIRST

With 41 percent of emails now being opened on mobile and more than 90 percent of B2B executives using their smartphone for business, designing with the mobile first in mind is no longer a best practice, but an absolute must.

To maximize messaging effectiveness, you'll want to optimize all of your emails for a mobile-responsive framework. There are many design elements that can help optimize a message for mobile, and you should pay attention to all of them. They include:

- Using bigger fonts (a minimum of 13 or 14 points)
- Using a standard format: multipart MIME (includes email content in both plain text and HTML)
- Using basic HTML for your template (as CSS may be blocked)
- Keeping images small in size, avoiding GIFs and Flash elements
- Staying under 600px when designing for Android
- Sticking to a one-column format
- Creating tappable CTAs with a minimum size of 44x44 points

 #79 AVOID THE SPAM FOLDER

To avoid having your emails end up in the spam folder, you should regularly familiarize yourself with spam rules and keep your emails within a design framework that avoids spam classification. Some of the rules under the US CAN-SPAM Act require that you never use deceptive language in email headers, "from" fields, subject lines, or in the body of emails. You are further required to include an unsubscribe link in all automated emails and to ensure that the link works for at least thirty days after the email is sent. You're also required to include your physical mailing address.

MailChimp's *How to Avoid Spam Filters* is a handy resource if you want to learn more about avoiding spam filters and email firewalls. It offers deeper insight into what can get you into trouble such as your email campaign metadata or issues with your IP address.

Here's a quick list of things that can get you in trouble with spam filters when designing and formatting an email:

- Enormous fonts or full capitalization (a font size between 8 and 14 points is best)
- Invisible, light grey or red fonts
- Repetitive keyword usage
- Misspelled words and garbled text
- Missing title tags
- Javascript and Flash elements
- Phishing links
- SPAM trigger words such as free, cheap, money, lowest price, lose, sample, deal, offer, prize, vacation, congratulations, urgent

An additional way to prevent your emails from being labeled as spam is to play it safe and use a double opt-in. That is, get permission for the different types of messages you are sending to your lists (especially if they're promotional messages) and never use purchased email lists. Also, always prominently display the opt-out link in all your messages.

 ## #80 PROVIDE AMPLE WHITE SPACE AND KEEP EYES ON THE LEFT SIDE

One of the simplest, yet most important, email design rules is to always provide plenty of white space. People get turned off by a crowded page, whether it's in a physical publication or an electronic message. Just the right amount of bullet points, short paragraphs, and easily skimmable content with images that support the main purpose are all elements in an email that converts. White space is not your enemy, it's your friend.

Marketing studies that focus on eye movement reveal that people will typically keep to the left side of a message's content when browsing. However, they will also readily take directional cues when provided, so tailor the position of your most important text accordingly.

CHAPTER 9

CRAFTING EFFECTIVE EMAIL COPY

The power of email is enormous, but it needs to be properly harnessed to encourage readers to open and take the desired action. B2B marketers have only six to twelve seconds to catch readers' attention. That's why every word counts.

Each detail in an email campaign needs to be thoroughly thought out, monitored, and A/B tested for improvement. Email content should tie ideas together seamlessly, tell a compelling story, and guide the reader to the desired CTA. Ideally, effective copy should make an offer that people can't refuse.

Here are ten clear-cut practices to spark readers' interest and convince them to absorb your message:

TRY THE "BEFORE AND AFTER" APPROACH

Chances are, your target audience might not even be aware that they have a problem your company can solve, and that's okay. This situation is a good opportunity to use a proven email approach known as the "before and after" tactic. This approach allows you to shed light on something that might be reducing their productivity or customer satisfaction, or to invite them to imagine how much better off they could be without a particular issue or problem.

Pleasure and pain are major motives for everyone, and they're certainly motivations for your potential customers. Identify the pain a target audience is feeling, and promise to relieve it. Explain how your solution will make the "after" state so much better for your audience. Concisely show how your product or service can take away pain points and make doing business a pleasure.

#82 ASK PEOPLE IF THEY FEEL LIKE TALKING ABOUT THEIR PROBLEM

Your potential customers might already be aware their problem exists. But they might not realize the extent to which it is affecting them, and they might not be accustomed to articulating it. If this is the situation, you can be the one to help them.

Compose an email that elaborates on the difficulties the problem is causing them. Try to prompt a discussion, or simply offer your sincere concern. This articulation of an issue they may be dealing with will get them thinking about what they can do to improve things. No one likes to experience difficulties, but when a problem is now painted as acute and solvable then they will begin to take action.

Unlike the "before and after" approach, you don't need to go into great detail about the after-effects of using your product or service. Instead, your goal is to make your readers realize that they have a problem, that it's okay to talk about the problem, and that the problem is one that can be solved. Then you can move on to highlighting the powerful benefits of your product and how it can help them achieve their goals.

#83 GIVE PEOPLE THE FREEDOM OPTION

It's okay to ask tasks of your customers (businesses do it all the time), but it's important that your customer always feels that participating is optional. For example, when asking customers to fill out a survey or retweet your blog post, always present it in terms of a favor. It's something they can do, but not something they have to do. You can pitch it to them that if they liked your product or service, an optional way to express that (which you'd appreciate) is to take action X or Y.

Psychological studies have shown that when customers are given the opportunity to potentially decline a request with no negative consequences, most recipients will feel at ease and be more likely to do what is being asked of them.

#84 PROVIDE FACTS, FACTS, AND MORE FACTS

Facts are powerful, and a tremendously persuasive marketing tool. When you need to make a case to an audience, especially when it comes to large purchases, it's immensely effective to use a chain of arguments containing facts.

When opting for a fact-based approach, start with a sentence that frames the situation by detailing the problem at hand. Then support your point with as much credible evidence as possible. A well-positioned and targeted string of facts do not necessarily need to include claims about your own business. The right set of facts can lead an audience to conclude that buying your product or service is the best (and only) way.

It's still good to conclude a fact-based pitch with a call to action, but it does not need to be forceful. If your presentation of the facts has been compelling, then it won't take much urging to get the reader to demo or purchase your product.

#85 PUT THE CLASSIC FOMO IN ACTION

Yet another effective approach to crafting emails is to rely on your audience's fear of missing out (or FOMO). It plays upon a customer's potential concern that they may be "behind the times" or that they have failed to use an effective solution that their competitors have already adopted.

When employing the FOMO approach, start your message with a personal greeting and briefly remind the reader of the perks that you are offering. Then, point out all the notable people or companies you've worked with, review all the industry leaders who are using your product or service, and then highlight the limited amount of time this product or service will be available. This will lend your offer an air of exclusivity, even as it gives your audience the impression that others in the industry may know something that they do not. This sense of FOMO will then encourage readers to take the next step and follow your call to action.

#86 USE STORIES BECAUSE THEY MAKE THE WORLD GO 'ROUND

Almost all good emails tell a captivating story. Whether simple or elaborate, stories connect with everyone. Stories are how we learn about the world and about ourselves. But to write a story that's effective in a business context, you'll want to write a compelling narrative that immediately triggers emotion. Emotions in a business context can include frustration with pain points, excitement accompanying a successful initiative, or fear of missing out on a solution that would make work easier.

Customer profiles and case studies can be an excellent delivery system for stories. You can even make up anecdotes about theoretical customers. The key is to make it feel true and relatable, and to remain focused on the story's purpose. "Why are you telling me this story?" an audience member might ask. The answer should always be, "This is the story of someone just like you, who had a problem that my company solved."

Storytelling as a marketing method has become increasingly popular in recent years, and there's a good reason for that. Stories stimulate our brains, stir our imaginations, and keep us interested. The overall narrative that your email is going to go on is up to you. But the important thing is to showcase how a challenge has been overcome thanks to your solution.

LEARN FROM *READER'S DIGEST*

Reader's Digest, a publication that has hooked millions of readers for more than one hundred years, is worth mentioning as a source of inspiration for successful email copywriting. It has a global reach and is the largest paid-circulation magazine in the world. So, what's the essential takeaway for marketing copywriting? *Reader's Digest* became so successful by running stories that are pithy, short, and get right to the point. This is not just what readers want in a magazine, it's also what they want in marketing communication.

You can adopt some of the best practices that have allowed *Reader's Digest* to stay so successful. Write condensed stories that are filled with facts. Use fewer adjectives and more numbers. Always give your audience the sense that you are here to get directly to the point and give them the information they need as efficiently as possible.

A successful marketing message incorporating *Reader's Digest* techniques will begin with something catchy and personal, and ignite curiosity in the recipient. Then it will quickly deliver facts and statistics in a straightforward manner, and these facts will lead the reader to an effective CTA at the message's conclusion. The reader will have the sense that their time is being respected, and only the most important and relevant information is being presented. No fluff. No extras.

 ## KEEP IT SHORT AND SWEET (AND HONEST)

Crisp marketing messaging focuses on creating short and simple messages. But there's an additional element to keep in mind, and that's honesty. If leaving out something vital will make an audience feel deceived, then you still need to take the time to include it.

Shorter emails are more likely to be read in full, but being clear about your request or expectation makes it easier for the person on the other end to take action. It's a delicate balance, but one that anyone in marketing can master. Keep it short and sweet, but always tell the whole truth.

#89 OFFER A COMPLIMENT

Who doesn't like being praised? You can often stir up interest among email recipients by starting off with a recognition of their work or with a straightforward compliment.

But never just leave it at that. After delivering a compliment, get down to business and persuade the reader to imagine their world with (or without) your solution. Use convincing cause-and-effect examples that activate the logical side of the brain. The recipient will be engaged both on an emotional and analytical level. Then present your offer to the recipient.

#90 MAKE IT A THRILL

One of the most powerful ways to get your readers' attention is to employ surprise and exhilaration. You can do this by introducing novel ideas or news items into your emails that your audience won't be expecting. A message employing this tactic should upset people's preconceived notions.

Our brains love unexpected positive surprises. They cause us to respond with excitement and engagement. Consciously or not, many of us seek daily thrills because we get small dopamine rushes from them. It can be challenging to formulate thrilling messages, but it's worth your time. Making your reader feel delighted and thrilled can be the first step to getting their attention and starting them down the path that leads to a sale.

PART THREE

PAID ACQUISITION

Any skilled marketer needs to understand paid acquisition. Knowing the basics of traditional pay-per-click is no longer enough. You need to understand how the field is evolving.

Practical advertising is exploding, and companies from all industries and of all sizes are taking advantage of it. Until recently, paid advertising was used only to display ads through desktop (mostly as website banners). Now it has found its way onto almost every type of touchpoint and channel—including video, mobile, and social media. In this section, we'll look at how marketers can harness these techniques to maximize impact at any level of investment.

CHAPTER 10

GETTING STARTED WITH PAY-PER-CLICK FOR B2B

Pay-per-click (PPC) is the fastest-growing and most dynamic industry within advertising today. Recent research indicates that 55 percent of marketers have bigger PPC budgets than they did a year prior, and that 64 percent of brands plan to increase their PPC budgets. From this, we can infer that the perceived importance of PPC is increasing among industry decision makers.

In the same survey, 74 percent of respondents reported feeling positive about their PPC success, while only 5 percent reported poor performance. This serves as a testament to this marketing method's efficiency in driving positive results.

Here are ten tips on how to improve your pay-per-click programs for performing best-in-class PPC:

#91 ESTABLISH YOUR PPC LIFE CYCLE

It's easy to feel at odds with your PPC strategy, but figuring out a PPC life cycle can tie those loose ends up. Follow a life cycle to optimize your effective campaigns, or set up entirely new ones to explore different approaches. Doing so provides a framework in which you can confidently take consistent and logical steps at each stage of your PPC journey.

A stable PPC life cycle includes the following six steps:

1	Audit	**2**	Research	**3**	Implementation (or launch)
4	Testing	**5**	Optimization	**6**	Reporting

Begin at the beginning. Perform an audit of your account (if you already have one) that can determine whether it's in need of improvement. A complete audit should include measurement of your KPIs and can be a large undertaking. But once you're finished with it, you'll know exactly what you need to do going forward.

After completing the audit, you'll enter the research phase. This research should provide the means to build tighter ad groups, write more compelling ads, and design stronger landing pages.

The next three phases are launching, testing, and optimizing your campaign. They should occur simultaneously: the idea is to implement, monitor, test, and implement again.

Finally, the reporting phase will allow you to draw conclusions about what works within your particular niche, and what doesn't. Once you know this, you can make the necessary corrections, while researching further campaigns.

#92 CREATE BRANDED CAMPAIGNS

Branded campaigns allow you to focus your efforts on a particular area and can emphasize your company's dominance in that area. Bidding on branded keywords can strengthen your name and its position in search results.

You can expect to see SERP (search engine results page) domination, cheap ads, and significant Quality Score improvement. Branded campaigns are also an effective way to promote new services and products. They offer the perfect opportunity to test brand messaging cost-effectively before rolling it out elsewhere.

Branded PPC campaigns can actually complement your overall paid search strategy as an inexpensive yet efficient way to build additional momentum.

 #93   **THINK BEYOND GOOGLE**

Google is certainly the dominant choice, but it's not the only tech giant when it comes to search engines. Don't get caught up in "Google tunnel vision" when implementing your PPC strategy. Competitors such as Bing, DuckDuckGo, Yandex, or Yahoo provide ready audiences and unique targeting capabilities.

Consider reviewing all available options before deciding on a PPC strategy. While Google drives the majority of search traffic worldwide, its competitors can offer a number of advantages, including:

Better targeting
More control
More transparency
Better social extensions

If you've only worked with Google in the past, you won't necessarily have to build everything from the ground up. You can import your Google Ads into Bing to compare a campaign's performance on each platform.

 #94   **RESEARCH YOUR COMPETITORS THOROUGHLY**

As the PPC life cycle model suggests, research is a vital component of any campaign. Research your marketplace and your competitors. If a competitor has effective PPC strategies, there's no reason that you can't adopt elements of it for yourself.

Researching competitors can help you determine whether your keywords have good commercial value, how to phrase your ads, where those ads lead, and how to structure your landing pages. Various paid tools can assist in this process by allowing you to track your competitors closely and automatically to get the best possible sense of their overall search engine marketing strategies.

 ## #95 USE GOOGLE DISPLAY NETWORKS TO REDUCE SPENDING

The Google Display Network (GDN) is a great tool to use for remarketing purposes, especially the Remarketing Lists for Search Ads (RLSA) feature of Google AdWords. You can run Gmail Ads through the GDN, which are then displayed in the Gmail Sponsored Promotions tab if it's active.

You can also display your ads on LinkedIn. Keep in mind that you'll be speaking directly to your audience, which makes relevance a high priority. GDN LinkedIn ads can acquire and nurture early-stage leads at a low cost.

 ## #96 FINE-TUNE YOUR LANDING PAGE

An effective landing page must contain a number of key elements in order to achieve the desired goal of capturing or converting leads:

User-friendly
Accessible
Persuasive
An establishment of your brand's credibility

Pay attention to landing page success factors during the design process, including how landing pages work in conjunction with paid ads and how you can increase the relevance of your landing pages.

#97 DON'T FORGET THE FORM

A successful landing page form increases conversion rates and attracts better-qualified leads. What you ask (and how you ask) your visitors should depend on their stage in the sales funnel. Those at the top of the funnel (or "TOFU") stage will typically not want to share too much personal information, so you're likely to collect only email addresses.

But as prospects progress down the funnel, they'll be willing to provide more information in exchange for premium content, demos, or other complementary materials. Finding out more about people who are middle of the funnel ("MOFU") or bottom of the funnel ("BOFU") is centrally important for your sales team. A multi-step landing page is a persuasive alternative to a form with multiple fields that can actually generate even more conversions.

In addition, platforms like Unbounce offer message match features that address each visitor differently, using unique URL parameters to produce text. This enables you to create highly personalized landing page experiences with only one landing page design.

#98 TRY THE IN-MARKET AUDIENCES FEATURE

AdWords' In-Market Audiences feature is particularly useful for a start-up. However, it can always deliver an additional boost to those who've been managing PPC accounts for a while and want to diversify their ads.

In-Market Audiences draws on information from Google concerning user behavior, preferences, and even intentions. You can market to people or businesses who are actively demonstrating an interest in your particular market. You can then begin to build lists to run through remarketing campaigns.

 #99 IMPROVE YOUR QUALITY SCORE

Don't forget to check your ad's Quality Score (QS). That score is an estimate of how effective your keywords, ads, copy, and landing pages are. The better your score (meaning how useful and relevant your elements are to users), the lower your costs, and the higher your rankings and click-through rates.

While the QS doesn't take into account auction-time factors, such as the user's device type or language preference, it does give a rough idea of an ad's quality. By checking your QS on a regular basis (and taking steps to improve it if necessary), you can increase your Ad Rank, which ultimately determines your ad position.

 #100 ADJUST DEVICE BIDS

Google has bid adjustment features in AdWords that allow marketers to target specific devices depending on audience behavior.

With over half of all searches handled by Google each year now on mobile devices, this change reflects the growing need to optimize for mobile. You can use this feature to adjust device bids to improve results or limit wasted spending.

CHAPTER 11

USING PROGRAMMATIC MEDIA BUYING

Programmatic media buying is the buying and selling of advertising outlets using computer algorithms in order to automate the process. It promotes hyper targeting and bidding on each individual user. Programmatic ad buying will eventually capture the bulk of all digital advertising spending, and become the majority of the digital ad spending market in the US.

Despite its growing prevalence, programmatic ad buying can be complicated and costly if done inefficiently. You'll want to do it right. Here are some of the best practices in the field that can set you on course for success in your programmatic efforts.

#101 HAVE AN INTERNAL PROGRAMMATIC CHAMPION

There's one thing that everyone with programmatic experience seems to agree on. That's the fact that it takes a big shift in thinking within the marketing department to use it properly.

Using programmatic ad buying requires a degree of "loosening" and a "hands-off" approach. The team needs to be able to sit back and allow computers to do their job without human intervention. This kind of approach may come as a shock, or "feel wrong" to marketing departments that have historically been very hands-on. The same culture shock applies to management, especially in companies where executives keep a close eye on every aspect of the business. Because of this, it is important to have someone internally who acts as an advocate of the practice and keeps an eye on how it is used.

Even if you work with external partners, having someone internally who can serve in a similar capacity is invaluable. This person should not only act as a change agent, supporting the mentality of the shift, but also serve as the point of contact for external partners and the authority on decisions about the programmatic efforts.

#102 UNDERSTAND THE BASICS

There is no other type of advertising that comes close to the high levels of scalability when it comes to programmatic ad buying. This is achieved through the use of algorithms, which can make the field seem inaccessible. However, you can typically grasp the basics even without in-depth technical knowledge.

Here's a brief guide to the initial steps of the process:

Marketplaces where programmatic buying can be used include:

- **Real-time bidding (RTB):** the process of conducting a per-impression auction for a given ad space. It happens in the time it takes to load the page where the ad will be displayed.
- **Programmatic direct:** removes the auction element, but keeps all other aspects of programmatic buying. The ad space is guaranteed and negotiated directly between the seller (publisher) and the buyer (usually a DSP, see

below), while incorporating the advanced targeting and measurement.

- **Open auction:** a public RTB process in which any seller and buyer can participate.
- **Private marketplace:** In some cases one (or more) publisher(s) may choose to organize an invitation-only RTB platform where they will invite only a select number of buyers to participate.

Agents include:

- **Demand-side platforms (DSP):** allow buyers to gain access to a multitude of advertising inventories and control and monitor their campaigns from a centralized location.
- **Supply-side platforms (SSP):** help publishers (especially large ones) keep track of and manage their advertising inventories effectively.
- **Ad exchanges:** places where buyers (through their DSPs) and sellers (through SSPs) meet one another. They facilitate the process through the use of automation and auctions.
- **Data management platforms (DMP):** data warehouses, storing huge amounts of (anonymized) data about users. DMPs add value by using the information provided by SSPs to help buyers improve their targeting and performance.

Familiarizing yourself with the basics of programmatic advertising buying in these bulleted lists can make the process less of a mystery and can increase your team's comfort-level.

#103 PLAN YOUR PROGRAMMATIC STRATEGY ACCORDING TO BUSINESS GOALS

Experimenting blindly with programmatic ad buying can turn out to be very costly. You should take the time to align your programmatic initiative to your overall business strategy, not just to short-term advertising goals. Then compare these goals against your overall business goals to have a better understanding of ROI potential.

Cost Per Action (CPA) is often used as a universal measure in digital advertising, yet its efficiency as a guide is not always reliable. Here are some cases in which other KPIs might be more relevant:

- **A business model is built on customer engagement and retention** (e.g., most subscription businesses). CPA might be low for such campaigns, but the business might still see some benefit. Comparing against a metric such as customer lifetime value (CLV) would be much more relevant in these cases.
- **Entering a new market**: CPA may initially appear high in this situation, but it does not include the positive impact advertising campaigns have on improving brand awareness. Look for the financial effect future customers will have. This is not just an exercise in manipulating statistics, but a real business investment.

#104 PROVIDE AND DEMAND TRANSPARENCY

You can and should employ the services of multiple DSPs in the quest to get the best possible ROI. However, you'll always want to make sure they provide (and receive in return) the highest level of transparency. You'll need free-flowing information to make the collaboration work.

It's crucial to understand how campaigns are structured in order to make sure you get the best result for your money. You have to be able to provide feedback on the structure of the campaign in order to avoid simple but costly mistakes.

For agencies and DSPs, getting timely information (i.e., more than once a week) from their clients means they can optimize their campaigns and provide better results. Even when working with multiple partners, it is always better to provide transparent information about the performance of each. Keep this need for transparency foremost in your mind as you deal with DSPs, and the results will speak for themselves.

#105 COMBINE ALL TYPES OF BUYING IN THE OVERALL STRATEGY

No type of auction is necessarily better than any other; the "best" auction will always be the one that gets the best results for you. To reach maximum effectiveness and be able to place your creativity in front of all types of customers, you'll want to integrate various ad marketplaces into your strategy.

For example, you can integrate RTB in open and private marketplaces along with programmatic direct inventories in your campaigns. This will allow you to execute campaigns with different end goals: identifying new audiences (prospecting), building trust with an audience (nurturing), or reaching existing audiences (retargeting).

#106 RUN CAMPAIGNS ALONG THE ENTIRE FUNNEL

You should run your campaigns along the entire funnel from prospecting, through nurturing, and into the retargeting stage. Buying media in this fashion generates multitudes of data and also greatly increases the speed by which the algorithms will "learn" and improve their own efficiency.

#107 USE PROGRAMMATIC FOR TESTING

Due to its speed and scale, programmatic ad buying is a great tool for testing every aspect of a digital media campaign. You'll generate plenty of "big data" in the process, and you want to make sure you get the most out of it you can.

So use programmatic to test your creative efforts. Overall messaging, as well as minor details such as colors, buttons, etc., are excellent targets for evaluation. Find out what's working, and what's not. Keep track, and tweak appropriately. Since context is very important to the success of any programmatic campaign, it's vital to learn how various creative assets work in a variety of different contexts.

It is also excellent for experimenting with strategic aspects of your campaign. Companies can "relax" their criteria when targeting certain audiences in order to discover new customer segments, which they may not yet be aware of. This kind of testing and experimentation can let you grow your target list in an effective way.

#108 TRUST THE MACHINE . . .

Relying on machine learning is the basis of programmatic buying success. There is simply no alternative to computing power in this type of marketing due to its high-speed and high-volume capabilities. To use these assets effectively, marketers must separate themselves from the instinct to always fiddle with the results, and let computers do their job.

In prior sections, we've reviewed the aspects of programmatic ad buying that can, and should, be tweaked. However, interrupting a campaign with constant manual input prevents algorithms from learning and improving performance. This hurts subsequent runs of the same campaign. Algorithms can discover new information, but only if you relax your criteria and allow the learning to happen.

#109 . . . BUT COMBINE DATA WITH MANUAL INPUT

The scalability of programmatic works both ways; it has the potential to multiply positive findings, but mistakes can also be costly on a greater scale. Keep a close eye on your operations, and take action if something goes amiss. We've just said to "let the machine learning happen," but when it appears that the machine is *not* learning, the time is right for you to investigate the problem.

Leaving it to the algorithms doesn't mean you can't observe and assess progress. Campaigns can be customized to stop running on weekends or avoid certain channels, such as Facebook. If your machine learning shows that such channels aren't right for you, for example, go ahead and pull the trigger on making a change.

#110 FIND RELIABLE PARTNERS

Not all DSPs are created equal. There is a huge degree of variability between them when it comes to how sophisticated, transparent, and ultimately effective they are. When it comes to choosing a DSP, you need to consider the following aspects:

- **Inventory**: The number of publishers offering ad space is almost infinite, and most larger DSPs have established relationships with the biggest ad exchanges.
- **Optimization**: Does the platform offer scalability? Is it based on line items, or does it allow dynamic allocation of resources for best results? Ask these questions to ensure your experience is optimized.
- **Targeting**: What level of targeting does the DSP offer? Is it possible to use cookies to retarget across the whole breadth of the inventory offered by the DSP?
- **Data**: Does the DSP have access to third-party data overlays? Without additional third-party data, any campaign is bound to be much less effective, expending valuable resources to run learning cycles that could otherwise be skipped.
- **Platform costs**: These tend to be variable based on how much a client is ready to spend. Most DSPs include the CPM

costs in their fees, and agencies add their compensation on top of this number.

- **Support:** If you are just getting started with programmatic, support will probably come from a partner agency, which will help you set up your campaign. It is always important to know what level of support the DSP has to offer, and if there is additional cost associated with it. Ask about support at the outset so you aren't surprised by charges.
- **Reporting:** Marketers rely on data in order to optimize their programmatic campaigns. Extensive and timely reports can be exported in one format suitable for further analysis, and that should be one of the leading requirements when choosing a partner.

While all these technical details are important, you should also inquire about the efficiency of your potential partners. Always ask "What is your win rate?" This is the ultimate measure when it comes to the performance of a buyer-side platform. All advances in the use of technology, algorithms, and third-party data amount to better win rates for the end buyer.

CHAPTER 12
EXPLORING THE BENEFITS OF NATIVE ADVERTISING

Native advertising consists of branded messages placed so well that audiences see them as an organic part of the content they are consuming. Instead of disrupting the viewer's experience on a platform, native ad placements blend into and can even enhance the platform's organic content. They still carry purposeful information that the brand wants to communicate, but it's delivered in a more unusual (and often more effective) way.

In the B2B sphere, purchasing decisions are rarely made spontaneously. Potential customers are usually working with a long buying cycle. By presenting audiences with native ads in the right spot and at the right time, you can gain the familiarity and trustworthiness that you need to close the deal.

Native ads are viewed more frequently than traditional ones, and they perform almost three times better than traditional advertising in terms of brand lift. It's no wonder, then, that an increasing percentage of B2B marketers are already riding the native ads bandwagon. If you'd like to join them, then here are ten tips to consider as you develop your native advertising plan of action.

#111 CREATE A STRATEGY ALIGNED WITH YOUR COMPANY'S GOALS

Your native ad efforts will only deliver impressive results if you set proper goals. Take the time to align your ad ideas with your overall inbound marketing strategy, from the type of content and language used, to the platform and timing.

Each piece of information you've gathered about your target customers should be used to inform your native advertising goals. Demographics, and your target audience's primary pain points, are especially important.

#112 TRY ADVERTORIALS AND SPONSORED CONTENT

Advertising and editorial sponsored content are branded content that are marked as "sponsored," but placed alongside the original publisher's content. It is often displayed in the same format and design to resemble the organic content.

For these advertising options, the media platform and the sponsoring company typically work in close collaboration to create advertorials. In some cases, it is launched directly by the brand, but most of the time it is launched through a media outlet. Either way, the goal is to avoid any interruption in the viewer's experience, while seamlessly informing them of product news and raising awareness about your brand.

When preparing your sponsored content materials, remember that they'll need to fit the organic media environment where they'll live. Your content should be relevant to the platform and provide real value to the audience. Keep the branding tone down and focus on serving the reader. This will mean the difference between a disruptive ad and a skillfully executed native ad.

#113 EXPERIMENT WITH PROMOTED TWEETS

Another intuitive platform for native advertising is Twitter. Eighty-nine percent of its users report utilizing the platform to discover products and services. You can use Twitter native ads to promote a specific event or product launch, or simply to boost brand awareness.

Twitter poses a unique challenge with its strictly enforced character limit. Although the recently launched Twitter Blue subscription offers users the ability to post tweets containing up to 4000 characters, only the first 280 are displayed in the feed, unless the reader clicks a link to expand the text. Therefore, any promotions on this channel need to be short and engaging. Its ad algorithm is what makes it an attractive platform for native ads. The algorithm assesses factors such as who people follow and their re-tweet history in order to determine which promoted tweets to display to them. This allows for very precise targeting, so your message can be served to people who are likely to connect with it.

#114 LAUNCH LINKEDIN SPONSORED UPDATES

Since LinkedIn is the most popular social network for B2B professionals, it's a logical choice to pursue native advertising there as well. You can employ LinkedIn sponsored updates to increase brand awareness and promote content such as articles, videos, infographics, events, or other campaigns. Your branded message appears directly in users' feeds, sandwiched between the regular non-sponsored updates they are reading.

When LinkedIn first launched the native ad option in 2013, tests revealed that sponsored messages achieved very solid results in terms of impressions and new followers. Expanding your audience on LinkedIn's professional network is a smart move. It gets results and allows you to easily reach a target group that's highly relevant to your business goals.

When it comes to creating a powerful LinkedIn ad, there's no secret; be sure to include a brief, catchy headline, succinct copy, and a strong call to action to suggest to readers what their next step should be. As with other native ads, high-quality visuals or even videos can make the content even more successful.

#115 EXPLORE PROMOTED UPDATES ON OTHER SOCIAL NETWORKS

Let's not forget that many other social media channels offer native advertising, including Pinterest, YouTube, Reddit, and Tumblr. Each of these networks can also offer different kinds of audiences that might better suit your marketing goals. You may find that your particular industry happens to have a larger following on one of them.

Another useful platform is Foursquare, which uses geolocation technology to display targeted messages from companies in the vicinity of the user. It's very accurate for local searches, so is especially handy for small or local businesses.

If you're excited to pursue an envelope-pushing strategy, try YouTube's new native ads, which allow for a seamless shopping experience right from a video. Thanks to YouTube's recent algorithm update, "product-centric" videos like tutorials and reviews are now embedded with links to the products featured. These ads are thus an effortless and cutting-edge opportunity for lead generation.

#116 INVEST IN SPONSORED LISTINGS IN SEARCHES

An alternative to social media native ads is creating sponsored listings on websites and search platforms. By buying a sponsored listing, your brand will appear in your viewer's search results. This means that, since your ad is displayed when a viewer uses search terms relevant to your product or service, the viewer is more likely to find your ad helpful. You can thus position your brand on important industry websites.

One of the most popular platforms for sponsored listings is Google text ads. These consist of a short, promotional piece of text and a link leading to a landing page on your company's website. When someone searches for the products and services you provide, they may be served your ad above organic results in their search, as well as in various other places across the Google display network.

#117 PURSUE INTERACTIVE CONTENT

Brands are progressively experimenting with more engaging content forms, and one type that has recently gained a lot of traction is interactive content. A great example is when General Electric promoted its participation in the 2013 Paris Air Show. The industrial giant partnered with BuzzFeed to create a series of sponsored content about aviation. They collaborated to develop and deploy a game called "Flight Mode," in which users could choose an article to read on BuzzFeed by flying a plane over it with their arrow keys.

Another way to use interactive content in your native advertising efforts is to embed ads in video content. There are two main choices for this available: instream and outstream.

Instream ads are placed before, during, and after the video stream and are already being used on well-known platforms like YouTube.

Outstream ads are an option in which video ads are placed among other types of content, such as text or imagery, instead of within another video.

#118 ADAPT ALL CONTENT FOR MOBILE

Mobile is extremely important for native ads. Conversion rates are much higher on mobile, so failing to optimize your content for mobile potentially means missing out on one of the most important parts of your campaign.

The challenge with native advertising on mobile is the size of the screen. Due to the relatively small size of phone screens, it's much easier for a user to perceive a mobile ad as intrusive and disregard it. Thus, you need to create best-of-the-best branded content for mobile and take extra care to provide a valuable user experience for viewers. Interactive content and other inventive formats are optimal, but so are videos and other forms of entertaining, visual content.

You'll also want to make your native ads easily shareable. Before you launch your campaign, test these ads thoroughly. And once it's deployed, track results and gather data that can inform your next mobile campaign.

 ## #119 LEARN TO SPEAK THE NATIVE LANGUAGE

If you want your branded messages to be seen as organic, you'll need to use the "native tongue" of your chosen platform. This is the only way to make your ad truly native, and not something that feels disruptive or disconnected.

Every channel has its own voice with which your brand should integrate. Choose your tone, content, and visuals wisely, and make sure they use the language people tend to use on your chosen platform. Then you can tell compelling stories in a wide variety of contexts. General Electric was playful and fun when published on BuzzFeed, but they tend to take on a much more sophisticated persona when they're in *The Economist*. This makes them most effective in both locations.

To blend your native ads with the channel's organic content effectively, don't make your brand the centerpiece of your messages. You certainly want to communicate your company's name and perhaps a few values and benefits, but focusing too much on these will defeat the point of native ads. Your brand should have presence, but should not be pushy.

#120 EMBRACE TRANSPARENCY TO WIN TRUST

When it comes to advertising, nobody likes to be tricked into believing something. The only way to truly gain the trust of today's consumers is through transparency. In this connection, you'll want to make sure you always include a disclaimer on sponsored content. Platforms usually indicate with an icon or a small note that certain content is paid, so be ready for this. Sometimes they even have a special page dedicated to the partnership between the sponsoring company and the media.

To ensure both transparency and optimal placement of your ads, choose platforms where native ads appear naturally. Twitter and LinkedIn are superior among social media channels for making ads noninvasive, as are Forbes and BuzzFeed in terms of advertorial content.

PART FOUR

LEAD GENERATION

For many marketing professionals, lead generation is the most complex aspect of B2B marketing. Perhaps this is because it can be so multifaceted. Yet, despite its complicated nature, effective tactics exist to address it. Marketers rate social media marketing, SEO tactics, and email marketing as the most effective forms of lead generation.

Whatever the approach, generating quality leads remains the biggest challenge. B2B marketers sometimes have difficulty articulating exactly where their leads come from because they often originate from sources that are not measured in a traditional analysis. For most marketers, about 20 percent come from unknown sources.

To convert leads into customers, you need an ongoing lead generation process that incorporates testing and improving campaigns in a continual fashion. Shortages of staff, budget, and time are the most common obstacles to marketers' success in this area. The same challenge applies to a limited ability to create content, which can also be a major stumbling block.

CHAPTER 13

UNDERSTANDING THE PRINCIPLES OF B2B LEAD GENERATION

Lead generation requires a strategy that focuses on building relationships in a meaningful way while continually evaluating each lead's potential for conversion.

A successful strategy focused on lead generation will typically employ predictive behavioral analytics, automatically adjusted nurturing outlets, deep CRM integrations, and a coordination of online and real-world tactics.

The ten tips in this section can provide you with an introduction to lead generation best practices to enhance the conversion rate and quality of your B2B lead generation campaigns, as well as to improve the ROI of your demand generation programs.

GET STARTED WITH A LEAD GENERATION EXERCISE

More than half of all marketing teams fail to take the important first step of matching their strategies with company needs. You can avoid this pitfall by using the elementary exercise below to reevaluate your company's lead generation strategy. Answering the questions below is a good way to start developing best practices.

Who is your audience?

Your audience should include the broadest demographic possible while still staying relevant. You need to narrow down your audience to just the right amount. One mistake B2B companies frequently make during lead generation is trying to reach an unsegmented audience. Because of this, they're not successful and they end up expending unnecessary resources.

What problem does your company solve?

Instead of relying on a mission statement, marketers need to determine a straightforward answer when it comes to the solutions they bring. What does your product or service do? How does it help people? Articulating a satisfying answer is a vital step in pursuing any lead generation strategy. Evaluate and reevaluate your answer to this question as needed.

What hasn't worked?

When it comes to lead generation, many marketers make the mistake of:

1 | Trying to ride trends and fads in the marketplace.

2 | Only doing what they've always done when it comes to developing leads.

Don't fall into either of these traps—now is the time to analyze your approaches honestly. Find out which methods aren't working, and put them on the backburner. Accept that "we've always done it that way" is a lousy reason to continue doing something in the future. Efficient lead generation requires willingness to be creative, to take managed risks, and to reevaluate the process at every step.

Life Cycle of a Lead

Omnichannel is an approach that incorporates all channels available to you. A solid adoption of the approach should include the following:

Content marketing
Paid search
Organic search
Webinars and live events
Social media programs and outreach
Email marketing
Content syndication
Marketing automation / lead nurturing
Programmatic campaigns
Mobile programs

With an omnichannel approach, you'll have the opportunity to stay in front of potential clients longer, engaging them in a variety of ways until they make a buying decision. Successful campaigns center on implementing strategies that not only generate but also nurture leads to the final sale.

Because it has many elements, building out an omnichannel approach certainly takes some upfront investment. However, when the hard work has been finished, both marketing professionals and sales teams will find themselves powerfully armed to engage with potential customers in a variety of effective ways.

#121 MAXIMIZE CONTENT MARKETING ASSETS

Developing quality content must be a priority for any effective lead generation campaign. Over half of the effort involved in nurturing a client takes place before a prospect ever makes contact with a B2B seller. Marketing assets have already been created and tweaked to maximize their effectiveness.

This means that content marketing is actually responsible for a large segment of lead generation. The top three reasons why B2B companies turn to content marketing are to develop brand

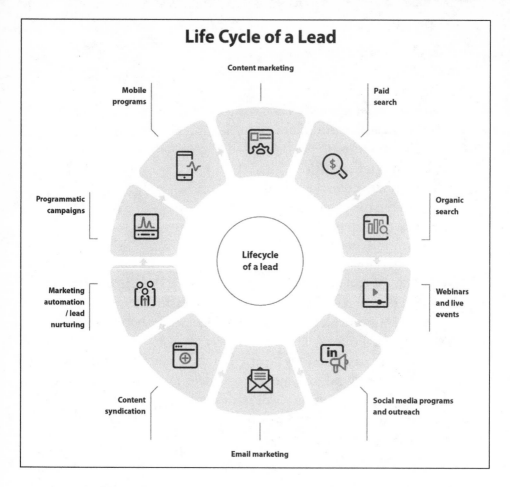

Life Cycle of a Lead

Content marketing

Mobile programs

Paid search

Programmatic campaigns

Organic search

Lifecycle of a lead

Marketing automation / lead nurturing

Webinars and live events

Content syndication

Social media programs and outreach

Email marketing

awareness, generate leads, and boost engagement. Effective marketing assets can help businesses do all three of these things.

Content assets include more than what has already been featured on a blog or a website. They contain new, more compelling, and more targeted information designed to connect with prospective customers. For your content marketing assets to be truly effective, you need to develop natural keyword usage and acquire inbound links from other sites. You should also focus on maintaining the quality and diversity of content assets. You'll have to apply a number of distinct content marketing approaches to reach your target goals for lead generation.

Here are some illuminating facts about how leading B2B marketers are using content assets from a recent report:

- 52 percent of B2B marketers report that their companies plan on increasing content marketing budgets
- Marketers still express difficulty measuring content ROI
- 97 percent of B2B marketers use LinkedIn as a content distribution channel
- 58 percent of B2B marketers use paid search engine marketing, and report that it is the most effective technique

Creating diversified content on a regular basis appears to be one of the biggest struggles that B2B marketers face. Build a physical document that details your content marketing strategy to increase adoption and success rates.

Content marketing should be a long-term strategy. The top metrics for determining the success of lead generation should include the quality and quantity of sales leads that are attributed to online content. Failing to capture these metrics does not indicate a failed strategy, but as long as you have metrics that evaluate interactions, you're making progress.

Effectiveness Ratings for B2B Tactics

Virtual events/webinars/online courses

Research reports

Short articles/posts (less than 3,000 words)

E-books/whitepapers

Case studies

Videos

In-person events

Long articles/posts (more than 3,000 words)

Infographics/charts/data viz/3D models

Livestreaming content

Podcasts

Print magazines or books

The most effective forms of online content, as rated in the Content Marketing Trends chart, include webinars, videos, blogs, case studies, and white papers. These types of content are best used when they feature in-depth industry information. Prospects who engage with them are more likely to become leads, who are then converted into sales.

Gated content, which requires prospects to provide contact information to access downloadable content such as white papers, webinars, and case studies, can benefit your strategy by providing quality lead sources. Gating content can also skew your lead results, however, so consider carefully whether adding a promotion to your gated content will benefit your marketing goals. Make sure to detail which content assets will be gated and which won't be in your documented content marketing strategy.

You can also use additional assets such as case studies and infographics, which around 70 percent of marketers say is valuable to their campaigns. These assets may or may not be gated, but are vital to a comprehensive plan.

#122 OPTIMIZE YOUR LANDING PAGES

Landing pages can serve as the first opportunity to convert a lead and present a solution to your target's immediate need. The purpose of your product or service should be highly visible, easy to read, and easy to understand. Landing pages are not intended to directly sell a product on their own. Rather, they are meant to serve as a touchpoint, which will guide the lead in the right direction along their buying process.

For optimal results, focus on creating a landing page that helps the visitor easily understand your company's purpose. Start with a succinct message that also highlights how your product offers outstanding benefits that meet the needs of your customers.

A clean environment is more likely to persuade a B2B customer than a page with content overload and overly artistic designs. Aim to streamline the page for easy scrolling and minimized page navigation.

The content your prospect is most likely looking for should always be visible and prominent on the landing page.

Links to webinar information and signups may pull in more attendees to these offerings and can be featured on a landing page. Case studies also serve as valuable links from a landing page; prospective clients will take them to management to make their case for a product. Give your potential customers the tools they need to pitch your product internally. Not to mention, glowing reviews from your customers will always help your company stand out.

Any other content that makes a prospect's research easier is worth displaying on a primary landing page:

FAQs
Cheat sheets
Product demonstrations
Ebooks
Gated content (such as white papers)
Video interviews

Remember that the person tasked with researching new products is not necessarily the same person who will make the final purchasing decision. So make sure you provide content both to educate the former and to convince the latter.

Here are some other important factors to keep in mind when developing a landing page:

- **Value proposition**—Your landing page can include the product statement and information.
- **Clarity and intuitiveness of a site**—Is the visitor receiving the right kind of visual cues when they visit your page, and is the information streamlined and complete?
- **Freebies**—Demos, ebooks, or newsletter subscriptions are good to include as additional content.

- **Calls to Action (CTAs)**—scattered across the landing page.
- **Minimal distractions**—All relevant information should be immediately available. A visitor who sees contradictory statements, or is left questioning an offer or a claim, can immediately lose trust in the company.

You can (and should) use the same principles as on your primary landing page to optimize other landing page environments. Your other landing pages may include the following:

Social media—LinkedIn, Facebook, and Twitter
Third party—Google search, your blog site, and ads
Microsites and mobile pages

An ad on a website that asks a user to visit or "like" a page and then takes that user to a makeshift or not fully developed social media page can appear unprofessional. Tailor landing environments to the inbound source. Ensure that landing pages for a mobile campaign are optimized for mobile devices. Don't rely only on video content as primary landing page content. Videos should always remain optional to the information written on the site.

#123 EXPLORE LEAD GENERATION METHODS AND CHANNELS

Developing useful quantities of high-quality leads depends on a thorough understanding of your target market. Often, B2B marketers say they find it difficult to create content directed at an individual's stage in the customer journey. That statistic highlights the importance of using various marketing personas.

Marketing personas are a useful tool that provides better visualization of a target market. You can create personas with information you already have concerning your current client base. Generally, it is useful to develop between three to five personas that accurately represent typical client demographics. These persona outlines can vary, but they should include at least the following information:

Job, title, and role
Demographics (age, gender, education, etc.)
Marketing style/pitch
Goals and challenges

Personas are also associated with real-time metrics to help steer B2B marketers toward the appropriate level of interaction. A basic profile based on market data and combined with a persona's engagement and purchasing behavior gives you a real advantage. Automated marketing software can be successfully leveraged in such situations, as long as you take the time to understand and apply the insight derived from the analytics. And if you use data-driven personas, you will be better positioned to make your product available to a prospect at the right time in the buying decision process

Omnichannel approaches to lead generation are typically distinguished by how seamless they appear. More B2B consumers now expect their interactions to be similar to their B2C interactions. A truly effective omnichannel approach will support their needs and continue as one fluid conversation across whatever platform the potential customers use.

The importance of seamless experience in omnichannel marketing:

- 73 percent of B2B buyers would feel satisfied with an experience similar to those offered to B2C consumers.
- Over 80 percent of B2B buyers now prefer placing orders and making payments through digital commerce and online shopping systems.
- The top challenges for B2B companies in omnichannel marketing are technology integration and customer data sharing.

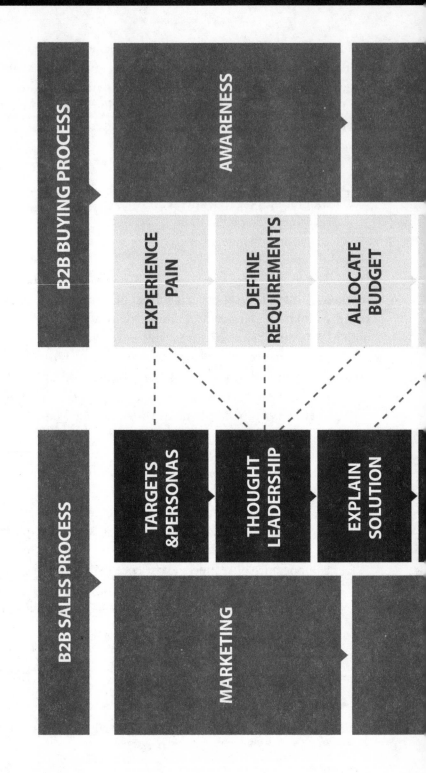

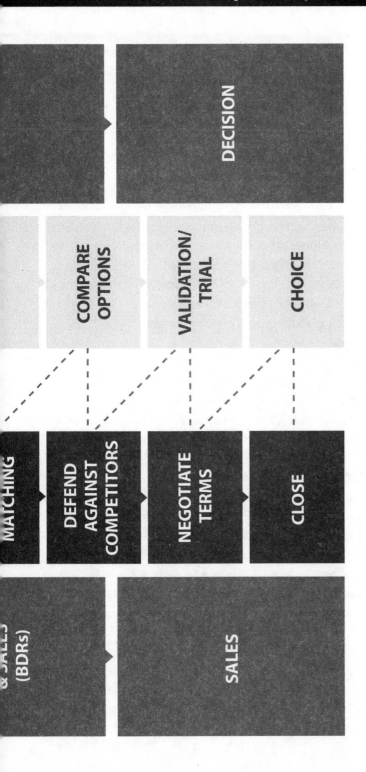

DECISION

COMPARE OPTIONS

VALIDATION/ TRIAL

CHOICE

MATCHING

DEFEND AGAINST COMPETITORS

NEGOTIATE TERMS

CLOSE

& SALES (BDRs)

SALES

- 90 percent of B2B buyers are more likely to buy after reading positive reviews, but only 20 percent of B2B marketers add these assets to their marketing campaigns.

Companies that embrace the changing omnichannel environment that consumers expect are able to enjoy higher quality leads, in greater quantities. Customers secured through a seamless and information-driven experience are proven to be more likely to remain loyal.

It's important to choose several distinctive approaches to generate leads. Keep the number of methods you employ under ten to ensure that your team can fulfill the obligations of each method. You'll always want to extract data from these methods to continually improve what works and change what does not.

The following methods are strongly recommended:

- **Paid Search vs. Organic Search**—Organic searches drive 53 percent of all website visits, while paid search only accounts for 15 percent. Considering that most B2B consumers start looking for products online, your best bet is to focus on improving site visibility on search engines and not relying exclusively on paid search.
- **Content Marketing**—Diversify content and focus on providing relevant information to personas.
- **Webinars and Live Events**—Event-based approaches are a great way to isolate interested parties from those who are just browsing. They also present an excellent opportunity for personal interaction in a way other approaches don't.
- **Social Media Programs and Outreach**—Social media is vital to personifying a brand. Prospects look to social media for genuine but non-invasive interactions. These platforms can also quickly spread important information regarding promotions and product features. B2B marketers regularly post content on six different social media sites on average, with LinkedIn and Twitter being the most frequently used.

- **Email Marketing**—This method still has an incredibly high ROI rate. Email marketing platforms also offer a valuable way to measure lead generation opportunities.
- **Content Syndication**—A measurable solution, it helps B2B marketers deploy information throughout the web. RSS feeds about a client or non-competitor's site are the most commonly used content syndication tactics. Pitches for syndication should always highlight why a site would find the information relevant.
- **Programmatic Campaigns**—These campaigns commonly include programmatic advertising and ad retargeting. Partnering with a programmatic specialist can improve the number of prospects a company receives while the automated campaigns take just minutes a day to monitor.
- **Mobile Programs**—Focus on providing content through informational apps. It's also a best practice to create a demo app so that prospects can improve their understanding of your product at their leisure. All app interactions are measurable, and the number of downloads will impart valuable lead information.

#124   IMPLEMENT LEAD VALIDATION TACTICS

A firm rule of marketing is that reliable leads equal a greater return. An omnichannel lead generation approach has many benefits, but it can also increase the likelihood of acquiring unreliable leads. Obviously, this is something you'll have to be aware of and address. You can combat this potential issue by implementing some lead validation tactics.

If you have a campaign that you're concerned could be fraught with unreliable information, the best approach is outsourcing lead validation. Outsourcing also saves valuable time that can then be used to focus on reliable leads that have been garnered through organic searches.

Outsourcing lead validation can be extremely useful if you are running large marketing campaigns. You may receive hundreds (or even thousands) of emails, names, phone numbers, or some combination of these inputs. Those contact cards will need to be checked out by a reliable source. Companies who work specifically in lead validation have access to huge databases that contain reliable and up-to-date contact information. The validation company can quickly provide you with an accurate report that can then be processed in your lead nurturing stream.

Possibly the most important tool for lead validation is the CRM system. It can flag individual leads that have been validated through a webinar so you can nurture them. It can also potentially do this for all organic search contacts.

Anyone whose information appears in more than one campaign platform should also be flagged. A well-maintained CRM system even has the potential to completely eliminate the need for outsourced lead validation services. Many CRM platforms will also integrate with email marketing, social media, and event management systems. The information is all compiled and analyzed in one centralized hub.

However, an underutilized system is virtually worthless in validating leads. CRM management, cleanup, and use must become part of the daily workflow in order for a lead validation system to be successful.

Unfortunately, the majority of CRMs on the market today do not have intuitive interfaces. This is changing, but the industry is not yet where it needs to be in terms of usability. Training and top-down mandated use are the most effective ways to successfully incorporate CRM utilization in a lead generation pipeline.

#125 EMPLOY LEAD NURTURING AND SCORING

An intimate understanding of the buyer persona is vital to the lead nurturing and scoring process. You have to be able to identify subtle signals in prospect interaction within parts of a campaign in order to take action effectively. You must always be ready to engage in a conversation with the lead at the appropriate time.

In this stage, a lead has been identified with either multiple site interactions on the same site or appearances in a variety of platforms. The lead may even have requested further information about a product, but indicated they were uninterested in pursuing a dialogue at the time. At this point, a lead should be scored, and either moved further down in the buying process or continue being nurtured.

Failing to properly nurture a prospect often limits the sales team's ability to complete the buying process. Build brand awareness for those in the nurturing cycle on a group level by creating and delivering content that is helpful to their decision-making process.

Over time, companies who utilize personas will often see patterns emerge. Certain personas will stay in the nurturing stream longer than others. Measure and use this information to determine how to approach future leads that meet similar persona qualifications when it comes to when and how you make contact, deploy content, and follow up.

Using Lead Scoring and Lead Grading

Lead Scoring → Takes prospect's activity & interactions into account → ✓ Great for measuring: **Interest**

Lead Grading → Uses information about prospect's size and industry → ✓ Great for measuring: **Fit**

Around 58 percent of B2B companies use some sort of lead scoring system. Lead scoring requires careful parameters created by knowledgeable people engaged in the sales pipeline. To be effective, you'll want to have predetermined categories representing a lead's level of interest in the company's product.

The point person who receives inbound requests ought to be the one who fits the lead into one the following categories:

Uninterested
Interested in learning more
Comparing different company products
Ready for a conversation

Some organizations use the terms *marketing-qualified* or *sales-qualified* to describe these stages. One prospect may go through a cycle several times before they are ready to be approached.

Along with scoring, you should make note of a prospect's role within a B2B prospective company. Is this prospect a decision-maker? A second-level manager? Or perhaps an assistant who has been tasked with gathering information? Let the person's level of influence guide where a company is placed into the nurturing stream. A personalized scoring system can be more beneficial than an auto-mated process for this purpose.

New buyers drive this process. They should be guided, not pushed, toward a higher level in the buyer's cycle. There may be prospects who fall from a point of readiness back into a nurturing stream for a time. It's okay if this occasionally happens; you just have to make sure that when a product is needed, your company is the one that comes to mind.

Before those closest to making a purchase are sent to the sales team, your marketing departments should work together to hash out the details on the prospective client.

Lead information can range from something vague (like the prospect's persona) to more specific data such as stats on the client's industry, role, and company revenue. This can also include detail about the lead's activities and interests. If you have this information at hand, you are more likely ready for a stronger buyer-consumer relationship.

#126 CHOOSE THE RIGHT BUSINESS DEVELOPMENT REPRESENTATIVES

Business development representatives (BDRs) have a unique role. They serve as a liaison between the company and the client. These individuals are always looking at the bigger picture, both for the company and for its potential growth. When used effectively, they create and maintain relationships with the goal of developing customer loyalty and retention.

Companies may structure their business development departments in a number of different ways, but whatever the structure, representatives should work closely with marketers and data analysts. They will often be called upon to interface with prospective clients at the moment they are ready to seriously consider the company's product.

BDRs should be both friendly and extremely knowledgeable about the product or service being offered. In most situations, their goal is to make a personal connection with a prospect and be a familiar touchpoint.

These representatives are the ones who work live events and may serve as the face of your company. Look for a BDR to run demonstrations or to visit a company for an in-person look at a product. Instead of focusing on making just one sale, they will focus on networking to find further prospects and on making connections with decision-makers in prospective companies.

The process for B2B sales is often drawn out over a period of months or years. Pitches that successfully convince a company to adopt a new product can take time. A BDR is in the perfect position to continue a higher level of prospect nurturing. They know when a company is ready and understand about waiting on the approval process.

Of all the people involved in a sales pipeline, BDRs need to have the best understanding of the marketplace. To do this, instead of using industry standard practices, they need to be looking specifically at their company's goals and matching those with the needs of their target markets. They may also be responsible for updating and adjusting the buyer personas as needed.

After a lead has been developed into a sale, the BDR's role is still not complete. They are then responsible for the final stage in the sales cycle, the one which leads to retention and loyalty. They need to follow up with existing clients, ensure product satisfaction, and coordinate any customer service needs. They are also responsible for informing existing clients about new product additions and future purchasing opportunities.

 ## #127 MAKE THE MOVE TOWARDS A SALE

Moving toward a sale can either enhance or destroy a lead connection. Because of this, knowledge of the client is vital when deciding to act. By the time you're ready to consider a move, a successful lead generation campaign will have already worked on a prospect from all angles in order to create a seamless buying process.

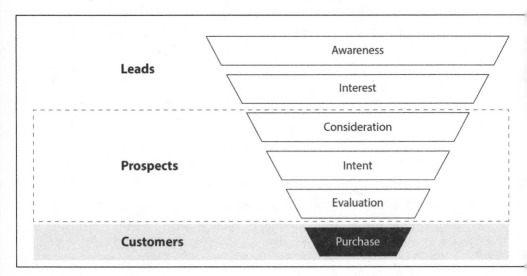

A distracted and shortsighted sales team can create problems for you. Ninety percent of sales and marketing professionals report lack of alignment with regards to strategies and processes. What are they doing instead? They're working in a silo. This leads to the loss of potential annual revenue growth of up to 39 percent. So one of the most important ways you can drive growth is by ensuring that marketing, business development, and sales all work seamlessly together.

A successful lead generation process should lead to a natural sale. Your team should include a mixture of professionals at all levels who can focus on one subgroup from lead identification to closing. Every individual who connects with a lead should be kept up to date on the lead's history.

Business development, sales, or a combination of the two are usually responsible for providing price points and negotiating the final terms of the sale. The reality is that, if a lead generation process has worked, the salesperson is only responsible for taking care of the details and answering any last-minute questions a customer may have. However, the sales teams can accelerate the buying process at this point in the sales cycle.

The average length of time for a lead to become an opportunity in a B2B buying cycle is eighty-four days. They also found that, from there, it takes an average of eighteen days to complete a sale. By the time a prospect gets to sales, the deal should be ready to close. And if a deal is ever lost in the sales cycle, then take the time to get feedback on the loss and use that information to improve the sales process.

CHAPTER 14

POSING THE RIGHT QUESTIONS TO YOUR LEAD GENERATION VENDOR

Many companies outsource their lead generation efforts to independent vendors. These vendors are experts in finding and establishing a relationship with potential customers who are an ideal fit for your business.

An increasing number of these vendors offer such services with varying degrees of success. If you're at the point of choosing such a vendor, it's good to know what to look for and how to make an informed selection. Start by asking questions that will give you a chance to get to know the company better. Make sure they have the experience and relationships that will help yield more customers for your business.

Here are the twenty-five most important questions you should ask your potential lead generation partner in order to make sure they will bring a positive impact to your business.

 ## #128 CHECK THEIR INDUSTRY EXPERIENCE

Your lead gen partner should know and have experience in the industry you operate in. Vet them for industry knowledge and experience in this connection. You'll want to make sure that the company you choose to work with:

A) Knows the people you want to target.
B) Knows how to talk to them in the language they actually use.

#129 INQUIRE ABOUT THEIR PARTNERS AND NETWORK FOR CONTACT DISTRIBUTION

Whenever you engage in lead generation, the quality of the publications where your content can appear is one of the most important factors for success. The vendor company you are considering should be able to present you with an extensive list of publishers with whom they can work at a moment's notice.

Develop a strong understanding of where your content is likely to appear and make sure the audience who will see it is aligned with your target segments. That way, your business is much more likely to receive new customers, thus increasing the ROI of the campaign.

#130 UNDERSTAND IF YOUR VENDOR CAN SPOTLIGHT YOUR CONTENT

It's not enough for your vendor to simply bring quantity; they also have to bring quality. Relevance matters. The volume of marketing materials published by companies today is staggeringly enormous. However, much of it is ineffective because of where and how it is positioned. Having your content featured in the right places can make all the difference.

Experienced lead gen companies have dynamic relationships with their partner publishers, which allow them to get their customers' content in front of the right eyes. As part of the deal, your partner should be able to guarantee that your content will be given premium placement on a number of sites.

#131 SEE WHO THEIR CURRENT CLIENTS ARE

Your prospective partner should be comfortable demonstrating some of the work they've already done. If they have experience in your field, they should be able to demonstrate that by mentioning companies in the same industry with whom they have worked. Be very cautious when dealing with a prospective partner who can't or won't do this.

You can follow up by asking for permission to speak with some of these customers; if the vendor is confident in the services they provide, they should be happy to provide referrals.

ASK IF THEY TURN DOWN CLIENTS

No one likes to miss opportunities to bring more revenue to their business, but every good lead gen vendor knows that their success depends on the success of their customers. Some customers are a bad fit, or simply beyond help. Your partner should be brave enough to say no if they feel their field of expertise falls outside the needs of a potential customer.

#133 READ THEIR SUCCESS STORIES, AND ASK ABOUT FAILURES TOO

It should be easy for a lead gen company to provide examples of clients that experienced great benefit from working with them. So certainly ask for case studies to learn more about the best ways to structure such campaigns.

However, you shouldn't forget to ask about cases where the vendor wasn't so successful in helping the client. Do not expect to see a full case study, but any honest vendor you're considering should be able to talk frankly and openly about such occasions and be able to tell you what they managed to learn from them.

#134 CHECK WHAT KPIs THEY WILL USE TO MEASURE THE SUCCESS OF CAMPAIGNS

Both sides of the partnership should be using the same performance indicators to measure the success of the campaigns you'll be running together. A number of standard metrics are generally used throughout the industry: downloads (of content), opportunities generated, and appointments set. Agree on a set of metrics that align with your business goals. If you are tracking different metrics, it might be because each side is after a different objective.

You can also use KPIs as a tool to measure the past performance of each potential partner in previous campaigns. This may be useful when comparing and assessing different lead gen partners.

#135 TALK ABOUT THE ORIGIN OF LEADS

Knowing how your potential partner collects data should be a top priority for a number of reasons. It can help you get an idea of how specialized they have become in your industry or area. It can also help you figure out how legitimate and experienced your potential partner is. In content marketing, seeing a list of the databases that your vendor uses can speak volumes about the level of their commitment in the industry.

#136 ASK IF THEY RE-SELL LEADS

Unique leads are of a much higher quality (and cost) than shared leads. In some cases, leads can be sold to a number of competing companies. Obviously, you do not want to put yourself in a position where your leads will be resold by a partner. The best way to protect yourself against this practice is by discussing who's going to own the final database.

Another method of reselling leads occurs when a company monetizes its database by sharing it with other lead gen vendors. You want to avoid companies who practice this at all costs, because the leads they provide to you will likely have much lower conversion rates. As leads get contacted by numerous lead gen vendors, they start to perceive such interactions as much more invasive (spammy), leading to a massive drop in engagement.

 ## INQUIRE ABOUT THE FILTERING AND #137 TARGETING OF CRITERIA THEY PROVIDE FOR LEADS

Ensure that your lead gen partner enables you to reach the right audience for your business. Find out what kind of filtering your selected vendor offers. This will have a huge impact on the success of your campaigns and your ROI.

 ## SEE WHAT INFORMATION THEY #138 COLLECT ON LEADS

Make sure you're not asking leads to submit the same information over and over again. Competent publishers and lead gen vendors should collect the bulk of all relevant information about readers upon sign up. They should also fill out their detailed request forms with this data. If you ask leads to fill out their details more than once, you are very likely to see a high drop in conversion rate, or a high percentage of fake information. Make sure your partner knows how to navigate this.

 ## CHECK IF THEY OUTSOURCE OR #139 OFFSHORE

There is nothing wrong with outsourcing part of the work on the campaign. Yet it is appropriate for you, as a customer, to know exactly how the campaign will be performed and managed. If you trust your brand name to your partner, it makes sense to know at all times who is going to be representing your brand, and what measures your partner will be taking to preserve its value.

Once you're done getting to know the company, move to more detailed questions about structuring your partnership with the lead generation vendor.

 ## #140 ENSURE THAT THEIR ONBOARDING PROCESS WORKS FOR YOU

Your lead generation partner will be representing your brand in its earliest phase of interaction with future customers. That's why it is so important that the vendor you choose has a clear understanding of your brand, your offering, where their efforts are going to fit in, and how they are ultimately going to complement your business processes.

Discuss and agree on how you are going to structure the initial training, so that your partner will learn the most important things about your business and your brand.

#141 GET AN IDEA ABOUT THEIR QUALIFICATION CRITERIA

No matter what method of payment you agree to (which will be covered in one of the following sections), the number of leads produced during the partnership is surely going to be one of the most important measures of your vendor's performance. Discuss and agree on a definition of what makes a lead a billable opportunity.

To make sure your partner gives you enough room to influence the process, don't hesitate to have your say. Otherwise you might end up being unhappy with the final results, even if they technically fulfill the criteria. Now is not the time to be subtle. Speak up and be clear on what you expect to pay for.

ASK WHAT KIND OF REPORTING AND STATISTICS THEY PROVIDE

Beyond knowing which KPIs your partner will use to measure success, you'll also want to measure the performance of your content personally (along different segments and groups). Having access to this kind of data can also guide your content production data, thus greatly increasing the efficiency of your campaigns.

 ## MAKE SURE THAT THEIR CHARGING SYSTEM FITS YOU

When it comes to compensation, there are two standard ways that the arrangement can be structured:

1 | A monthly fee   **2** | Pay per performance: the vendor is paid based upon the number of warm leads/appointments/opportunities generated

Neither compensation structure is inherently better than the other. The one you employ depends on past history, personal preference, and on the specifics of your campaign. If you choose to pay per performance, be very careful with the definition you agree on when it comes to what makes a billable lead. And with a periodic fee, it's essential to develop a service level agreement, which is a set of commitments made by both sides on the minimum work to be done during the billing period.

 ## DOUBLE CHECK IF THERE ARE ADDITIONAL OR SETUP FEES INVOLVED

Some lead gen vendors charge additional fees as part of total campaign compensation. Educate yourself on this during your research process, so that you can take this information into account when comparing providers and making a final decision. A fee should not necessarily be a deal breaker, but nobody likes an unexpected surprise.

#145 SEE IF THE CONTRACT TERMS SATISFY YOU

There's a good reason why most folks are resistant to long-term contracts. Beware of vendors who want to lock in a lengthy commitment without any flexibility even before the partnership takes off. Serious lead gen partners should be happy to get the chance to prove the value of their efforts by leaving the arrangement open-ended. Even if everything looks and sounds great at the outset, don't jump into a long-term relationship too soon.

#146 ENSURE THAT THEIR SYSTEMS INTEGRATE WITH YOUR SOFTWARE

Make sure your vendor's solution can be linked to your systems for quick and easy transfer of leads to your sales department. The lead delivery format from your lead gen company should be able to link with your current CRM solution. Without this kind of integration, you are likely to spend countless hours manually adding leads from spreadsheets into your platform. Let your vendor know what system you use, and ask them how they will accommodate this.

#147 AGREE ABOUT OWNERSHIP OF THE FINAL DATABASE

Get a commitment that identifies you as the final owner of the information you receive during the partnership. This will help you guarantee that the leads collected during the campaign won't be resold later to another client after your partnership has run out.

This will also give you peace of mind that the leads you're getting are not themselves being reused from a previous campaign, thus lowering their general quality.

#148 GET CLARITY ABOUT WHAT HAPPENS WHEN A LEAD IS TRANSFERRED

In addition to the integration between your partner's systems and your own software, you should also discuss what additional information will be passed along with the lead and in what format. Every aspect of the process should be outlined.

#149 DISCUSS EXPECTATIONS ABOUT THE TIMING OF THE FIRST LEAD

Let's say you've finally made a decision on a lead generation partner and agreed on all details of the partnership. Now your sales team is ready to take those opportunities and turn them into loyal customers! But unfortunately, they have no one to talk to yet, because you haven't managed their expectations.

You can avoid this kind of situation by clarifying with the vendor how long it is going to take for the campaign to start producing leads and then preparing your sales team for that timeline. Make sure to check with your partner about what they expect to be able to deliver.

#150 SET RESPONSIBILITY FOR UPDATING CONTENT

Your marketing collateral should be constantly monitored and updated to ensure it remains relevant and attractive to your target audience.

Consider outsourcing this process (or at least part of it) to your lead gen partner or to another industry expert. As your content inventory grows, keeping it up to date is likely to become increasingly time-consuming. Using a trusted partner's assistance can be the support you need to keep things updated.

#151 DEFINE HOW YOU WILL GRADE SUCCESS OR ADJUST IN CASE OF UNDERPERFORMANCE

As they do in so many situations, things often look the most promising before you actually start the work. At the outset, we hope that campaigns work well and produce the results we want without any extra effort.

Unfortunately, that's not always how it goes. Hope for the best, but be prepared for worst-case scenarios by agreeing on a project timeframe with your partner. That way, you can be prepared to make adjustments if you aren't happy with the results.

#152 ASK WHY YOU SHOULDN'T DEVELOP LEAD GEN INTERNALLY

Insourcing is always a possibility. Play devil's advocate and ask a potential partner why you shouldn't just do it yourself. The question gives your potential partner the opportunity to explain how they are going to add value to your business. And look out for business partners who get defensive when you ask this question. It might signal they are not so confident in their ability to create real value for your company.

Lead Gen Vendors Cheat Sheet
Questions for Partners

1. What's your industry experience?
2. Who are your partners? Where can you place my content?
3. In how many places can you ensure my content will be spotlighted?
4. Who are your current clients?
5. Do you ever turn down clients? If so, why?
6. What are your biggest success stories? How about your biggest failures? What would you have done differently in those situations?
7. What KPIs do you use to measure the success of your campaigns?
8. Where are your leads currently coming from?
9. Do you resell leads?
10. What kind of filtering/targeting criteria do you provide for leads?
11. What information do you collect on leads? Do you pre-populate forms?
12. Do you outsource/offshore? If so, what aspects of the campaign?
13. What is the onboarding process going to look like?
14. What are the qualification criteria going to look like?
15. What kind of reporting/statistics do you provide?
16. How do you charge your clients?
17. Are there any additional/setup fees involved in a campaign with you?
18. Do I need to sign a long-term contract to do business with you?
19. Will your systems integrate with my software?
20. Who will own the final database?
21. What exactly happens when a lead is transferred?
22. After we sign a contract, when can I expect the first lead to come in?
23. Who's going to be responsible for updating content?
24. How are we going to grade the success of the campaign and make changes if it's underperforming?
25. Just to play devil's advocate, can I ask why we shouldn't just develop lead gen internally?

CHAPTER 15

AMPLIFYING ACCOUNT-BASED MARKETING

O ver the last few years, account-based marketing (ABM) has emerged as the preferred B2B marketing tactic. According to a recent report by ITSMA and ABM Leadership Alliance, 71 percent of marketers who utilized ABM in their strategies reported a higher ROI than traditional marketing. This would be one of the many reasons why more people globally will start to adopt ABM as a strategy.

Therefore, to remain competitive, you need an effective ABM strategy. However, the true challenge with ABM is not implementing it (you're probably already doing it to some degree), but expanding your capabilities to the point where you use it effectively on a larger scale.

In the following pages, we'll explore just a few of the techniques that you can use to engage with these target accounts digitally.

WHAT IS ABM?

ABM adds value to your business by focusing on accounts that are more likely to convert or generate higher revenue.

Instead of trying to acquire customers from a large pool of leads, ABM marketers start by identifying the best possible customers (down to the actual companies) and chasing only those. Many professionals compare the two strategies to fishing. Inbound marketing is like casting a wide fishing net with the hope that at least something edible will bite, whereas ABM is like fishing with a spear, focusing on one (tasty) target from the beginning.

In conventional demand generation, marketers use several tactics to reach the widest possible audience. Their hope is that there are at least a few good leads in the larger pool that will convert into customers. In essence, it looks something like this:

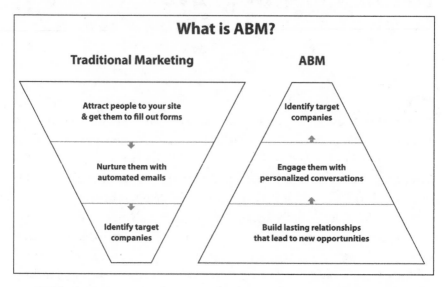

With ABM, your resources are focused on a few prospects that promise more significant returns. By creating personalized, targeted messaging and content that will help attract and engage your target accounts, you can maximize conversions and help reduce wasted time and budget.

WHY ABM WORKS

Marketers have recently adopted ABM for its ability to perform two key tasks:

- Understanding the needs and goals of current and potential customers.
- Tailoring the interactions you have with those high-value prospects based on the knowledge you have about their requirements.

It Is Efficient

Some experts even call it "zero-waste marketing" because of how efficient it is. By focusing only on the most lucrative prospects, ABM marketers avoid wasting resources on leads that will never convert.

Creates a Strong Relationship between Marketing and Sales

The ABM approach is great at creating strong alignment between the goals of the sales and marketing teams. By getting everyone on the same page, ABM creates a strong bond between those people on your team who are responsible for identifying the leads, and those who are closing them.

Helps You Deliver Better Customer Experience

- ABM allows you to focus on the individuals who participate in the decision-making process.
- The content and campaigns your team creates will be personalized to the specific individuals within each account.

What you end up with is a custom-made approach that helps you understand your customers better and form strong relationships with them, thus delivering a better experience.

Generates Higher ROI

ABM helps businesses attract higher-value customers because you're focused on identifying your ideal prospects and then figuring out the best ways to close them. Unlike with previous tactics where you would spend a lot of time and energy on many different clients to barely see the results, with ABM, most of the time and resources spent will yield results.

#153 THE SECRET TO ABM SUCCESS IS DATA

Collecting and leveraging data is key to ABM success. Here are some of the ways that data can improve your ABM campaigns:

- **Selecting better targets:** Access to good data and the ability to analyze it allow you to find the highest-yielding targets in your audience.
- **Measuring the success of an ABM program:** Because ABM is so detailed, you can build models and come up with a set of KPIs for each specific target. Then you can use this data to understand the overall effectiveness of your strategy.
- **Personalization:** ABM relies heavily on delivering high-quality content and using it to convert key targets into customers. However, that would be very hard to achieve without personalizing each campaign to meet individual customer needs. Data delivers insights that help marketers deliver the right message to the right prospect at the right time.

#154 HOW TO SCALE YOUR ABM PROGRAM

Finding the right set of accounts to target with your ABM program is just half the battle. Identifying the right channels that will allow you to connect with these accounts is just as important.

Following are some of the best channels for companies using ABM to connect and engage with customers digitally.

#155 USE PAID SOCIAL MEDIA

Social media advertising on Facebook, LinkedIn, and Twitter is an effective way to get your brand and content in front of the right account contacts because of its superior targeting capabilities.

Facebook allows you to create custom audiences for your advertisement based on several factors, including email address, phone number, name, and location. This tool can help you expand your targetable market and find new accounts that have the potential to become high-value customers. Then, you can deliver highly targeted content to those leads right in their news feed.

Facebook also offers powerful remarketing tools, such as Facebook Pixel, a snippet of code you install on your website. Using this website traffic data, you can present ads to target accounts that have expressed interest in your brand by visiting your website.

Twitter provides similar advertising opportunities with Tailored Audiences on Twitter. You can upload a list of emails or @handles and use that to target only relevant leads or influencers. Website tags and conversion tracking allow you to connect with customers who have visited your website or taken specific actions inside your app.

LinkedIn is one of the best platforms for B2B marketers, especially for those engaging in ABM. Like other networks, LinkedIn provides opportunities to target users based on fixed criteria. One of the most useful aspects of LinkedIn advertising is the option to target people from specific companies. You can use this feature to find and connect with the key influencers within their target accounts.

#156 CONTENT SYNDICATION TO EXPAND YOUR AUDIENCE

Educating leads, thwarting objections, and answering questions are just a few of the things that can be achieved with content. However, over the last few years, getting that content in front of its intended audience has emerged as one of the biggest challenges in this area.

Content syndication allows you to expand your reach and get your content in front of the right people at the right companies. It is also a cost-effective tactic because content syndication is generally priced on a cost-per-lead (CPL) basis. This means that when you provide your target account list to the right content syndication network, you will only pay for leads who match all your criteria (including company name and title) and have interacted with your content.

Before you start syndicating content, you will want to be very precise with your targeting. Think about which syndication networks will help you reach your ideal audience as well as the specific types of content that will appeal to the key stakeholders. You should also consider what type of syndication will be most beneficial for your ABM campaign. Some publishers or syndicators will host the content on their site while others will house just a snippet or include a link back to your own site.

#157 MULTICHANNEL LEAD NURTURING

When you think about lead nurturing, the first thing that comes to your mind might be email marketing. However, it is important that you go beyond creating email campaigns, so a multichannel approach is typically most successful. This will put you in touch with the target account's key players and stay top-of-mind while building a solid relationship.

Traditionally, these channels include email, blogs, and social media. But increasingly, we are seeing brands succeed through the use of chat. This way you have several opportunities to reach your audience while providing valuable content that nurtures your relationship. Remember, any engaging content that you promote through your multiple channels should be targeted to your audience with topics and language that appeals to them most.

Moreover, you need to make sure you provide an experience that's both customized to their needs and consistent across channels. Predictive analytics, marketing automation, and chatbots are invaluable tools that allow marketers to engage with their customers at scale.

By implementing an analytics tool, you can collect and analyze the behavior of individuals within your target accounts across channels. This will help you understand not only what topics they care about, but also where they spend their time.

#158 WEBINARS AND VIRTUAL CONFERENCES

Hosting a virtual event or webinar is the perfect way to engage key players in this current climate, no matter where they are located.

However, that doesn't mean that the one-size-fits-all approach works with webinars. The virtual event should be informative and offer the attendee something they may not be able to get anywhere else. For instance, you might invite a special guest to speak and provide advice, but you need to make sure that the content is valuable for all who attend. This is where audience segmentation becomes valuable; instead of creating one event for all of your target accounts, you should segment your account list into different audiences and create events that are relevant to each segment.

When planning the event or webinar, consider what the greatest pain points are for your audience. Though you may want to transition into a soft sell at the end, keep in mind that this is not the main purpose of the event. Instead, you want to work on building goodwill and fostering relationships with your audience so that they come to trust your company and value its expertise.

#159 MAKING ABM WORK FOR YOUR BUSINESS

The majority of B2B marketers claim that ABM is vital to their business and that ABM's ROI outperforms other marketing investments, so developing and implementing an ABM campaign should be on the forefront of all marketer's minds.

However, to be truly successful with ABM, you need to implement a scalable strategy. The tactics we've discussed in this book are the ideal starting point to create an ABM program that drives your company.

CHAPTER 16

THE B2B MARKETER'S GUIDE TO INTENT-DRIVEN MARKETING

We live in a time where brands are vying for the attention of customers from every digital and physical corner. As a result, many consumers have become resistant to the messages that businesses employ to attract target audiences.

In this environment, intent has become the secret ingredient for creating meaningful relationships with audiences and seeding deep customer loyalty. Research indicates that three out of every four business buyers expect companies to understand their needs and expectations, but only a small proportion expect that companies can identify those needs.

This clearly shows how brands need to understand and leverage buyer behavior to personalize their marketing and deliver campaigns that achieve higher conversion rates and ROI.

In the following sections, we'll examine the basics of intent: what it is, how it is used in a B2B environment, and how to incorporate it into your digital marketing strategy.

WHAT IS INTENT-DRIVEN MARKETING?

Intent-driven marketing helps businesses to focus their resources on prospects that have a proven need for their product or service. This type of marketing goes beyond simple demographic and behavioral data. The aim is to create highly sophisticated (and automated) experiences driven largely by the needs of the audience.

To understand what potential customers need and where they are in the buying process, businesses can track and analyze buyer intent. Using this intel, marketers can determine what the prospect is looking for and then create and serve personalized content that directly appeals to them.

However, before you get to the point where you can capture or generate demand, you need to excel at identifying and understanding the intent signals that your target audience generates.

WHAT ARE INTENT SIGNALS?

Marketers with SEO experience are probably familiar with intent signals. Every time someone searches for something (for example, "CRM software for digital agencies"), they're demonstrating a specific intent. For years, SEO experts have been using keyword research to create and optimize landing pages to align with audience intent.

Search engines are not the only source of intent data. Website behavior, content consumption (for example, tweet engagements, blog post reads, or white paper downloads), queries over the phone, chat, and social media are all signals of specific interest or need.

There are three types of intent data:

- **First-party data** is information collected from direct interactions with customers or prospects.
- **Second-party data** is first-party data from another company.
- **Third-party data** is unsourced data collected from the web.

Given that first-party data is both predictive and unique to your brand, it is the best source of reliable information. However, with the ever-increasing number of connected channels and devices, it's crucial to have adequate technology and processes in place to collect this live data.

WHAT GOALS CAN BE ACHIEVED WITH INTENT MARKETING?

One of the biggest advantages of intent-driven marketing is that it allows marketers to pursue and fulfill very specific and relevant business goals. Rather than casting a wide net, hoping to capture as many customers as possible, they can safely focus on a small segment, knowing that those prospects are more likely to convert.

#160 UNDERSTAND AND ENGAGE ALL DECISION-MAKERS

There are often several people who influence the final decision in an organization. Using intent allows marketers to understand the varying motivations and needs of all actors that influence the decision-making process at a target company. Furthermore, they can use this information to engage their prospects in meaningful communication and guarantee their buy-in.

With intent-driven marketing, organizations become better at linking prospects (and their behavior) across platforms and understanding the common factors that drive their purchasing decisions.

Knowing the characteristics shared by most of your customers allows you to design a model of your ideal client. This model can be used to identify the leads with the highest potential and focus your resources on converting them into customers.

#161 IDENTIFY THE BEST PERSONAS/ SEGMENTS IN YOUR AUDIENCE

Existing customers can provide significant and meaningful information about your audience. By analyzing the pre-conversion behaviors and actions of your best customers, you can determine the intent signals of a promising lead. For example, you might discover that one of the signs of high-value customers is that they download and engage with sales enablement content (white papers, case studies, etc.) early in their relationship with your brand. Therefore, you can build your nurturing campaigns to focus on converting prospects that have consumed one or more pieces of sales enablement content.

Over time, this type of analysis will help you uncover the most attractive segments within your audience. It will also help you understand how each group's behavior differs and the signals that indicate that they're ready to convert.

Data surrounding buying intent can also help B2B marketers keep their personas up to date as targets and company strategies change.

#162 IDENTIFY THE BEST CHANNEL FOR EACH PROSPECT

To engage with prospects and nurture them through the funnel, you need to be able to reach them wherever they are. However, with numerous channels and devices available today, picking the right mediums can be a daunting task.

Using intent data, you can determine which channels effectively reach your target audience. These insights can show you the channels used by your best customers so that you employ the same combination and reach new prospects.

#163 OPTIMIZE MESSAGING AND VISUALS

Observing and analyzing how your audience reacts to brand messaging is central to intent-driven marketing. It presents a unique opportunity to optimize brand communication and how it's delivered to potential customers.

With intent marketing, content optimization is no longer based on trial and error. Rather, this tactic enables you to easily produce content that meets your audience's specific needs. By understanding your prospects' intent, you can identify which stage of the buyer journey they're in and produce compelling, informational content that entices them towards a purchasing decision.

Creating a keyword strategy that aligns with buyer intent is one of the strongest ways to optimize your content. By identifying keyword opportunities and prioritizing them using buyer intent, you can construct a more effective content map.

#164 DATA COLLECTION AND ANALYTICS

The first thing you need to do is to make sure you've set up your data analytics in a way that can provide ample information about the intent of your visitors.

Google Analytics, one of the most common tools to analyze user behavior, is a great platform for capturing buyer intent. By defining goals, which are configured at the view level of the platform, you can identify users who have visited a certain page (e.g., your pricing plans), or who have downloaded a specific piece of content (e.g., a price comparison chart, signaling that they're in the decision stage of their journey and considering a few competing products).

You can leverage Google Analytics features, such as Google Tag Manager, for even more robust data collection options. With advanced tracking abilities, these tools provide additional insights into site engagement and interactions.

Multiple third-party tools take this even further and allow you to build comprehensive profiles of your visitors that include demographic and behavioral data (page visits, content consumed, etc.).

#165 PROGRAMMATIC BUYING

Programmatic buying refers to the process of algorithmic high-frequency auctioning of digital advertising. Every time there's an opportunity to show an ad (such as when someone loads a web page that contains a banner or some other type of ad space), an automated auction determines which ad gets displayed.

Combining programmatic buying with intent data can create a powerful lead generation engine, which feeds your funnel with a significant number of relevant high-quality leads.

#166 REMARKETING

Digital advertising works even better when it's targeting people who have expressed interest in your brand or the product you're offering. Using remarketing allows you to take advantage of this. With this tactic, you can retarget people who have visited your website.

For example, a potential customer visits your website, spends fifteen minutes browsing the product page of your tool, and then leaves without completing a purchase. By leveraging this behavioral intent data, you can display an ad to remind them about your solution next time they visit their favorite news or social media website.

Remarketing is growing in popularity because it is proven to convert customers at a higher rate compared to traditional display advertising. At its core, it relies on intent signals—namely, expressing interest in a brand by visiting its website.

#167 MACHINE LEARNING

Given the amount of data that marketers have access to nowadays, it's natural for them to use algorithms to uncover insights and optimize the use of marketing channels and tactics. INFUSEmedia has previously explored how machine learning can be used to improve a website's conversion rate. And much of the optimization is driven by the analysis of past user intent.

For example, by analyzing the behavior of the most profitable customers, an AI-powered conversion rate optimization tool might identify lucrative prospects early in their buying journey. Next, it can provide relevant offers that would make them more likely to convert.

In a broader context, machine learning can be used to identify the best prospects within your audience and the combinations of messaging (copy, visuals, etc.) and channels that are best for converting them.

#168 LEAD NURTURING (WITH MARKETING AUTOMATION)

Lead nurturing is a tactic that reveals the full potential of intent-driven marketing. Up to 96 percent of all leads are not ready to commit to becoming customers when they first engage with a brand. That's why B2B marketers use specialized tools to take their prospective customers through a series of touchpoints aimed at maximizing the chance of conversion. The intent demonstrated by leads is key when building lead nurturing campaigns.

With effective lead nurturing, marketers can account for each leads' behavior and leverage those insights to decide their course of action. For example, if a lead is actively engaging with brand content, it will be handed off to the sales reps, who will then call the target company/individual and try to close the sale.

If, on the other hand, the lead appears "cold" (i.e., it hasn't demonstrated any intent to adopt the solution offered by the brand), the lead nurturing mechanism might put them into another nurturing track where they're offered case studies of similar companies who succeeded by using the solution.

#169 ALIGN YOUR MARKETING STRATEGY TO YOUR CUSTOMERS

The trend toward making marketing more intent-driven is only going to become stronger. With recent technological innovations, we have access to more intent signals and the ability to apply these insights through automation.

Rather than marketing to customers based on timing and strategies, intent-driven marketing focuses on the buyer's needs and expectations. It's about following the digital footprint of your targets—which pages they visit on your website, which blogs provoke them to read and leave comments, what questions they want to have answered when they engage with your brand on social media, and learning what your prospects or customers care about before communicating with them.

PART FIVE

CUSTOMER AND PUBLIC RELATIONS

Customer relations and good public relations (PR) are absolutely vital for success in the marketplace. However, with the digital revolution, the traditional press release, conventional media channels, and classic strategies for marketing a brand have all been turned on their heads.

Yet at the same time, these digital changes have also increased brands' abilities to better connect with their audiences. Since "social" came onto the scene, brand communications have become more dynamic and personal than was previously possible.

In this new environment, knowing exactly how your B2B clients are making decisions is increasingly important. But that doesn't mean that it's easy to find this information; our customers' choices will largely be influenced by your marketing efforts, all of which are backed up by your unique selling points and the emotional appeal of your brand.

That's where influencer marketing comes in—it can make a direct impact on decision-makers at your target B2B companies. The opinions and recommendations of peers, experts, and professional networks are what nearly every B2B professional trusts most. In 2022, a survey identified that 85 percent of marketers expect influencer marketing to enjoy increased attention in B2B marketing. Expect this trend to continue and for the focus on marketing and PR to remain a vital tool going forward.

CHAPTER 17

ACING YOUR DIGITAL PUBLIC RELATIONS

Thanks to the introduction of "the digital age" into public relations, the lines between traditional PR and digital marketing have become blurred. Consistently reaching out to websites, building relationships with bloggers and influencers, and publishing materials externally are practices consistently used within both digital PR and inbound marketing.

The main difference between the two comes down to what each approach emphasizes. PR, which of course stands for "public relations," focuses on building a brand's recognition and reputation. Digital PR (sometimes called "strategic PR") is an extension of content marketing that focuses specifically on putting a brand's content in front of larger audiences, whether or not leads are generated.

Inbound marketing, on the other hand, places greater emphasis on using digital to generate leads with the right content for the right audience at the right time. Inbound marketing and digital PR serve the same purposes through the same approaches—although somewhat differing in their focus. However, they generate the best results when they work together.

Here are ten PR practices for successful B2B marketing in the digital age:

 ## #170 BECOME A THOUGHT LEADER

The ability to position yourself effectively (and authentically) on the basis of real expertise is one of the strongest PR assets you can add to your brand. Strive to get the word out about your services, products, or innovative ideas, but don't forget to tell the story of your own expertise and do so in an authoritative voice.

Thought leadership establishes you as someone worth listening to in a noisy environment. It also places a responsibility upon you to protect your brand and preserve the value of your name. Your status as a thought leader can also be valuable in times of crisis. When your company receives criticism, your reputation will be stabilized by the counterpoint from your positive image and years of authentic work.

#171 CONNECT AND BUILD STRONG RELATIONSHIPS

In order to get the word out about your brand, you'll need to build strong relationships with the right people and the media channels. Social media is one of the most important ways to do this. It allows brands to connect with their target audiences, even in a B2B environment.

In addition to potential B2B customers, industry journalists are constantly monitoring a variety of social platforms such as Twitter and Facebook and following events in real time as they occur. These channels support their work in a variety of ways, enabling them to find experts, to research stories, or to start discussions that may inform their writing. If you are positioned as an expert in the social sphere, you can find yourself benefiting from the attention of these reporters.

The combination of social platforms and traditional media holds a power that few PR channels can offer. Social media strengthens and amplifies mass media by putting you in front of more outlets and providing many more options for getting your story attention.

That's why building strong relationships with social influencers, famous bloggers, and other entities with an established media presence is an important way to enhance brand awareness. These affiliates will help you gain the greatest access to your target audience and can extend your influence far beyond your own followers.

#172 PERFECT YOUR PITCH

Establishing relationships with influencers can take place in a number of ways. The first step is usually writing a great pitch. How your pitch lands is crucial because it opens the door to determining whether or not your brand gains recognition with media contacts.

Unlike the traditional, more formal PR pitch, an online pitch is usually much less stringent. Being conversational and personal is often preferred. Along with establishing a personal tone, you should make an effort to get to know the person you're approaching. Become familiar with their brand voice, and show them that you understand their world.

When communicating with influencers, don't hesitate to say what you want and why you want it, but also make clear what you're offering in return. While you may at times stumble upon people willing to feature you *pro bono*, a pitch usually proposes an exchange, whether it be financial compensation, a free trial of your product or service, or free exposure.

 #173 CREATE STRONG CONTENT THAT ENGAGES

"Storytelling" has become a PR buzzword in the last few years, and it's one of the most potent forms of digital PR and marketing for brands today. But it's more than just telling a story with text. An interactive, engaging, and immediate brand experience is something users are looking for, and storytelling is the perfect way to offer it to them. The more "human" your brand appears, the easier your potential leads will be able to relate to it, even in a B2B context.

Also, make sure your content is *useful*. Whether it's content that tells a compelling story or simply one that informs usefully, the usefulness (or lack thereof) of a piece of content is often what makes (or breaks) it.

What will people in your industry find useful? How will they find information in the first place? Most of them will probably find you through the internet, so a great first step is to read the in-depth document released by Google that specifies its search quality guidelines in great detail and explains how website content is rated by Google according to page quality (PQ) and needs met (NM), among other criteria. While this is particularly relevant for the content on your own website, this information provides insight into what Google deems important and the direction it's taking with regards to the exposure of online content.

PROMOTE YOUR CONTENT IN THE RIGHT WAY

Paid promotion and social ads continue to rise in popularity as very efficient ways to deploy your content through various channels. Seventy-two percent of marketers who utilize paid advertising report leveraging social ads to build awareness. Search engine marketing (SEM) is also a common marketing tactic, utilized by 46 percent of B2B marketers. The use of promoted posts on channels like Twitter has grown steadily.

Promoting your company's content through these means seems like a no-brainer. The challenge, though, is to find effective, new, compelling ways to promote your content across social channels, as well as to optimize existing forms of promotion to better target the right audiences.

LISTEN AND RESPOND TO YOUR AUDIENCE

Online reputation management (ORM) is a key aspect of digital PR and marketing. Brand awareness, engagement, customer retention, and customer loyalty are all outranked by lead generation, nurturing, and sales as organizational goals.

News travels fast, people respond in real time, and content often goes viral in unexpected ways. What someone says in relation to your brand can make a huge impact.

Monitoring what is being said and devising a strategy about how to respond to it are both important PR practices. Take time in advance to clarify questions about company transparency, attitudes toward criticism and praise, and devise a strategy for how you'll deal with reputation management failures. Take control of online conversations by answering questions, offering support, and expressing gratitude to ensure your brand outshines its competitors.

#176 WATCH AND LEARN FROM YOUR COMPETITORS

Don't forget to follow your competitors closely; learn from their wins, and from their losses. Some of your best sources of new information (and media connections) can be the same places where your competitors are getting mentioned in the press.

Sticking only to a particular niche of your online space (or to the connections you're already familiar with) greatly limits your outreach and how many businesses are going to hear about you. You can be sure your competitors are also working on increasing their own brand awareness, so you'll need to do the same—only better.

Along with tracking your direct competition, make it a regular practice to also track other high-performance leading brands in similar industries. This will allow you to find more ideas that you can apply to your own digital PR strategy. There may be ideas and tactics that have been successful in other industries, but simply haven't been tried in yours. Analyze what types of content leading businesses promote and precisely how they promote it, then consider whether it could work for your brand as well.

TRACK AND MEASURE SUCCESS

Once you've created and implemented a digital PR strategy, begin measuring its effectiveness. Measurement is vitally important because it provides you with hard facts and data about the impact you're having on your audience.

There are several tools you can use to assess the effectiveness of your marketing endeavors. For example, a great approach is to utilize a simple four-criteria measurement in which you determine:

How many times your content was shared
What the quality of the engagement was
Whether you gained any links
Whether your campaign or content influenced sales

 ## OPTIMIZE YOUR CONTENT FOR MOBILE

As the desire for instantaneous content (such as live video coverage on social media) picks up, brands will need to react by responding in real time themselves. This requires catering to an increasingly mobile audience, since more and more real-time interactions are happening via mobile. Your own social and web presences should be tailored accordingly.

Mobile-optimized websites need to be accessible and easy to use. This is an area where marketing and PR coincide in their approaches and goals. Along with an optimized site, you will also want to develop apps that offer even more mobile benefits to your customers. Consider what time of day your buyer personas are using their smartphones, so you can distribute your content during these periods for maximum impact.

#179   DON'T FORGET THE TIME-SAVING TOOLS

From workflows for planning, creation, distribution, and amplification of content, to triggering and tracking engagements, there are plenty of powerful tools to help you track how well you're accomplishing your PR goals. You need to know what these tools are and make sure your team members know how they work.

Here are two helpful resources for finding the best tools out there:

- Stephen Waddington, former chief engagement officer at Ketchum, offers a great sample of effective tools used by contributors to his ebook, along with their insights and tips.
- Prezly's excellent guide featuring 140 digital PR tools provides a broad spectrum of tips that are not to be missed.

Finding and implementing the right tools for *your* organization will simplify your digital PR efforts and free up more time for you to sharpen your skills in other areas.

CHAPTER 18
CREATING AN EFFECTIVE ADVOCATE MARKETING STRATEGY

When considering the best approach to acquiring new customers, most marketers believe that a referral lead is far more likely to convert than a lead gained through inbound marketing. After all, most people would be more likely to purchase a product if a trusted friend recommended it to them, rather than if they read a testimonial from a stranger on the internet (no matter how compelling or well-written it might be).

This rule of trusted recommendations holds true for many types of purchasing decisions, but it can become even more complex in the B2B buying process. Every B2B company can benefit from adding advocate marketing to their marketing mix to boost customer retention. While 83 percent of satisfied customers are willing to become brand advocates, just 29 percent of them actually do.

Recruiting customers to be part of your advocate marketing efforts isn't easy. Figuring out a good place to start and developing a long-term strategy can also be challenging. But the following tips can guide you through the basics that you need to know.

 **#180** **RECOGNIZE WHY BRAND ADVOCACY WORKS**

Although most people won't endorse companies purely out of kindness, most of them aren't holding out for something like money, either. Rather, a true brand advocate is someone who goes out of their way to promote your company because he or she gains a personal or business value from your services or products and wishes to share this.

Once you've provided a value that your customer might wish to share with others in their circle, you're on the right track to winning over trusted brand advocates. How you go about the process of cultivating your brand advocates depends on many factors that ultimately determine which advocate personas will be worth your time to target.

#181 SET UP BUSINESS OBJECTIVES

You can't approach advocate marketing without first identifying clear business objectives. But once these objectives are identified, you can begin to consider how promoters for your product or service can help you to reach them. The power of brand ambassadors to refer new customers should not be underestimated. A brand advocate is 50 percent more likely to convert than a referral from a non-advocate. And 86 percent of buyers consider word of mouth to have the greatest impact on their purchasing decisions. It is clear that when properly harnessed, brand advocates are going to be an incredibly powerful tool.

You'll want to harness this power early in the process in order to obtain a maximum impact. I encourage you to consider implementing advocate marketing as early as during the product development phase. Brand advocates know your company and its products better than most people and their sincere feedback can drive the very evolution of your product itself.

#182 UNDERSTAND YOUR ADVOCATE PERSONAS

When you first launched your inbound marketing strategy, you undoubtedly put a lot of thought into understanding your buyer personas—who they are, what their pain points are, and how your products and services can solve their problems.

You need to approach understanding your brand advocate personas with the same level of attention. People who are willing to vouch for your company have a vested interest in it because of problems that have been solved thanks to *your* products. Recognizing the specific ways in which you have helped make your customers' lives easier will put you in a stronger position to approach them.

You'll also need to take into consideration your advocate personas' job titles. For example, a senior level executive and an HR manager might both be enthusiastic about your product, but they would probably have different reasons for becoming brand advocates. Likewise, the impact of a recommendation from a senior executive will be different than one coming from an HR professional.

#183 PREPARE YOUR TEAM TO DO ADVOCATE MARKETING

Successful advocate marketing is everybody's job; the success of your strategy will depend not only on your brand advocates, but how your employees use these advocates.

Your own content team should always be in close communication with your brand advocates. Your content should be regularly updated to ensure it reflects and conveys these testimonials. Brand advocate content could be a short piece on social media highlighting your product's best features, or a downloadable PDF on how to maximize benefits from your product or service.

Involving a product development team can also have great benefits, as they can quickly respond whenever brand advocates identify patterns of customer feedback. Make sure everyone on your team understands how brand advocates can impact their work.

#184 NARROW DOWN YOUR LIST

Now that you've done your homework, how do you begin pursuing your first relationships with brand advocates?

Start with the low-hanging fruit; target satisfied customers who've given positive feedback or who've already provided your sales team with customer testimonials and references. Other potential advocates could be people who've mentioned your company on social media or bloggers who've featured you in a post. Keep in mind that these people may not be as ready to become brand advocates as loyal customers would. You may need to put in more effort to convince them.

Don't rush the relationship. Most customer testimonials will require brand ambassadors to sign a release giving you permission to use their story. They may also need to provide you with photographs for your team to use. Don't lead with this; begin the contact by acknowledging that you're recognizing special customers by inviting them to become featured brand "all-stars." Letting a customer know that you want to "profile their excellence" can open more doors than pitching it as an opportunity for them to help you.

#185 MOVE BEYOND CUSTOMER REFERENCES

While a testimonial provides proof that someone is satisfied with your company, it doesn't immediately make them a brand advocate. You'll need to put in some extra work for that to happen.

Start with a small group: If you approach too many people at once, you won't have the resources to connect with all of them in a personalized way.

The key is to offer rewards and incentives, but not money. It's widely recognized that offering to pay threatens to formalize the relationship, makes it feel more like a business transaction, and can cast doubt on the genuine nature of the testimony.

#186 LAUNCH A CUSTOMER REWARDS PROGRAM

Gift cards and discount coupons are a good start. Think of creative ways to make advocates feel like they're part of the team, like publicly recognizing their achievements or providing bonus features before they're available to anyone else.

Whichever approach to customer rewards you choose, it makes a big difference to express gratitude for their input. Sometimes even a thoughtfully written thank you note will do the trick.

#187 ENGAGE EMPLOYEES AS BRAND ADVOCATES

You don't only need to look externally to find brand advocates. Your own employees may have a different relationship to your business than your customers, but they can be just as powerful advocates as your clients.

Incentives can help grow this internal advocacy. For example, Google offers perks to its employees that motivate them to talk positively about the Google culture. Granted, not every company has as many resources to spare as Google, but most can do *something* to boost their employees' loyalty and encourage them to become brand advocates.

A clear advantage your employee advocates have over your client advocates is an understanding of your company from the inside, including its strengths and weaknesses. Encourage them to express their full range of thoughts about the business, across the spectrum.

Once your employees feel like they're part of the company and personally connected to it, brand advocacy will follow naturally. Forty percent of the public already regard employees as the most important factor in a company's success.

 ## #188 SUPPORT THE PROCESS WITH SOFTWARE

Given the amount of effort needed to get an effective advocate marketing strategy off the ground, you might assume that you'll need to dedicate an entire team to the task. While this is a viable option, an effective software solution can often lessen manpower required and streamline the process.

The best software solutions are able to combine all aspects of your advocate marketing strategy into one solution. It should provide the option to automate and gradually upgrade your rewards program. This becomes useful as your brand advocate list begins to grow. With software, you should also be able to find more references across the web, generate buzz, and receive feedback.

 ## #189 DON'T SKIP ON MEASURING THE RESULTS

As with any marketing strategy, the inability to measure ROI renders your brand advocacy strategy useless. Track not only metrics that relate to your bottom line (such as the number of referrals), but also metrics related to brand advocate recruitment (such as the engagement rate). This way, you can easily see the number of leads referred by each advocate, along with their conversion rate and average value.

You can choose an attribution model to see which channels bring in revenue. Which case studies are downloaded from your website? Which testimonials are viewed most frequently? Which are liked and shared the most on social media? If one is performing better than the others, you'll know where to increase your budget and emphasis. Identify weak spots so you can improve them.

#190 DEEPEN YOUR RELATIONSHIPS WITH BRAND ADVOCATES

Once you've established a working advocate marketing strategy and recruited a number of influential brand advocates, the process doesn't end. It's really just beginning. You'll want to ensure your team attends closely to these relationships and nurtures them going forward.

Don't let your relationships with your brand advocates become stagnant, or you'll risk losing touch with them or even losing contact entirely. Consistent communication is the best strategy, but it may not be possible with every brand advocate. If this is the case, and the bandwidth for regular communication is a challenge, pick the most committed advocates and make a point to maintain communication with them on a regular basis. The return on investment will be worth it.

Treat your brand advocates the way you would loyal employees. There's no better motivation than genuine appreciation.

CHAPTER 19

EMPLOYING INFLUENCER MARKETING

Influencer marketing works so well for B2B companies because it accurately reflects the way people make decisions on a day-to-day basis. Our family and friends and the people we view as experts in certain fields can powerfully influence us. They have influence not only because we trust and value their opinions, but also because we subconsciously want to fit into certain social groups. Studies show that 92 percent of consumers trust earned media such as personal recommendations and word of mouth over other types of advertising.

First, identify those who are most likely to affect the decisions of your target audience. Who do they know? Who do they want to learn from? These are your target influencers. When you have this background knowledge at hand, there are nine crucial steps you can follow to increase your chances of success in influencer marketing.

#191 DO YOUR HOMEWORK

Thoroughly research the important people in your field; these should be the individuals your customers look up to: industry leaders, journalists, bloggers, market analysts, and knowledgeable experts.

In order to identify the influencers who matter most, start by talking to your sales department and to current customers with whom you have a positive relationship. They should be able to provide you with insights into what makes your audience tick. Attending industry events is another hands-on approach that can yield effective insights. The thought leaders in your field often speak and present at conferences.

Next, do some investigative work online. Select a number of keywords related to your business and run them through search engines to give yourself a better idea of potential influencers in your field. Then move on to Twitter and LinkedIn to find out more about the people you've identified, as well as the possibility of connecting with them.

Innovative influencer marketing solutions have been thriving in recent years. Use platforms that harness social media stats to pinpoint the people your customers trust. They can provide you not only with the right names, but also with additional details about each influencer.

#192 BOOST YOUR SOCIAL CREDIBILITY

It's difficult to win people's votes when they haven't even heard of you. The same goes for persuading influencers to talk about a brand they're not familiar with. So before you start engaging with influential figures in your field, there's one more thing to take care of.

Your social credibility needs a boost so that you're able to establish relationships with the top people who can impact your customers' decisions. How can you achieve that? Well, it certainly won't happen overnight, but with consistency and commitment, you can take steps to build up awareness of your brand.

First of all, make sure your social media strategy is being executed thoroughly and that your profiles are up to date with all the proper information. While you're at it, don't forget the power of curated content, which gives you the opportunity to share and comment on your influencers' work, setting the stage for future collaboration even as you enlarge your social reach.

You can position yourself as a thought leader in a number of other ways. Preparing and sharing useful case studies and white papers that inspire people in your field, speaking at industry events, and engaging with your community both on and offline are all proven methods of building trust and elevating your brand.

#193 START BUILDING RELATIONSHIPS THAT MATTER

Once you've taken action to increase your brand's reach, you can launch the lengthy but rewarding process of building relationships with media and influencers. Simply having the right names on your radar isn't going to get you those important connections. You need to get out there and actually develop rapport with your target influencers.

It might be best to select targets who are already interested in your brand in some way at first. Start with a few interested influencers and thoroughly research their passions and interests. Look for the commonalities between your brand and their expertise in order to establish a relationship, and make a case for how you both can benefit from it.

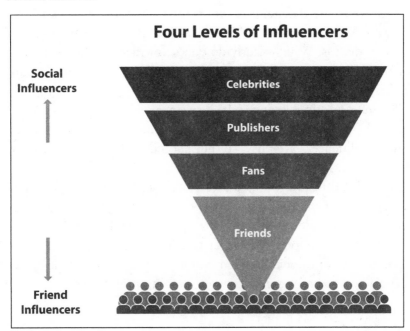

After you've become acquainted with them, make the first contact by posting insightful comments on the influencer's blog posts or other articles, or by taking part in online forums they're engaged in. Follow them on social media, but do so in an active way and always keeping an eye on what they're sharing and who they interact with.

Once a mutual affinity has evolved naturally, you'll be ready to launch direct communication. Prepare tailored emails for each influencer so you can show your sincere interest in what they're doing. Let them know you've been following their work, and introduce yourself and your brand with a short but compelling pitch.

#194 ENGAGE INFLUENCERS THE RIGHT WAY

You've now made your name known to your target influencers and taken the first step in building meaningful relationships with them. Now it's time to find the right approach to engage those who can make a difference for your B2B brand.

Based on your thorough research of their work, make an offer or proposition that suits each individual, conveying to them a few important details. What exactly do you want them to do? What's in it for them? How do you see your relationship progressing? Be sure to include all of this.

The relationship is going to be a two-way street. When someone agrees to help you, make sure you create the best possible experience for them. Influencers are busy, so they should find working with you to be a seamless process.

Naturally, offering your products or services for free can improve the likelihood of maintaining strong relationships with influencers. In some cases, people are open to being paid to speak at your event or contribute to your ebook. Whatever you choose, the best approaches involve maintaining personalized communication with each target influencer so you can learn what your mutual interests are.

#195 BUILD BRIDGES WITH RELEVANT BLOGGERS

Among the different types of influencers available to you, bloggers can be particularly helpful for building B2B brands. If you develop solid connections with bloggers, they can write about your products and services, share content for your outlets, and spread the word about your work using social media.

As with any other influencer, before you approach any bloggers, you need to delve a bit deeper into their work. First, identify the people who write about topics that are closely related to your own content and interests. Then engage with them directly at industry events, on social media, online forums, and their own blogs.

After making initial contact, nurture that relationship by sharing their articles or offering them free services or other promotions. Suggest placing a backlink on your own blog. You can also engage them in more elaborate campaigns that will promote their work, along with your own brand. Help them understand from the outset that a relationship with you will be a two-way street.

#196 GET GUEST CONTENT FROM INFLUENCERS

An alternative way to develop your relationship with influencers, and more specifically with bloggers, is to invite them to directly contribute to your own media channels. This will allow you to diversify your blog's content for your readers and social media followers, while at the same time establishing thought leadership that will benefit your brand's presence across deployment channels.

Getting an expert to share their insights by writing a guest post can give your brand greater exposure and higher social authority. This can open new doors for collaboration with even more renowned influencers. Select top influencers so that their efforts will truly benefit your content flow. You can also minimize their workload by offering them a draft text or talking points.

Besides increased traffic to your website, guest bloggers can also share content they've contributed on their own channels, potentially republish your content on their own blogs, and talk about your brand in their communities in whatever format they'd like. The authorship remains with them, which means it's not a sunk cost on their part.

#197 DON'T FORGET ABOUT STRUCTURING YOUR STRATEGY

But once you've gotten a firm grip on each process, wrap them all up into one simple strategy with a formalized structure.

Through a structured approach, you'll have a strong overview of your actions and tactics, and of the ways in which you'll measure success. Since you've already invested time in the initial research, it's useful to document everything you've found out, including details on your target audience and the circles of target influencers. Don't forget to keep track of the relationships you've started building and the different activities you've engaged influencers in.

Whether you launch a campaign or get involved in guest blogging, it's pivotal to track how it's performing. Then you can evaluate whether your efforts are actually bringing in new visits, creating introductions, garnering social media attention and mentions, and ultimately, qualifying leads.

#198 ENSURE CONSISTENT PRESENCE, NOT SPORADIC PUSHES

Cultivating relationships is similar to growing some plants. Turning up occasionally to water them means they probably won't blossom. They need constant care and attention, much like influencers do.

With consistent communication and fair collaboration, you can cultivate loyalty and truly inspire influencers to become your brand's ambassadors. Never forget to praise them publicly, and express your gratitude. Additionally, it's smart to engage with influencers in person. Suggest meeting them at an industry event, or invite them out for coffee if they're local.

Set up automated reminders for yourself to follow a schedule for touching base with the various influencers, in order to avoid sporadic contact that's based only on your marketing needs. Just like any person, influencers enjoy regular attention and care.

#199 CONSIDER HIRING AN INFLUENCER

Here's a more unconventional idea. If an influencer is especially knowledgeable, experienced, and respected in your trade, it could be worthwhile to get them on board with a formal relationship. Social hires are becoming a prominent recruiting tactic. Your company can benefit greatly from the expertise of an established and recognized specialist, and a small investment can potentially yield a big return.

In terms of brand awareness, formally bringing an influencer on board can also increase the credibility of your work and the respect for your brand. Your company should be focused on bringing together a team of qualified experts. And remember, you can also meet new connections and potential collaborations from the influencer's professional network.

PART SIX

EMERGING BEST PRACTICES

The adoption of new technologies is creating chances for marketers to explore new channels and reach new audiences. Mobile, video, and events are just a few of the exciting opportunities marketers are starting to explore.

It's becoming even more important to have a highly skilled team to implement these new technologies, and to commit to measuring the experiences your customers are receiving. In this section, we'll review the best practices in some of the emerging areas of digital marketing that I believe will come to dominate the field in coming years.

CHAPTER 20

ESSENTIAL CONVERSION AND EXPERIENCE OPTIMIZATION TECHNIQUES

Conversion optimization has emerged as the primary field for investment in online marketing. Professionals across all industries have discovered that putting effort into it can yield high returns, especially on websites that enjoy high traffic.

Yet focusing only on one detail of the conversion experience (such as page copy or design) is unnecessarily limiting. That is why we're seeing a shift toward optimizing the experience of customers across all interactions with a brand. This is true both on and offline. There is no secret mathematical formula you can apply across your site to ensure success. However, by following these ten best practices, you get started on the right foot with optimization techniques.

 ## #200 OPTIMIZE ACROSS ALL TOUCHPOINTS

Conversion optimization arose from the need to increase website performance. Marketers realized there was a potential to improve web business performance by improving the copy and design of a web property. Yet early efforts showed there might be a limit to what these improvements could deliver.

As this initial excitement passed, another philosophy started to take root. Behind the percentage points, it was acknowledged that there is also a human need for much more than a catchy headline and the most eye-pleasing color for their CTA button. There is a human who brings thoughts and feelings to the purchasing choice they may be prepared to make.

Experience Optimization: Think about the total sum of the interactions your customers have with your brand. They come to your website, read your social media updates, and receive your emails. They meet you in person at conferences and trade shows. Maybe they even call you on the phone and speak to you and your representatives.

Ask yourself: Are you providing a consistent experience across all these platforms? Are you making promises on one and not delivering on them on the others? You'll want to ensure that you are following through in order to create a complete and consistent experience for the user.

To do this, start the optimization process by mapping out all touchpoints a customer can have with your brand. Then audit all your actions across those interactions. When you've completed this process, you will have an excellent base to start optimizing these experiences in a consistent way.

EXPERIENCE	MARKETING GOAL	POSITIVES	AREAS FOR IMPROVEMENT
Landing pages	Convert traffic into sales	Good SEO performance, stable traffic	Conversion rate across all pages
Email drip campaign	Brand awareness, generate leads	Good open and clickthrough rates	Small size of email list

Use Personalization Strategically: Using your customers' first names in your email campaign is important, but it will not do the job on its own. This kind of personalization is so rudimentary that no one is likely to be impressed by it.

The advances in our ability to collect, store, and quickly analyze large amounts of customer data, together with the cheap access to new analytics technologies, means we now have a much better ability to provide personalized experiences to customers. We need to act on these new abilities.

Invest in finding out as much as possible about your customers. What are their particular wants and needs? Set out to fulfill these needs and give them valuable information in the context where they would be best suited to consume it. This could be as simple as a basic drip campaign in MailChimp, or something much more complicated and personalized that uses advanced analytics, segmentation, and automation software.

Align Messaging Across Platforms: Your customers are humans who expect a consistent experience from your brand. One of the most widespread mistakes marketers make with paid advertising is to use one message for the ad, but show a completely different value proposition on the landing page:

#201 ADOPT DATA-DRIVEN MENTALITY AND TESTING

If you want to improve your conversion optimization, you have to become comfortable with collecting, analyzing, and understanding data, and then making decisions based on it.

Being data-driven also helps with leading a team; making decisions becomes easier, and no one feels slighted because you'll have an impartial way of showing why you've made these decisions. You'll have an easy answer to every question that comes up regarding your optimization strategy. In most cases, that answer will be: "Let's test."

"Should we have a long or short landing page?"

"Let's test!"

"What copy works best for this CTA?"

"Let's test!"

Learn How to Perform A/B Testing: A/B testing is an art unto itself, so performing it correctly is an imperative step toward success with your optimization campaigns.

Knowing what to test, how long to test it for, when to trust the numbers, and when to run additional tests are all essential. To get the most out of your testing, research and explore some of the excellent online resources and tools that are available before you start testing.

Perform Live Usability Testing: A/B testing is a helpful tool, but in some cases it can fall short because it doesn't always provide an explanation as to *why* users are acting a certain way. In fact, the optimal way to understand this is to live test with customers.

If focus groups are too difficult and expensive for you to organize, don't give up. There are easy, affordable online services that allow you to collect feedback.

#202 UTILIZE THE "ABOVE-THE-FOLD" AREA

"Above the fold" refers to the area of a website that users first see when they land, before they do any scrolling. In other words, it's the section of each page that is seen by 100 percent of your visitors. Optimization experts often call this "the prime real estate" of a website.

Despite the opportunities presented by above-the-fold web positioning, even large and sophisticated brands can make poor use of this on their sites. There are still far too many cases of businesses using flashy photos and gaudy copy that grab attention, but do not do anything to convert the average visitor.

Yet there is an even bigger problem that is surprisingly common: Not placing a CTA in the above-the-fold area.

Urge visitors to fulfill the ideal goal you have set for the page, and give them the opportunity to do so immediately. Ultimately, you want everyone who visits this page to take action. There is no better place to put the button for this action than the area where everyone who visits your site will see it.

#203 MAKE COPY YOUR ALLY

On-page copy is one of the vital factors in conversion optimization. It is useful for both visitors and search engines, and has crucial impact on how well your content ranks. Most importantly, it can make the difference when it comes to a visitor becoming a client.

All text should be compelling, but use as little as possible on your home page and landing pages. Try adding bullet points instead of long, visually intimidating blocks of text. This will drive more customers to take the action you desire.

The rules for good web copy aren't complicated. Write in plain, simple language and avoid fancy terms. Even if you are dealing with a highly sophisticated audience, keeping complexity to a minimum is always beneficial.

Also keep in mind that audiences are often driven by emotion rather than by rational arguments. Use this to your advantage. Learn to use language to connect with the emotions your visitors may be experiencing. Does a current event in their industry have them feeling excited, or on edge? Can your product help them solve a problem? Overcome a fear? Or just make them feel and look better?

Whatever it is that you are selling, asking someone to hand you their money is always likely to elicit one overriding emotion: worry.

"Is this right for me? Is this website legitimate? What if I stop using this in a month?"

These are just a few of the questions prospects will have running through their heads when considering your product. The copy you use on your site is one of the best places to provide assurance for potential customers.

The ultimate goal of every page is to ignite the reader into some kind of action. That is easier to achieve when the copy you use on your website is heavily action-oriented. Diffuse worry, create incentive, and drive your customer to take the action you want them to. Headlines and calls to action are naturally suited for action-heavy vocabulary words, but most high-converting pages incorporate that vocabulary into every piece of text. Follow that model for optimal results.

Make sure your headlines are as specific as possible. Adding detail to your headlines serves two purposes:

1. It allows visitors to obtain a better understanding of what to expect from the content that follows.

2. It immediately tells your reader that you are an expert on the topic.

Consider the following titles:

- "How to Grow Your Site Visitors"
- "What I Learned about Content Marketing from Publishing 150 Blog Posts and Growing My Site to 11k Monthly Visitors"

Which one would you be more likely to click on? Does the second example make you more likely to trust the author and her expertise? Numbers in headlines work much the way that specific details do. They set a framework and then build credibility for your content.

The headline "The Seven Best Tools for Product Managers" gives readers a short and distilled version of the information they need. But notice how the headline "Teams That Use Our Product Save $400 per Month on Average" is much more convincing than simply saying, "It saves you money."

The copy in your call to action is a great place to highlight the qualities of your product or service one more time. Instead of a simple "Buy" or "Subscribe," feel free to implement copy that is rich in benefits, such as "I'm Ready to Get More Quality Leads."

People are inherently driven by the fear of missing out (FOMO) on something good. You can benefit from this psychological trait by adding urgency to your CTAs. You often see businesses apply this leverage by offering flash sales targeting visitors who are about to leave their website with special one-time discounts.

#204 WRITE EXCEPTIONAL CALLS TO ACTION

Calls to action are important for your conversion rate, so they need to be exceptional. They are the things that make a block of text or a webpage into a true marketing asset. You could have the perfect web design or copy, but without an eye-catching CTA, visitors to your site may still leave without becoming customers.

Everything about a CTA is worth adjusting, especially when it comes to size, color, and copy. Obviously, every site is different, so you can experiment and find the CTA that works optimally for yours.

CTAs have a visual element, but whether your CTA is blue, orange, or black is not important, as long as it is distinct from the background. Use colors that contrast your CTA against the page background. This will allow your buttons to stand out.

Do not limit yourself to just one CTA button. Certainly, place CTAs in areas that a visitor sees when they first land on your page (above the fold), but don't be afraid to use multiple buttons.

As you employ this tactic, also use the Google URL builder to customize the links you place on the buttons, so that you can keep track of how each separate button is performing. This will help you know for certain which CTA buttons are working most effectively.

#205 USE MULTIPLE LANDING PAGES

Landing pages are an essential element in the personalization of your business's offerings to the different customer segments you serve. They allow you not only to offer a customized product/service, but also to use different language and messaging that can target specific audiences.

Additionally, customized landing pages can boost your SEO efforts, allowing you to incorporate key terms you may be missing on your home page. Research shows that conversion rates tend to improve exponentially with the number of landing pages you use.

When you want to build landing pages for your website, start with your target customers. Use data that you have already obtained from surveys and conversations with existing customers to understand the problems they have. Pay close attention to the language they use and isolate it.

Next, start creating a template for your landing page. With the information you have collected from your customers, you'll know what questions to answer on the page and to address their needs in a way that feels natural.

Finally, make sure the landing pages you create are at least 90 percent unique, especially in terms of the copy used. Otherwise, you risk having your site marked for duplicate content, which can result in a penalty by major search engines.

#206 DON'T ALLOW FORMS TO TURN INTO A CONVERSION KILLER

If you are operating a business with online elements, there's no doubt you'll run into the need to use web forms. These are great for collecting visitor information, but should be crafted with extreme care since they have the potential to negatively impact the conversion of your website.

In general, always aim to have the lowest possible number of required fields on a form. The final number depends on many factors, including what industry you are in, and what your goal is for each form. You want to aim for requiring the least possible effort on the part of the customer. For example, if you are using your corporate blog to collect emails, do you really need more than one contact field (email) on your form? Probably not.

You can collect information about your visitors progressively when you know they are likely to come back to your site. Ask them for the minimum amount of information the first time, then gradually request additional information on successive visits.

Ensuring data integrity is also important when dealing with online forms. Whenever you have the chance to validate the information your visitors are providing, you should do so without waiting for them to submit their details before you check them.

Even without knowing a customer's specific email address, you know what it should look like. Do not wait for them to click "Submit" before asking them to fix a mistyped address.

You can take inline validation to the next level by dynamically filling in forms for which you already have the data. For example, once a customer enters their zip code, you'll know which state they are in, so do not ask them to choose it from the list, just fill it out for them.

#207 REDUCE DISTRACTIONS

Too often we see landing pages with hundreds of distracting options—main menus, drop-down submenus, numerous links to social media, case studies, and so on.

Many businesses do this, thinking that providing their audience with more options automatically makes it more likely to turn visitors into customers. The reality is that the more distractions and possibilities you provide, the easier you make it for users to veer off course.

If you want visitors to make a purchase on a certain page, do not give them the option to subscribe to your email list or download a white paper. This will only distract them and give them an excuse to postpone a purchase decision.

#208 USE EVERY OPPORTUNITY TO BUILD TRUST

Trust is important for every business, but it's even more important for an internet business relying on a web page to convince a stranger to take an action that involves spending money. Use every opportunity to build trust with potential customers. Here is a selection of popular and effective trust-building tactics:

Social proof: "100 of the Fortune 500 companies use our software."

"10,000 happy customers can't be wrong."

Everyone knows that utilizing social conformity can be a benefit to business, but you can take it to the next level by employing personalization. Apply the information you already have about a visitor to incorporate social proof that may have a higher impact on them.

A decision-maker from a marketing agency may be more convinced by the fact that you have a number of other similar agencies as clients, rather than the more boastful (but generic) message that you count big Fortune 500 companies as customers.

Testimonials from customers can always be helpful, especially when they answer critical questions that a user may have about your product. If you are selling a software package, feature a user review that explains how easy it was to get started. This can help convert a reluctant prospect worried about the complexity of your product.

Endorsements from professionals who are perceived as authorities in their industry likewise allow you to "borrow" from the trust these authorities have already built with your audience.

Address users' concerns about keeping their payment profiles secure by including **guarantees** on payment forms. When the user is asked to submit payment details, that's when they are most likely to be worried about the security of their data. Be sure the reassurance elements are added in just the right context, and at just the right place.

Another good example of this tactic is the free trial/money-back guarantee method, which helps ease customers' uncertainty when they are wondering if a solution is right for them (and if it comes from a trustworthy source).

 ## #209 MAKE CONVERTING AS PAINLESS AS POSSIBLE

One reason conversion is so tricky is because we are essentially asking visitors to do something they would rather not do: take a risk. We're asking them to risk doing business with us, and to trust that doing business with us is the right move for them.

To improve the likelihood of getting the user onboard, you can do two things:

| **1** | Improve the quality of what you are offering in exchange for their buy-in. | **2** | Ask them to start with a smaller commitment. |

Think realistically about the smallest possible commitment you need a user to make (in each separate interaction) in order for them to continue their journey toward becoming a customer. Asking them for their credit card information on their first visit may be too much, but getting their email with a promise to deliver relevant and useful information in the future is probably likely to succeed.

FOUR BONUS PRACTICES!

 ## USE A LONG-FORM SALES PAGE FOR PRICEY OR COMPLICATED PRODUCTS

Some products require more effort than others to convince consumers they're worth checking out. That is why many marketers have begun to utilize long-form pages when dealing with certain products. They use the extra space to build a stronger case.

This practice is particularly widespread when selling online courses taught by email. Here is an example of what it looks like in practice.

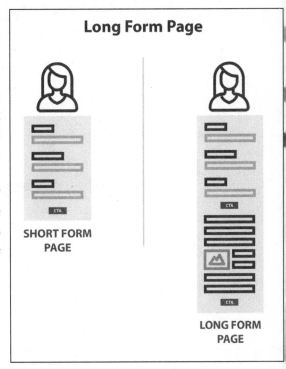

Long Form Page

SHORT FORM PAGE

LONG FORM PAGE

Notice how the page is structured in a way that targets all customer segments. Those who do not need much convincing have the chance to convert right at the beginning by using the form and CTA at the top. For those who make it to the bottom of the page, there's still another CTA that affords an additional opportunity to convert. It even explicitly addresses the fact that the visitor is hesitant to convert.

Although this tactic runs contrary to the view that landing pages should always be short, utilizing long-form sales pages can be quite successful in reaching more reluctant purchasers via a long fuse.

#211 AVOID FALSE BOTTOMS

Make sure you structure your page (especially if it is long-form page) in a way that doesn't create a false impression that the page is over before it really is. Here is what a false bottom looks like:

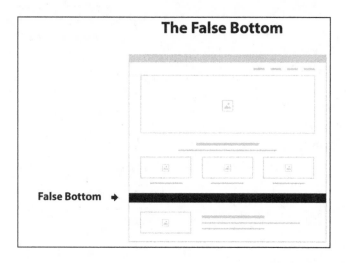

As you can see, the design of the page does not make it immediately obvious that it continues below.

By implementing scroll mapping technology and analyzing the performance of your pages, you can see if a disproportionately high number of visitors are leaving before the end of the page. If this is the case, chances are it will be an example of a false bottom.

To stay on top of this issue, make updates to these pages and track how conversions, scrolling, and bounce rates improve.

#212 USE INFORMATION GAPS TO CREATE CURIOSITY

Curiosity can be a central motivator for your visitors. A strategically placed gap can help you move customers from one channel to another—from an email you sent them to a landing page, or even between the top and bottom of the same page. But remember, once you create a sense of curiosity, you have to deliver on the promise you created. Make them curious, but then satisfy their curiosity.

#213 USE TWO-STEP CONVERSION

Once they have made a commitment, people naturally feel obligated to follow up on the promise they have made. Some marketers take advantage of this by using a two-step conversion. You can use a simple question to get readers to commit, then ask them to deliver on their commitment by entering their email.

Be careful not to insult your readers' intelligence. The questions in the opening step of your campaign should relate to what they care about. It should show you have done your homework. You still need to offer something of substantial value in the second step in order to convince them to convert.

Consider, but be cautious, when applying this tactic. If you do decide to adopt it, run an A/B test vs. a conversion box with only one step and see which performs better. Some sites actually see a much lower conversion rate from a two-step opt-in form. That is not so surprising considering this tactic goes against the conventional wisdom of including as few barriers and steps to a conversion as possible. You may want to test out both and see what works better for your site.

CHAPTER 21

INNOVATING WITH MOBILE MARKETING

I n 2015, mobile search officially beat desktop search in prevalence. This was a strong sign for marketers that mobile marketing is now an absolute must for any company that wants to remain competitive.

Although mobile marketing has already been adopted by the vast majority of B2C companies, not all B2B companies have realized the need for it. Part of the reason B2B companies have been less enthusiastic is that they feel mobile yields unconvincing results. Although the buying process is longer, more complicated, and relies more heavily on relationship-building than in a B2C environment, B2B marketing will soon be impossible without the use of mobile tactics.

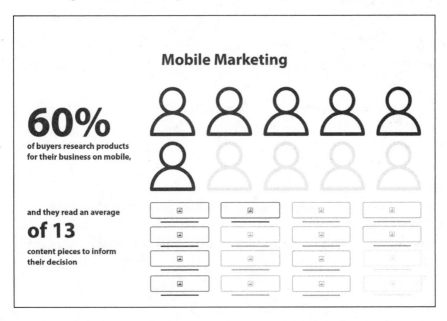

Mobile Marketing

60%
of buyers research products
for their business on mobile,

and they read an average
of 13
content pieces to inform
their decision

B2B buyers read an average of 13 content pieces before a buying decision, and 60 percent of those buyers report having utilized mobile devices in their last purchase. Since the buying process in B2B is longer, mobile can help bridge some of the gaps in engagement and speed up the decision-making process. It can be used with equal success during lead generation, lead nurturing, and in the closing cycle of the sale. Here are ten tips that you can view as a roadmap when implementing a mobile marketing strategy.

 ## #214 OPTIMIZE YOUR WEBSITE FOR MOBILE

Whether or not you have a comprehensive mobile marketing strategy, a website that's optimized for mobile is an absolute must. In fact, Google will penalize you in its search rankings if your website isn't mobile-friendly.

To design a web experience that's optimized for mobile, you need to put yourself in the shoes of the user. Mobile internet is slower, so you should focus on building lighter pages that load faster. Therefore:

> You can't use Flash, but you can create similar effects with HTML5.
> No pop-ups, either.
> Make sure all buttons are easy to press (even by people with large fingers) without the need to zoom in or out.

You'll also need a responsive web design, meaning that people on different platforms and devices must be able to view a version of your website that's customized for them. This is especially important on landing pages, where you gather valuable information about your visitors.

Many website builders may not give you the option to create landing pages with responsive design. You can use a third-party application which builds landing pages that have the same look and feel as your regular website, so that you don't feel like you're sacrificing quality.

#215 MAKE MOBILE CONTENT LOAD FASTER

As B2B buyers increasingly conduct research on mobile devices, there remains marked room for improvement. One study found that a staggering 61 percent of users would never return to a website displaying poor mobile performance. If you want *your* website to make the cut, make sure it loads quickly and provides a user-friendly experience. Nobody wants to wait for a page to load and then be forced to navigate a cluttered layout, only to have to zoom in and scroll horizontally to read the content.

Talk to your developer about what changes they can implement to make your content load more quickly. These changes can include compressing images and text files, caching, keeping JavaScript use to a minimum, and much more. After you've finished implementing these changes, check the speed using a different Google tool, and then perform small tweaks until you get it right.

#216 MAKE VIDEO MOBILE-FRIENDLY

Mobile is a great format for watching video. Statistics show that 70 percent of B2B buyers consume video during their buyer journeys, and that 59 percent of these decision makers prefer video over text content while researching.

YouTube should always have a place in your video marketing strategy, but remember that, ultimately, you want to send people to your website. To do this, you'll want to build video landing pages optimized for mobile. Whatever player you use to integrate videos on your website, confirm that it's responsive. This means that videos should be able to expand or shrink depending on whether the user is watching on a smartphone or on a tablet.

A good rule of thumb is to make it your goal to create big, easily noticeable splash screens and an enticing CTA. Don't rely solely on your video to serve as a CTA, because only a small proportion of users will watch it all the way to the end. So give them suggestions to interact with your brand outside of the video box.

#217 DESIGN EMAILS FOR MOBILE

Forty-one percent of all emails are now opened on a mobile device, so the design of your emails must be optimized for mobile. Otherwise you risk losing half of the audience that opens your emails.

Again, your main consideration should be implementing responsive design. This can sometimes be tricky for email. For example, the Gmail app does not support responsive design when used on iOS devices. That's why it's best to design your emails using a single column. Many email marketing automation tools provide responsive templates to choose from in this format. An additional way to get around this issue is by using fluid design for emails. This automatically resizes to fit the screen using percentages, rather than predetermined fixed measurements.

Keep the subject lines clear and concise. Mobile users are often impatient, and you don't want your email to be quickly dismissed as frustrating or (worse) mistaken for spam. As for the body of the message, use A/B testing to find the perfect ratio between text and images. Always place a clear call to action in each email that instantly draws in the reader and persuades them to click.

#218 EXPLORE MOBILE PAID SEARCH

Marketers are increasingly finding that paid search has a place in B2B mobile marketing strategies. In fact, 70 percent of all paid search impressions come from mobile devices.

While B2C paid campaigns focus on specific products, B2B campaigns tend to focus more on the person doing the search. To avoid irrelevant clicks, use long-tail keywords with exact match and negative keywords as well. If you're offering software solutions to big enterprises, you might want to include negative keywords such as *small business* or *startups*. That way, you ensure small businesses looking for small business software solutions will not land on your page. To become even more specific, think about adding a local element, like "mobile marketing agency in Seattle."

The ad should take users to a mobile-optimized landing page that gives them a solution to the issue your ad copy addresses. When brought to the landing page, mobile users don't want to spend time filling in boxes. Keep contact fields to a minimum. Be sure to also include a click-to-call option, as 57 percent of C-level and VP buyers across different verticals prefer contact via telephone over other channels.

#219 USE GEO-TARGETED ADS

Geo-targeted ads have become a mainstay for B2B marketers, and for good reason. They allow you to target users located in potentially useful places like hotels, airports, and shopping malls. If your business provides not just online but local services, then it's a great way to find potential customers.

Geo-targeted ads have grown progressively more sophisticated. Not only can you adjust targets by location, but also through a variety of demographic categories, to make sure your dollars are well-spent. For even more precisely targeted ads, consider geo-targeting at conferences and events you would normally attend or which are relevant to your industry. In case you're utilizing geo-targeting at several different locations, you can see where your ads are performing best and place your larger bids there.

USE TWITTER FOR MOBILE

As I've said, LinkedIn is undoubtedly the most popular social network among B2B marketers. And although Twitter comes second for mobile, it still might be a more sensible choice for your brand.

So how do you optimize Twitter for your B2B mobile marketing? Consider the following:

- Twitter is a great place to establish yourself as a thought leader by interacting with influencers.
- You can employ social media monitoring tools to gauge how your brand is perceived based on how people are talking about it. It's the most honest kind of feedback you can get.
- It's an excellent tool for boosting traffic to your blog.
- Posting several times a day won't be considered "spammy" on Twitter, as long as your posts are varied. Plus, you can easily reach beyond your followers with hashtags.
- Be on the lookout for Twitter chats related to your industry, where you can pitch in with your own advice and expertise. Hashtags are also a convenient way to connect to people in real-time during conferences and events.

 CONSIDER DEVELOPING A MOBILE APP

Developing mobile apps is yet another area where B2C companies are comfortably in the lead, as many brands have been using mobile apps to streamline their customers' experience for years. App users are frequently rewarded for their loyalty with special offers and discounts.

As you would with optimizing your website, begin by putting yourself in the shoes of your customers to find out what their true needs are. Perhaps there's a communication process that can be made easier through a mobile app. Or, if your business works in such a way that clients often order products, you could create an app to facilitate the ordering process.

Another frequently used idea is to create an ROI calculator, which can be beneficial in the consideration stage, or an event map (for occasions like conferences) that attendees can use for orientation, finding information, and networking.

You can also gain input on the best way forward by running a quick survey by your loyal customers, since they're the best people to ask for tips and feedback on which features of your product or service could benefit from an app.

 ## THINK OF MOBILE FOR YOUR NEXT EVENT

There are many ways to incorporate mobile at your next event. At conferences and other gatherings, you can use mobile for event apps, Twitter chats, and geo-targeted ads, just to name a few possibilities. Since a wide array of potential customers will be gathered in one place at these events, the opportunities to have an impact with mobile are huge.

Consider how mobile can bridge the gap between offline and online marketing during a conference. Let's say you have a booth where you're showcasing your products. Even a simple gesture such as handing out brochures and business cards with links to mobile presences can do the trick. You'll want attendees to be able to immediately find out more about your company and its offerings. If you don't provide them with that chance right away, they may forget about who you are and what you do. In addition to a web URL, consider adding a QR code on each of your print assets to make it easy for them to scan and load a content offer.

Don't want to miss out on connecting with attendees who don't have a QR scanner? Get in touch with an SMS provider and try SMS marketing! SMS can be just as effective as email marketing or other digital approaches.

#223 TAKE YOUR CUSTOMERS' PRIVACY SERIOUSLY

Everyone is concerned about web security these days, so you need to get serious about maintaining privacy for your potential customers. Ninety-one percent of people now won't do business with a company if they feel that company is not taking steps to protect their sensitive data.

So what can you do? A great first step is to make your privacy policy mobile-friendly. A surprising number of businesses don't optimize their privacy page for mobile devices. But you can easily create a short mobile version that links to the original version for those who want to take the time to read it.

You should always feature your privacy policy in order to give users peace of mind and convince them to continue using your website. And your policy can't be empty words, either. You might remember the controversy surrounding Snapchat's privacy leak, which cost them not only a hefty FTC fine, but also caused a serious dent in their reputation.

Many websites just copy and paste their privacy policy, and never think twice about it. But consumers are increasingly wary of this tactic. In addition to crafting your own policy, you can further reassure your clients by receiving independent privacy certification from a third party. Some popular options include TRUSTe and the CIPP certificate from the International Association of Privacy Professionals.

CHAPTER 22
MEASURING YOUR RESULTS WITH WEB ANALYTICS

Every company with an online presence regardless of its size, industry, or clientele needs a comprehensive web analytics strategy.

A typical B2B buying cycle can range between six and twelve months. That's a long period of time (and potentially wasted time) if you're not using your business analytics properly. Analyzing the right KPIs can give you valuable insight into where you may be going off course, so you'll know what to adjust to offer the best user experience possible.

Some marketers feel overwhelmed by the functionalities and options that web analytics tools provide. Because of this, they rush into the analysis and try to track everything, instead of focusing only on what matters. This approach is shortsighted and can water down their reports. The result is often that some of the most important KPIs get overlooked.

To help you get started, check out these nine helpful tips for optimizing measurement.

#224 SET THE RIGHT EXPECTATIONS

Some people expect Google Analytics to be able to read their minds. They think it can automatically sort and display all the most relevant data they need from the start. This is far from being the case. If you want to enhance your marketing strategy using Google Analytics (or any other tool), you'll need to first define your objectives.

Unlike B2C companies, which can easily track their top goals via the Google Analytics Ecommerce Tracking feature, B2B businesses will need to come up with their own algorithm. A typical B2B customer's buying journey is far longer than that of a B2C buyer. People may visit your website and do nothing, only to come back three months later to get more information and contact you.

Prior to setting up any sort of tracking and analytics tool, you need to understand the buying habits that are standard in your industry and get prepared to set expectations accordingly.

#225 DO YOUR KEYWORD RESEARCH

To attain maximum visibility, maximizing organic search results should always take priority. Once you start driving traffic to your website organically, you'll be able to rely less on paid search and other forms of advertising.

This is where thorough keyword research comes into play. You may have a grasp on which pain points you're trying to solve for your customers, but it's also crucial to identify what people are actually looking for when they use search engines.

Let's say your company provides marketing solutions to other B2B companies. A quick search shows that the keyword "digital marketing agency" has 14,800 monthly searches and high competition. Investing in such a competitive keyword might be unwise, as you'd have little chance of successfully ranking for it. Investing in a more specific aspect of digital marketing would be much more likely to yield better results for a much smaller cost.

Use keyword research to understand what issues your potential clients are trying to solve. That way, you'll not only deliver value by giving your solution visibility, but your site will be much easier for them to discover.

#226 USE AUDIENCE REPORTS

Let's take a look at several reports and metrics that are relevant for B2B businesses, starting with audience reports: a powerful tool that shows whether you're targeting the right audience.

196

Audience Reports: Contain basic demographic data, including the gender, age, and location of your visitors, as well as the device they're using. If you aren't attracting enough mobile traffic, the information provided by these reports will clue you in.

Cohort Analysis: Audience reports have a lot more to offer than just data. Using this tool, you can segment your users based on shared characteristics. You can then analyze specific cohorts to see how they contribute to your revenue.

Lifetime Value: An analysis tool which shows the effectiveness of each of your marketing channels. By comparing the lifetime value of users across multiple sessions, you can determine whether your email marketing is generating more revenue than your social media marketing, for instance.

In-Market Segments: With this tool, you can analyze users based on their in-market behavior and purchasing intent (that is, whether they're low or high in the buying funnel).

New vs. Returning Users: Since B2B buying cycles are notoriously long, this tab can help you keep track of whether your users are coming back and converting. It also enables you to see how effectively your strategies for acquiring new visitors are working.

#227 FOLLOW THE MOST RELEVANT B2B REPORTS

Content is bigger than ever for B2B companies, with B2B buyers spending up to 70 percent of their buying journeys engaging with content before reaching out to sales. Also, 55 percent of these buyers report relying on content to inform their purchase decisions more than in the last year (2021). Hence you need the **Content Drilldown** and **Landing Pages** reports. These allow you to analyze the individual performance of each of your pages. Look for pages with high bounce rates and compare them to those with lower bounce rates to identify what can be improved. Then think about ways to improve them. Do they need a better call to action? Or perhaps more content?

Site Search shows the search terms that users type into your site's search functionality when looking for something, while **Click Maps** reveal where exactly users click on the page.

The **In-Page Analytics** report includes a handy feature that's similar to A/B testing called enhanced link attribution. If you have two CTA buttons on one page that have the same destination, you can use this to see which one is clicked more often.

#228 TRACK THE RIGHT GOALS

Since they're aimed at attracting other businesses as customers, your products or services may not have straightforward buying cycles. Tracking the right goals is actually more pertinent in B2B industries than it is for B2C.

The goals you choose to track will depend not only on the nature of your business, but also on the content you're using to attract and convert visitors. Landing page forms on your website are the first places to start. If people are visiting your website but not submitting requests for more information, then it's likely your content isn't up to par, or that it's just not being promoted well.

How is goal tracking beneficial? Using video as just one example; you can calculate the number of views by installing an event tracking code and then observing how many visitors play it. Then see if those who played the video went on to check out other pages of your website or request more information. If they've taken further action, consider promoting the video to encourage more people to play it, or consider moving it to a more visible place on your website.

Seventy percent of B2B buyers watch video throughout the buying journey. Remember this and deploy your own video content accordingly.

#229   INTEGRATE GOOGLE SEARCH CONSOLE

When it comes to improving organic search, one way to gain more insight into your website's performance is to use Google Search Console, which can be integrated with Google Analytics to easily access all of your data in one place.

As vital as keyword research is, you can't just be academic about it. You have to take what you learn and use it to improve your rankings in the search results. With Search Console, you can pick any page on your website and see how well it ranks and for which keywords. If they aren't keywords you intended to rank for, you can then consider revising the content. Try entering a sample search query to see if your page is displayed for it, and at what position. You should also try seeking out additional relevant information, such as the number of impressions and click-through rate.

Google Search Console is the best tool for seeing how Google crawls and indexes your website. If there are any issues, it'll present suggestions for improving pages. And, if you ever receive a manual action penalty, Search Console is where to find out about it.

#230   TAKE ADVANTAGE OF GOOGLE TAG MANAGER

Marketing would be impossible without web developers. And yet, most marketers would probably agree that it'd be easier to implement changes without having to ask for a developer's help every time! What's the solution to this?

By using Google Tag Manager, you can place tags on a page without having to write any complicated code. Once you set up a tag and choose when you want it to fire, Tag Manager will produce the code for you. All you have to do is enter the code after the opening body tag in the HTML of the page. Google Tag Manager then replaces all tags with a snippet of code, meaning your page becomes lighter and loads faster without sacrificing analytical capabilities.

Page speed is crucial for your website not only because Google now factors it into its ranking system, but also because it impacts user experience. There's strong evidence. Consider this: A mere 0.1-second delay in load time can lower total conversions by up to 7 percent. Plus, nearly half of all users now expect a page to load in fewer than three seconds.

#231 OPTIMIZE YOUR PPC CAMPAIGNS

Some marketers are skeptical about how much pay-per-click actually benefits B2B marketing because of the long buying cycle involved. But PPC campaigns can be very effective for driving B2B conversions, as long as you continually monitor and tweak them.

As with any type of marketing, the first step should be identifying your goals. Do you want your PPC campaigns to generate leads at the top of the buying funnel, so that you can nurture them over time until they convert? Or would you prefer to generate sales-ready leads?

While many people would instinctively be tempted by the latter option, before you select it, ask yourself whether it makes sense for the particular product you're selling. After all, how many B2B buyers would jump into a purchase that costs several thousands of dollars immediately after clicking a paid ad? Probably very few. On the other hand, you might be offering something less intimidating than an expensive purchase, such as a 30-day free trial.

The pivotal role content plays in converting leads also applies to landing pages. Identify your top-performing content and use it to create a landing page, making sure it corresponds to the ad copy that convinced the user to click your ad in the first place. Otherwise, you risk a high bounce rate. Make it clear from the beginning what the call to action is, and be careful not to distract from the overriding message with unnecessary details.

No matter how good your PPC campaign is, it won't pay off in the long run on its own. You'll need to execute your campaigns in conjunction with a solid organic search strategy to achieve optimal results.

#232 CREATE CUSTOM DASHBOARDS

Many of the strategies I've recommended up to this point may take some getting used to, but once you've mastered them and grown accustomed to them, I think you'll be ready for more. When you reach that stage, you'll be ready to consider custom dashboards. These give you even more flexibility and freedom when it comes to reporting and data analysis. But what exactly should your custom dashboard be used for?

You might want to include a custom dashboard dedicated to SEO, where you'll collect your top organic keywords, along with your bounce rate and overall number of visits. You could also incorporate top-performing landing pages, plus key metrics like goal completions and goal conversion rates.

Another custom dashboard could focus on site performance. Given the importance of page speed, metrics for this dashboard could cover things like average page load time, server response time, page load time on mobile, and load time by browser.

Based on your objectives, you can include as many custom dashboards as you want. They can each center on a different aspect of your strategy, from mobile and ecommerce to social media and geographic distribution.

CHAPTER 23

EXPLORING THE APPEAL OF VIDEO MARKETING

E ver since viral videos became the norm for B2C brands, B2B businesses have taken notice and begun to utilize the full potential of visual content for themselves.

These numbers should come as no surprise; the power of visual storytelling has long been a strength of content marketing. Ninety percent of the information people receive daily is visual. Simply put, we are much better equipped for processing visual information quickly. Our brains perceive it 60,000 times faster than text. It's only logical that video is the top choice for consuming information not only for entertainment, but also for work and training.

Video content is not only faster to process than text, but also more emotionally engaging. That's why 91 percent of B2B marketers have included video in their content marketing tactics, and another 85 percent believe video is effective for B2B marketing.

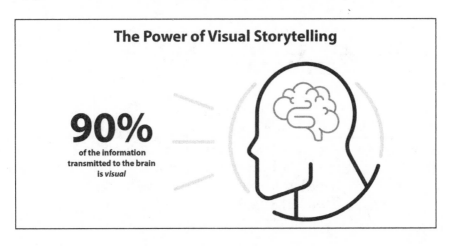

The Power of Visual Storytelling

90%
of the information
transmitted to the brain
is *visual*

But how do you get your audience to click "play"? Let's take a look at the top ten best practices to create engagement for your B2B video marketing efforts.

#233 BUILD A STRATEGY FOR LONG-TERM SUCCESS

One-hit wonders can sometimes happen when you experiment with video, and it's great when something goes viral. But if you want to reliably build your B2B brand through video, a detailed, targeted video marketing strategy is essential. Of equal importance is to track relevant metrics and monitor how your video campaigns are performing.

Besides adding structure, a video strategy can help you define your goals as a business. The best strategies provide in-depth details about your target audiences so that the messages within your videos are tailored to address their pain points.

Your video marketing strategy serves another vital function: It helps ensure that any campaign you launch is aligned with your overall branding and visual identity.

Decide from the start how you'll track the success of your videos. Your strategy defines the metrics you'll use to keep an eye on how well your videos are performing, and that's vital to their success.

#234 CHOOSE THE CUSTOMER-CENTRIC APPROACH

Take a step back and consider the details of your company's marketing approach, and you'll probably find that you do what you do because your customers are interested in how your offering solves a problem that's troubling them. The best way to get people to watch your videos is to showcase problem-solving tactics in a creative, engaging way.

To stand out from the crowd, make sure your video is as customer-centric as possible. Gone are the days when marketing was just about brand. Today, potential customers expect a personalized approach that focuses on them specifically. Your commitment to the plan should be reflected in your B2B video marketing.

Executing customer-centric visual storytelling means embracing empathy and highlighting what your company helps others achieve. How do the solutions offered by your product or service make your customers feel? How does it empower them? Sharing your brand's successes is also meaningful, but the main goal is to make your target audience feel like they run the show.

#235 CREATE EMOTIONAL CONNECTIONS

Visual storytelling is an intricate art with many unwritten rules, but keep in mind that regardless of what your end goal might be, creating emotional connections with your audience should be a top priority. Emotional relatability is crucial because video content is more emotionally evocative and impactful for your viewers than text.

Forging brand loyalty is also key. If you haven't already, it's time to let go of the rigid idea that each marketing effort of your company should be solely focused on bringing in sales. Videos can boost your audience's emotional connection with your company. In the long run, this will mean more loyal customers, as well as increased sales and a more recognizable brand.

There are a number of storytelling methods you can employ to make your brand's narrative resonate. They include telling stories that are both relatable and personal, and using striking video footage and carefully pairing copy to go with it.

#236 GIVE VIEWERS A FIRST-HAND EXPERIENCE

What makes video such a powerful medium is its ability to immerse viewers in the story being told. If you can't be somewhere yourself, watching a video is the next best option. It generates the feeling that you're still participating and getting as close to a first-hand experience as you can.

Customer interviews and testimonials have been the go-to for many brands for directly conveying what people think about a brand, and how they experience that brand's products or services. But explore other ideas, such as "Day in the life of..." videos that follow an employee or a customer, showing what their world is like, and how your product or service has made it a better place. Or how about shooting a short film that provides a behind-the-scenes look at a production location or your offices? You can even shoot something from a first-person point of view by using a GoPro. Or put a personal spin on educational videos.

DON'T RULE OUT HUMOR

Humor has been used sparingly in B2B, yet video marketing is helping to reverse the misconception that B2B customers should only be fed dry, straightforward content. Most people enjoy a good laugh: 53 percent of viewers are more likely to remember advertisement which leverages humor.

It's not about the quantity of humor you use, but rather the way you integrate it into your video marketing campaigns. You don't need to produce an entire comedy show to make your message stand out. Simply adding an entertaining story or a humorous (or even satirical) perspective to your videos can make what you're promoting more relatable.

MASTER THE CALL TO ACTION

Throughout the video production process, remind yourself of your video marketing goals, and make sure you're still aligned to them. As long as you keep this alignment, you'll come up with an engaging video that clearly highlights your message in the right way. Crafting a strong call to action to wrap up your video is the best way to capitalize on that message and drive it home.

This final component of your video can take different shapes depending on your target audience and on the content of your message itself. It's appropriate to tell your audience to take an action, try out your product, subscribe to a newsletter, or take part in a campaign, competition, or webinar. Or, simply, to get to know your brand better by checking out your website.

The call to action is where you need persuasive copywriting to be the most powerful during your video production process. You have a fine line to walk. Your copy should be simple and straightforward, yet also compelling and engaging—and strong enough to motivate someone to take a step. As with any marketing communication, its ultimate purpose will be to lead your viewers to take the next step down the marketing funnel.

#239 DELIVER THE RIGHT TYPE OF VIDEO

Once you have grasped the basics of video content, big questions about style and length come up. Should your videos be short, bite-sized snippets? Or in-depth, ten-minute explorations of a topic or issue? Should they include heavily scripted scenes or animated explanations, or be simple with modest production value?

There's no single answer to these questions. The step that's right for you will depend on your video marketing campaign's goals. There is not complete alignment on exactly what the most effective video asset looks and feels like. For example, 36 percent of executives prefer videos that are between one-to-three minutes, while another 27 percent favor videos between four-to-six minutes.

In fact, a mixture of different types of videos may be the best approach for you. For example, you can construct longer explanatory videos to show how your product works. Then, mix things up by introducing shorter brand-driven videos and ads, along with a number of other kinds of branded videos. Choosing the right option is all a matter of what best fits your marketing priorities.

#240 KEEP UP YOUR BRAND CONSISTENCY

In addition to coming up with engaging ways to tell your brand's story, keep branding in mind when creating your company videos. An otherwise successful video will miss its target if it isn't rooted in your brand strategy and visual identity. If something looks and feels inconsistent with your brand voice, look, and feel, it's less likely to connect with your audience. That's why brand consistency is critical to executing your B2B video marketing strategy.

A coherent brand identity is paramount for forging emotional connections with your audience and, ultimately, converting them into brand ambassadors. Your core brand values need to be aligned with how your videos look, the stories they tell, how they're told, and how they make your viewers feel.

Your goal is to avoid predictable and boring videos, yet ensure consistency that nurtures brand awareness and boosts the success of your marketing efforts.

#241 OPTIMIZE VIDEOS FOR DISCOVERY

Video marketing isn't the easiest marketing asset to craft and deploy, especially with numerous technicalities to consider before diving in, including SEO, which is crucial because it defines how your videos are presented and published online.

What are the basic rules for optimizing your videos? There are a few:

Include an optimized title.
Feature relevant keywords.
Add tags and a full description if applicable.

You can also upload a full transcript or embed closed captions. This text-based information can help direct traffic from your video to a landing page or your blog.

#242 GET YOUR VIDEO SEEN

Even the best videos won't make a big splash if nobody watches them. Thus, effective distribution efforts, paired with video optimization, are key to making your B2B marketing campaign a hit.

But how to do this? The best distribution channels include your own website and blog, as well as your YouTube account and similar video hosting sites. You can share your video marketing campaigns on practically every major social media platform.

Consider additional promotional tactics such as asking viewers to share your video, promoting it via influencers' blogs, and including it in your email newsletter campaigns. Offering free trials and other incentives can also make your videos more shareable.

CHAPTER 24

IMPROVING YOUR IN-HOUSE SKILLS WITH MARKETING TEAM TRAINING

Even if you already have a highly effective marketing department, making sure your team is up to date with the newest and most effective marketing trends is still paramount for delivering successful results. Ensuring your team is equipped with the best tools and expertise will give your marketers the advantage they need to expand the influence of your B2B brand.

The process of acquiring the essential marketing team skill set starts with a thorough understanding of the needs and "experience life cycle" of your customers. It closes with a focus on your audience through community building and engagement. Knowing how to apply the key techniques and tools from this skill set is what can give your company a competitive advantage.

So what's of utmost importance for *your* marketing team's skill set? Here are ten of the most significant tactics from recent years that can be immediately useful to your marketing team.

UNDERSTAND YOUR CUSTOMER'S JOURNEY

The first step in successful marketing training is achieving alignment between the teams responsible for marketing, business development, and sales. Only through ensuring all of these teams have a proper understanding of the business strategy and sales goals of your company can you then properly set marketing targets that will move you collectively closer to your goal.

Once you've executed internal alignment around goals and tactics, it's time to deploy proper training in customer journey mapping and the creation of buyer personas. Customer insight, segmentation, and profiling are essential skills for marketers to develop.

After completing in-depth customer journey training, your marketing team will understand how to:

- Use a customer mapping tool to identify the points of interaction between potential customers and your product's presence
- Conduct customer research to pinpoint the pain points and needs of your target audience, addressing them through brand messages and adequate product representation
- Craft semi-fictional buyer personas that can represent the typical customers your brand targets or wants to attract
- Navigate the customer experience life cycle in order to take your customers from the awareness stage to full engagement and even brand advocacy

Acquiring these skills leads to a better understanding of the actual needs that your product is satisfying. Observing the way customers interact with your brand through your social networks, company website, email, paid search, and ads is crucial to making the right marketing decisions when it comes to where to invest your time and resources.

#244 NAIL YOUR VALUE PROPOSITION

Once your marketing team has become intimately acquainted with the struggles, needs, and attitudes of your customers, it's time to craft a value proposition unique to your organization. An effective value proposition must be based on what you've identified as your customers' biggest pain point, as well as the overall market research findings you've obtained. With all this information in mind, create a value proposition that offers a sharp and effective solution, expressed in a powerful way.

Value proposition training can be a tricky undertaking, as it combines skills from a variety of fields: business development, sales targeting, and copywriting, just to mention a few. It also requires close collaboration between teams within your company to make sure the proposition is optimally aligned with business opportunities and the current market landscape.

Your team members will be better equipped to formulate a strong value proposition if they're trained in using a system such as the value proposition canvas, which identifies the best matches between customers' needs and the marketing messages that will build a successful relationship with the target audience.

Your B2B marketers will also benefit from learning about the work that goes into nailing down a strong value proposition, the step-by-step process of achieving it, and the analytical assessment of its quality. These insights will help your team to strive for top market fit, and to tweak their efforts effectively.

#245 GRASP LEAD GENERATION 101

With a solid value proposition in place, the next step your marketing team needs to take involves successful lead generation training. This concerns the actual process of engaging potential customers, offering them useful and educational information about your product and the playing field, and then leading them through the different stages of your sales funnel.

In order to create a lead generation strategy that fosters quality leads and conversions, your team will need to cultivate the ability to:

- Spark interest in your customers through engaging content, campaigns, and customer relations
- Guide potential leads through the stages of the sales funnel

- Educate prospects by explaining the problems they're facing, and showing how your solutions can solve those problems
- Nurture high value prospects through personalized emails and premium content
- Measure quality leads to help assess ROI

TRAIN IN SOCIAL MEDIA MARKETING

A crucial element of lead generation is mastering communication on social media and in other online outlets. To excel at this, your team must stay on top of social media marketing trends and best practices.

The social media approach not only allows businesses to talk directly to the buyer, but also the peer community influencing the decision of the buyer. But in order to take advantage of this new social media landscape, your team needs to gain skills in influencer marketing and social sharing.

Coming up with a thorough B2B social media strategy is another must. A strategy is not static. Rather, it should be frequently updated and adapted to fit new market trends and communication styles. Your team should also conduct social media audits to assess objectives and results.

Besides your boosting lead generation efforts, social media marketing can be useful in many other aspects of business development. Through social media monitoring, you can find valuable information about your customers and the channels they use. You can then obtain immediate feedback on your products or solutions and use that to inform your product development cycle.

#247 GET GOOD AT B2B COPYWRITING

Making the most of your company's social media presence in the B2B space includes sharing valuable and relevant content with your potential customers. While everyone on your team may not have a hidden Hemingway inside of them, everyone can benefit from training in B2B copywriting.

The top skills that your in-house copywriters should cultivate include copywriting techniques specific to B2B audiences, as well as those aimed at SEO optimization and lead generation. It's best to choose a training course that details both the practical sides of copywriting (such as content structuring, editing, and formatting), as well as the overarching B2B language. Technical knowledge of search engine optimization can take your content efforts to an even higher level, so it's also highly recommended as a part of the training.

Content marketing strategies can bolster the strength and effectiveness of your team even further, as the overall content approach is crucial for the success of individual content campaigns.

#248   ENGAGE WITH B2B STORYTELLING

When it comes to engaging your audience, content writing alone might simply not be enough. Since there's an overwhelming amount of content being produced on any given day, your B2B marketing team can gain a competitive advantage by mastering B2B storytelling.

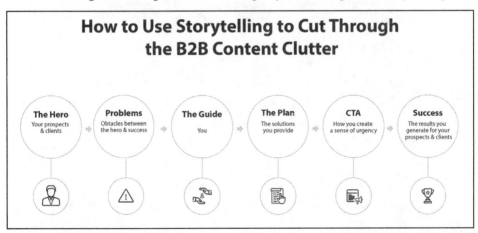

How to Use Storytelling to Cut Through the B2B Content Clutter

The Hero	Problems	The Guide	The Plan	CTA	Success
Your prospects & clients	Obtacles between the hero & success	You	The solutions you provide	How you create a sense of urgency	The results you generate for your prospects & clients

Storytelling is a highly engaging way to educate and captivate your B2B audience, because everybody loves a good story. Learning about the effective "good ol' storytelling techniques" that narrators have been using since ancient times—and their applications today in modern business scenarios—can give you powerful methods for creating buzz around your brand.

To engage your B2B customers with a story in a consistently effective manner, your marketing team will need to cultivate storytelling techniques that include finding your unique brand story, utilizing social media for storytelling campaigns, and brand building through narratives.

#249 BENEFIT FROM THE POWER OF VIDEO MARKETING

Eighty-seven percent of marketers report that video marketing efforts have helped them increase sales. With some basic skills in video making (or by collaborating with a video production house), your marketing team can create inspiring brand videos that give you another exciting chance to "wow" your audience.

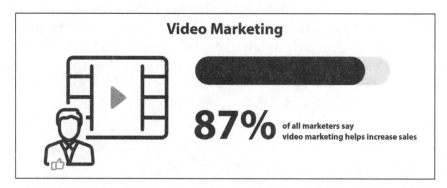

Video Marketing

87% of all marketers say video marketing helps increase sales

Explore the top trends in video marketing to guide your choice of stories, format, and execution. As with all content, the correct distribution is essential for video marketing. But how can video truly become a powerhouse for your brand? After all, that's the ultimate goal, right? You need to give your team members the tools they need to master and engage the top channels for circulating video content. That's what leads to truly memorable campaigns.

#250 ACE THE ESSENTIALS OF EMAIL MARKETING

Email marketing is an essential distribution method for B2B businesses. Time and again, it has been proven to be one of the top B2B communication channels. Taking advantage of the vast reach of email marketing methods can be very important for growing your brand, so empowering your marketing team to optimize their email marketing skills is a wise move.

Even the slightest nuance can make or break your marketing campaign. To ensure they craft effective and powerful email messages, your marketing team will need specific training in:

- Understanding the role of email marketing throughout the customer journey, particularly in lead generation, lead nurturing, and customer feedback
- How to manage email lists and integrating with email marketing automation software
- How to master the right words and messages through B2B email copywriting
- How to evaluate email efforts and measure success

Unleashing the full potential of email marketing starts with laying out a strong strategy. Once your marketing team learns the intricacies of producing sharp email content, finding the right recipients, and proper timing, your company will be well on its way to gaining the broad exposure through email that can really make a difference.

 ## #251 ADD MARKETING AUTOMATION IN THE MIX

When correctly applied, all of the latest marketing tactics can bring about amazing results. And with marketing automation, the entire process can be faster and more efficient. That's why it's worth investing in automation tools, and the time and expense it will take to bring your team up to speed with them.

The most basic and essential asset for your team will be learning the technical application of automation in nitty-gritty detail. To get to that stage, your marketing crew needs to understand how these tools fit into the big picture. Automation creates a shortcut to executing lead nurturing, lead scoring, email marketing, and an array of other essential marketing tactics.

Marketing automation training can provide your team with the technical skills it's missing. This training is useful if you've already started utilizing such tools but have perhaps been slow in adopting them, or aren't using their most essential features. In most cases, your automation tool provider will be able to supply basic training. If needed, you can reliably find alternatives for more advanced coaching that go beyond the specific solution you're using.

 **BUILD AND ENGAGE YOUR COMMUNITY**

Your marketing team can benefit greatly from training in segmentation and audience targeting techniques, as well as in multichannel marketing. Great things become possible when marketers understand and tap into the customer journey. That's why it's so important for them to learn how to use programmatic advertising to exponentially scale the number of people interested in interacting with your brand with minimum time investment.

It's only logical that quality content, effective B2B storytelling, mastery of social media marketing, and a coherent content strategy all contribute powerfully to effective community building and high engagement with your brand. Every element of your marketing team's training will contribute to keeping your customers happy and engaged. The effect is cumulative, so remember this as you train your team on the tools to foster engagement.

CHAPTER 25

PERFECTING YOUR SALES AND MARKETING ALIGNMENT

Sales and marketing work best when they work together. Aligning them can help you achieve an average of 20 percent growth in annual revenue, or a 36 percent increase of customer retention rates and 38 percent sales win rates.

In addition to being more profitable and efficient, internally aligned organizations also provide a better workflow for employees. Alignment brings greater clarity, better understanding of company strategies, and an improved perception of one's job and colleagues for employees. So here are ten best practices that will help you get started.

Marketing	Demand Generation-Lead Sourcing **(Inquiries)**	**Demand Generation**
	Marketing Captured Lead (MCL) **Inquiry** sent to CRM	**Lead Management**
	Marketing Qualified Lead (MQL) Qualified by LDRs as **match to ICP**	
	Sales Accepted Lead (SAL) Qualified by **BDRs**	
Sales	Sales Qualified Lead (SQL) **Opportunity Created**	**Opportunity Management**
	Won "Closed/Won"	

#253 DEFINE KEY CONCEPTS

Effective alignment should begin with defining the common vocabulary your teams are going to use. Marketing may have one notion of what a "qualified lead" is, while sales may see things differently. Not sharing definitions is one of the biggest potential mistakes that can be made when aligning marketing and sales teams.

Definitions of terms are always going to be linked to the sales cycle. Teams must make sure they're referring to the same sales stages as they map out the vocabulary.

Some examples of key terms that always need to be clearly defined are:

> Unqualified Lead
> Prospect / Qualified Lead
> Marketing Qualified Lead (MQL)
> Sales Qualified Lead (SQL)
> Opportunity

Keep in mind that while you should be aligned on terms, you don't have to use the exact same terms as everyone else. Some companies only have MQLs, SQLs, and Opportunities. Others have more granular categories to track leads even more precisely.

The only hard rule for naming is that both marketing and sales teams should be able to map definitions onto the overall sales cycles adopted by the company. That way, the lead handoff process will be clarified, and the teams inside the company will be able to effectively cooperate.

DEFINE SHARED KPIS

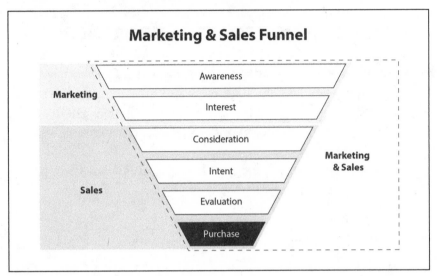

Marketing & Sales Funnel

Shared key performance indicators (KPIs) help sales and marketing teams work together. However, note that "shared KPIs" do not mean "identical KPIs." Instead of aiming for a 1:1 correlation, you should strive to devise KPIs that achieve the goals of each separate team. For example, both sales and marketing teams could have a "conversion rate" KPI. For each of the teams this might mean something different, but it should be related to the other team's KPI.

Expecting sales and marketing to go along with an updated KPI system may prove difficult at first. However, there are solutions to the common challenges to sales and marketing KPI accountability that will make teams feel empowered and excited about KPIs:

- Automate data entry
- Grant access to relevant KPI data
- Incentivize team communication
- Run holistic contests that concern all KPIs and involve the whole team
- Recognize strong KPI performance

These tactics should help make the adoption of KPIs more palatable to both sales and marketing teams.

 #255 DEFINE STRATEGY TOGETHER

It's easier for someone to adopt something that they themselves had a hand in creating. To help align sales and marketing around strategy, have the two teams define their strategies together. For example, sales and marketing can collaborate on the lead generation strategy or the content strategy.

The lead generation strategy will help teams align their understanding of the buyer persona behavior:

> Interests
> Needs and pains
> Goals and motivators
> Role in the decision-making process

Sales and marketing can begin to devise lead generation strategies to capture leads based on these characteristics. A content strategy may also be defined together. Initially it can be done in broader terms, and then given more specificity as alignment between teams increases.

Other strategies that can be defined together include lead scoring methods, as well as service level agreements (SLAs) during each stage of the cycle. SLAs have particular requirements and criteria that need to be passed on a stage-by-stage basis. These include protocols for handling, scoring, and handing off leads. SLAs will also assure that processes are documented and that steps can be replicated, providing teams with yet another source of future data and insights.

#256 COORDINATE CONTENT CREATION AND CAMPAIGNS BETWEEN TEAMS

Sales representatives spend plenty of time speaking to prospects or closing deals. They have an idea of what gets people excited, what prospects need to know before they can proceed, and what consumers want to get from the product or service the company is selling.

You can capitalize on this knowledge for your content creation efforts. Sales can help coordinate the content creation strategy with the marketing team. Marketers, in turn, can notify sales in advance of launching a campaign and can request feedback from them.

Once the campaign is launched and leads are being generated, the marketing team can also provide sales with further information regarding effective processes. They can provide talking points such as stats, business use cases, and "how to" advice which can be offered to prospects. The marketing team can also create a nurturing email template which sales can use to engage new leads or renew old conversations.

#257 INTRODUCE LEAD SCORING AND IMPROVE THE LEAD HANDOFF PROCESS

Lead scoring is the process of ranking leads according to their progress in the sales cycle and their "sales readiness." Agreeing on the proper way to score leads is an important component of creating marketing and sales alignment.

Leads can be scored a number of different ways, including:

- Demographic scoring
- Asset scoring
- Behavior scoring
- Product interest scoring

Once lead scores are in place, the lead handoff process should be examined and regulated. Some businesses choose to use SLA for the lead-handoff process. That way, when a lead is handed over to sales, there is a high degree of certainty that this is not just any prospect.

#258 REPLACE THE TRADITIONAL SALES FUNNEL WITH A REVENUE CYCLE

The traditional sales funnel has become outdated for a number of reasons. For one, it's based on the idea that the sales cycle is one of several distinct stages. First, marketing does its job, then sales does its job, and hopefully, at the end, the deal gets closed. This model also sees the customer as a passive participant who gets pushed around and directed towards the goal. This model also divides the work of teams rigidly—too rigidly, in fact. It may sometimes even pit teams against each other because of different goals, KPIs, and definitions.

Customers today behave differently than they did five or ten years ago. Modern business buyers do more research before they engage with brands and are far more proactive than traditionally understood. They need to be engaged differently and taken through different stages to establish new types of relationships.

Marketo and other marketing automation experts have suggested that the traditional sales cycle can be replaced with a revenue cycle. It is called a "revenue cycle" because revenue is a shared and major goal for both teams, but also because both teams affect the revenue outcome. The stages within this cycle are separated by key "conversion points" of varying importance. Conversion points are more distinct, based on particular interactions between marketing/sales and customers. Customers' movement from the top of the funnel to the bottom is not passive. It is a result of active engagement from both the company's and the customer's sides. When definitions are clear and each team owns a set of conversion points, greater cooperation will move the customer toward the end goal.

With benchmarks and metrics in place, progress along the revenue cycle can be tracked, reported, analyzed, and tweaked according to each situation. Ownership of the entire process is shared, even though marketing may take the lead for some conversion points and sales for others. Opportunities, successes, challenges and errors are collectively assessed and solutions are shared.

#259   GET EXECUTIVE SUPPORT TO MAKE CHANGES

Since sales and marketing likely share the same C-level executive, getting them involved can have a powerful positive impact on the degree of alignment. Executive involvement should not be too hard to get, since execs should already be invested in the success of the whole process.

A formal executive agreement about the need to achieve greater alignment can sometimes speed up the process and get managers and leaders from both teams on the same page. To get executives more involved, support your request with research data and a demonstration of what benefits their input may bring. Provide them with a vision of what could improve if they were to offer their active support.

Securing C-level support can give you opportunities for making changes in processes and introducing exciting new technology, such as integrating a marketing automation platform to be used by both sales and marketing.

#260   TRAIN THE TEAMS TOGETHER

Training can empower both teams and bring them closer to understanding their shared goal(s) as defined by the revenue cycle.

Trainings can focus on:

- Effective deal closure tactics for sales
- Creating leads with high closure rates for marketing

- Proper hand-off of leads for marketing and proper response to shared leads for sales
- Generating new business
- Introducing and mentoring new sales representatives
- Using content effectively during the sales process
- Understanding the target buyer and the revenue cycle
- Enabling sales and working through difficult use cases in a group environment
- Updates on products and services, and best practices for how to align strategies between the teams

Training can also help teams build on their core competencies. This can bring teams closer and help them share information and know-how, in addition to building team spirit.

#261 HAVE REGULAR MEETINGS

It might seem obvious, but regular meetings within and between teams can create the solid foundation which enables training sessions to be efficient.

You can organize and hold meetings on a weekly or monthly basis, such as:

- An onboarding "marketing" meeting during which marketers get to know new salespeople, and vice versa. Marketers can explain and demonstrate how they will support the sales process and what to expect from them.
- Weekly sales meetings during which the sales team briefs the marketing team on their progress, their quotas, and their goals. Marketers can share promotion plans for upcoming campaigns, content, and other offers. Sales can suggest how to optimize the lead gen process, while marketers can share suggestions concerning the follow-up process.
- Monthly sales and marketing manager meetings to analyze results. Teams can comment on metrics at conversion points

such as lead generation, MQLs, and SQLs, and examine the conversion rate. This meeting can also focus on reviewing, evaluating, and even introducing changes to SLAs.

- Weekly brainstorming sessions for marketers only (and/or brief sessions with sales where they are asked what kind of content they find necessary for improving the sales process).

#262 ENABLE SALES AND MARKETING TEAMS THROUGH AUTOMATION

Marketing automation is a net positive technological change. Among its many other benefits, a good marketing automation platform will fine-tune the lead scoring process to a greater degree than has been possible previously. More precise scoring all but guarantees to sales that leads from marketing are truly qualified.

Marketing automation solutions can also be connected to all your information channels. This helps all parties stay on track and keep pace with customers. Both teams will make more informed decisions and have better chances of reaching their goals when they are better connected in this way.

CHAPTER 26

IMPROVING YOUR EVENT MANAGEMENT

A combination of effective event management and marketing can quickly propel a brand to wherever it needs to go. Among executives surveyed, 19 percent report using in-person events as a marketing asset in the last twelve months, and 37 percent state that these events produced optimal results. The Content Marketing Institute identified virtual events, webinars, and online courses as the most effective and most commonly used of all B2B marketing tactics.

Effectiveness Ratings for B2B Tactics

- Virtual events/webinars/online courses
- Research reports
- Short articles/posts (less than 3,000 words)
- E-books/whitepapers
- Case studies
- Videos
- In-person events
- Long articles/posts (more than 3,000 words)
- Infographics/charts/data viz/3D models
- Livestreaming content
- Podcasts
- Print magazines or books

Brands that don't dedicate time to event marketing and management are not tapping into their full potential. Even those that have already adopted event marketing to some degree usually have room to improve their results by combining or adding different marketing tactics.

So how can event marketing work for your brand, and how will it affect the marketing strategies you already have in place? Here are ten best practices to help revolutionize your event management and marketing goals.

#263 FIND THE RIGHT AUDIENCE THROUGH INBOUND MARKETING

Inbound remains the main driver of all things marketing. Its power can be harnessed to help you attract the right people and get them to register for and attend your event. The right content is vital for making that happen.

To create content that engages the right people, start by establishing your target buyer personas. These should be based on data collected through market research. Once you have a good understanding of what your buyer personas are, your content marketing campaigns will be easier to plan and measure.

Inbound is a living, ongoing process which will continually yield new data that you can use to adjust and fine-tune your strategy, which is crucial for event marketing. All too often, event organizers don't use well-defined personas. Accordingly, their events are irrelevant to their targeted potential attendees, resulting in a low registration rate and lower attendance. In order to find the right attendees and see an increase in registrations and engagement, put inbound and lead generation at the heart of your event marketing.

#264 USE MARKETING AUTOMATION TO GENERATE LEADS

You'll need a way to handle all the information you're going to acquire during event organization, especially if you're expecting an influx of data from registrations from your content. Marketing automation is ideal for this purpose. It will aid in collecting, processing, and segmenting data before, during, and after an event.

Initial landing pages, such as your registration page, will capture information about the attendees. And once you have your buyer personas mapped out, you can use automation to segment attendees based on the information they've provided.

Marketing automation's potential goes even further. It can be used for setting up autoresponders at each stage of the lead acquisition process, and even for more complex tasks like importing and assigning leads to various follow-up email campaigns based on which buyer persona they fit.

#265 AUTOMATE EMAIL CAMPAIGNS FOR FURTHER LEAD GEN AND NURTURING

You can create successful campaigns that are fully automated. They can be adapted to a variety of purposes, such as encouraging participants to come to an event or scheduling appointments. Depending on where a lead is in the buyer's journey, automated campaigns can do everything from capturing the lead to nurturing it along.

Drip campaigns are another important component of automated email marketing connected to nurturing. If you input all your leads into a CRM tool and assign them different labels based on the persona or buying stage they represent, then drip campaigns can periodically remind the lead of your upcoming event, send the lead relevant material, or nurture the lead after the event (if they aren't quite ready to commit to the sale).

#266 DEVELOP A VIRAL SOCIAL CAMPAIGN

Creating a campaign that has the potential to go viral isn't an easy task. Yet, ultimately, its impact is worth the work and investment. It's also important to know what you're doing. Seventy percent of marketers now consider viral campaigns extremely important. Yet only 37 percent feel they know how to create them effectively.

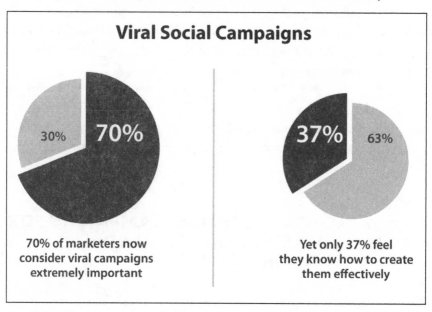

Viral Social Campaigns

30% 70%

37% 63%

70% of marketers now consider viral campaigns extremely important

Yet only 37% feel they know how to create them effectively

Before an event, I recommend using social networks to drive attendance and build awareness and engagement. Then, during an event, use social media to post photos and announce event-related information or contests. And afterwards, publish content that summarizes event highlights, as well as leverages influential customers and industry leaders to help give it viral properties. This is also an ideal time to start promoting your next event.

In order to get the most out of viral campaigns, don't forget to segment your audience when distributing targeted content.

#267 DON'T FORGET TO UTILIZE HASHTAGS AND SOCIAL AMBASSADORS

Hashtags can go a long way in a social campaign. They're a great way to break the ice, engage your followers in conversations, and increase the visibility of your posts.

Make event hashtags easily recognizable, simple, and short. Ideally, your hashtag will catch on with other users. Then all you'll need to do is monitor the conversation, respond to comments when necessary, and jump back in to get the discussion going again whenever it dies down.

Simply sharing your event online and getting a few people to share a post isn't enough. You'll need extra support. That's where your advocates' and ambassadors' endorsements come in. They humanize the experience for other followers, making your brand and event even more recognizable. After the event, thank your social ambassadors by promoting their work in return.

#268 CREATE DIFFERENT TYPES OF CONTENT

Just as you'll need to employ a range of social media strategies, you'll also need to offer varied types of content and segment them accordingly, depending on the stage of your event. There are two main kinds of content to use for an event: informative content and buzz content.

Informative content includes information about an event such as registration dates, the location, and the featured speakers. This content is helpful in responding to any questions prospective attendees might have, and is directly related to branding, awareness, and education.

Buzz content is the content you want to go viral. It can be anything that creates excitement or anticipation. This is where your hashtag fits in perfectly. Devise games, awards, and giveaways to get your audience's attention. If you like, utilize user-generated content that you cross-promote through different channels. This type of content is more concerned with lead generation, customer engagement, and upselling than it is with comporting useful information.

Both informative and buzz content require an editorial calendar. Start planning it well in advance of an event to gradually build awareness and momentum. The goal is to create immersive experiences that people want to pass along. In other words, your content has to be shareable, likeable, and pinnable. Include visuals, compelling copy, and a strong CTA at the end.

#269 REUSE CONTENT TO GENERATE AND NURTURE LEADS AFTER THE EVENT

After the event, you'll have the opportunity to generate more leads or turn existing leads into customers by nurturing them with event-related content.

There are many ways to repackage, repurpose, or recycle extant event-related content. Anything that shows how successful the event was, including videos (presentations, interviews), podcasts, or even blog post recaps will help keep your leads warm during this "afterglow" period. Ask attendees to take part in surveys or studies to get a better idea of how you can improve the event next time.

Whenever you hear from a satisfied participant, follow up and offer them premium content in hopes that they'll turn into a lead. This premium content could come in the form of infographics that show the event's successes and number of attendees, or as white papers and ebooks relevant to the conference's theme. You can also make specialized content assets available exclusively to attendees through their registration number or a gated form.

#270 IMPRESS ATTENDEES WITH DIGITAL ASSETS

Some digital assets are more compelling than others. Event apps, digital swag bags, and cashless payment options are some of the most effective ones you can use. Event apps are not only great substitutes for guides and program schedules, but also can function as networking tools with built-in chat, messaging, and live-streaming capabilities. Since networking is among the most important reasons folks attend any event, providing your attendees with tools to enhance their networking experience will get you a lot of credit.

Cashless payment options are also especially suitable for medium-to-large sized events where there are likely to be long lines. These apps allow people to quickly make or accept payments through their mobile devices.

Virtual swag bags can complement or even take the place of physical goody bags. Not only can they create buzz, but they also give you another opportunity to collect the information of potential leads.

#271 COLLECT DATA AT EVERY STEP

Whether it's through registration forms, app activity, or correspondence at the event itself, you should gather as much useful data as possible that can either be turned into content or used to analyze the event's success.

Types of data you can collect include:

- Session attendance and booth visit stats
- Content engagement (before, during, and after the event)
- Social media activity (check-ins, app usage, and tweets)
- In-app surveys and poll results
- Appointments made as a result of the event

- Instances of expressed interests in meeting and discussing business possibilities
- Overall mobile engagement

 ## #272 MEASURE EVENT ROI DRIVERS

Measuring your return on event (ROE) is one of the most important steps in assessing the success of an event. But to do this, you'll need to know which metrics are relevant to your marketing goals. One metric you might want to track is customer lifetime value (CLV), which provides hard data on how profitable your event was.

In addition to metrics, your goals should likewise be concrete. Whether it's acquiring a particular number of leads or converting a specific number of leads into customers, identifying your goals will help you better assess how you've performed.

If you're able to benchmark your data by comparing your event to those of your competitors, you'll be able to determine the impact of your event's effectiveness against theirs and against your industry cohort as a whole. You'll also be able to benchmark against your previous events to see how you've improved (and where you might still need improvement).

CHAPTER 27

BOOSTING YOUR BRAND'S LINKEDIN PERFORMANCE

Gone are the days when LinkedIn was only viewed as a platform for headhunting and showcasing elaborate resumes. Ninety-two percent of B2B marketers identified LinkedIn as their most used social network.

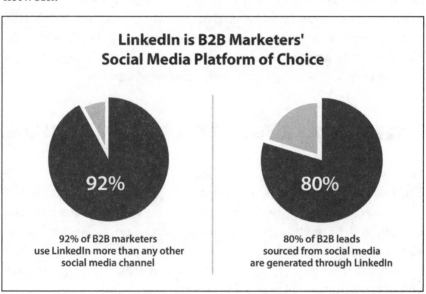

**LinkedIn is B2B Marketers'
Social Media Platform of Choice**

92%

92% of B2B marketers
use LinkedIn more than any other
social media channel

80%

80% of B2B leads
sourced from social media
are generated through LinkedIn

Eighty percent of B2B leads sourced from social media are generated through LinkedIn. So you can see the value for the great opportunities that it offers for branding, content promotion, thought leadership, and, ultimately, lead generation. But of course, it also provides a platform for facilitating valuable connections with influencers and prospects, as well as for executing social CRM and social listening tactics.

Whether you're ready to launch a LinkedIn strategy or already executing one, the ten best practices outlined next should help guide your LinkedIn efforts on the path to success.

 DETERMINE THE BASIS FOR YOUR BRAND'S SUCCESS

The first step in shaping your B2B company's success on LinkedIn should be building a solid foundation for your branding and marketing. That starts with optimizing your personal and company pages using consistent language, visuals, and overall branding.

Next, establish yourself as a thought leader on LinkedIn by utilizing Pulse, LinkedIn's integrated publishing platform. Using this platform, experts and professionals can share their views, potentially giving visibility to both their personal brands and their companies. You can write articles for Pulse to tap into LinkedIn's potential for the specialized targeting of your self-published content.

 MAKE YOUR COMPANY PAGE SHINE

Go visual on LinkedIn by following the example of other successful social media channels. As I've noted, people are able to process visual information much faster than words, which means that you can tell a story more efficiently with images and video. So besides showcasing your brand's logo and visual identity, you can also use your distinct branding in banners, Pulse article images, company videos, and infographics or other promotional assets.

How your brand speaks to your intended audience is also important, so use SEO techniques to research the right keywords, and then integrate them into the company description section of your LinkedIn page. This is key for developing a solid brand image and getting your page discovered by the right people. Bring your page to life by completing the Products and Services tab, Careers tab, and

Company Page FAQ. It's worth your time. Also, be sure to regularly post company updates that are visually rich.

After updating your Company Page, think about how you can start promoting it. There are simple tricks such as adding your company page URL to your email signature, website, and Twitter accounts, so you can create multiple opportunities for people to explore it.

 ## USE THE POWER OF SHOWCASE PAGES

Besides perfecting your main Company Page, you'll want to create separate Showcase Pages for your products or services to target specific segments of your audience. These become niche pages for each of your distinct offerings. Even though they're linked to the main Company Page, these pages enable you to segment your target groups and engage your buyer personas with more relevant, interesting content tailored directly to them. Plus, you get performance tracking analytics for each page.

Your Showcase Pages need to carry the distinct branding of the product or service they're presenting. As with your Company Page, it's worth sharing different assets such as educational materials, product videos, and presentations on these pages.

 ## FORMULATE YOUR CONTENT MARKETING PLAN

LinkedIn is now the top channel for content distribution; it has been proven to drive the most traffic to B2B websites and blogs. In light of this, dedicating a special content plan for LinkedIn would be a wise step.

The best content strategies for LinkedIn start with an analysis of which type of content will perform best on your Company and Showcase Pages. Since each of these pages targets a specific segment of your audience, you have the best chances if you produce articles, ebooks, case studies, and visual assets that address each segment. The focus of the content should always be on giving your audience actionable, useful advice rather than promoting your company.

Creating LinkedIn Groups on industry topics also helps drive engagement and establishes your brand as a thought leader. Groups are the perfect place to share your branded content and spur conversations around it.

 ## #277 SPREAD THE WORD ABOUT YOUR B2B BRAND

Next, explore the most effective ways to distribute your assets. Content promotion, as well as social media campaigns, can bring traffic to your LinkedIn profiles and your website and blog. These elements can work in sync to build your brand.

Share an update containing a link at least once per day from your Company Page at a time when your audience is most likely to engage (probably during the workday). Although you might not have enough of your own original content to share daily, you can still post relevant articles and white papers produced by other experts. Employ content curation to keep a constant and coherent story flowing through your LinkedIn channel.

As an extension of the LinkedIn Groups strategy, you can also create and run thematic groups of your own and participate in existing industry groups. These groups often have tightly knit audiences that are interested in a specific topic. By deploying your own high-value content there, you'll give further exposure to your brand.

 ## #278 GET HELP FROM SPONSORED UPDATES

Once you have a grasp of outreaching opportunities available on LinkedIn through its non-paid features, you'll want to test out

Sponsored Updates, LinkedIn's native advertising format. It can boost your branding, your relationship-building, and your lead generation efforts by reaching an audience that exists beyond your own connections on the platform.

Sponsored Updates allow for a high level of targeting when promoting your best blog posts, white papers, infographics, and videos. You can choose between cost-per-click (CPC) and cost-per-thousand impressions (CPM) models when it comes to payment, and set budgets depending on your campaign's goals.

You can select from a range of different targeting options:

Followers or non-followers
Locations
Industries
Job titles
Skills, gender, age
Membership of particular LinkedIn Groups

Obviously, the capability to be this targeted can bring great advantages. However, it's only worth investing in Sponsored Updates if you're genuinely confident in the quality of the content you plan to share. Sharp copy, attention-grabbing titles, and impressive images are all must-haves for a winning campaign. The persuasiveness of your overall campaign, and especially your calls to action, can make the difference between turning off your audience and eventually converting them into customers.

#279 REACH THE RIGHT PEOPLE WITH SPONSORED INMAIL

With Sponsored InMail, your messages will go straight to the inboxes of your target customers and influencers.

InMail is a function included with LinkedIn Premium accounts. With it, you can send messages, updates, and other announcements to the followers of your Company Page. However, there are limits to the number of people you can reach with basic InMail. However, with Sponsored InMail, you can take your lead generation a step further.

Sponsored InMail gives you the opportunity to perform highly focused targeting that works the same way Sponsored Updates do, allowing you to reach exactly the right people whether they're leads you're nurturing, potential brand advocates, or another target. Your InMail will be delivered to a recipient's inbox only when they're online, ensuring they'll see your message in real time rather than having it buried in their crowded inboxes. Needless to say, this is a tactic you may find well worth the expense.

#280 AMPLIFY YOUR PRESENCE WITH SOCIAL PROOF

Over time, your brand's influence on LinkedIn will grow as your activity on the network becomes more frequent. An element that can help you grow more quickly and effectively is social proof.

Social proof means using social networks to deploy testimonials. The most direct approach to influencing people's views of your company is to actively seek customer reviews and testimonials for your LinkedIn pages. After all, what's more convincing than actual customers recommending your products or services? Customer testimonials are considered a highly effective content marketing tactic on LinkedIn. To take this tactic even further, work with your most loyal customers to write case studies. They provide an opportunity to showcase how your product has helped other B2B businesses.

#281 TRACK YOUR PROGRESS ON LINKEDIN ANALYTICS

No B2B LinkedIn strategy is complete without a working method to track your performance. By following the right metrics, you'll be able to A/B test and swiftly adapt your approach in pursuit of the best results. LinkedIn offers built-in analytics you can use as a starting point for measuring success and tailoring your strategy.

Thanks to this component, you're able to see KPIs for each update you've posted via your Company Page, including impressions, clicks, interactions, and engagements. There's also aggregated data based on time, reach, and different forms of engagement by users. You can even access details about your followers, including growth and engagement rates, as well as demographic information like their respective industries and positions.

Another important feature is the Analytics tab, which lets you track metrics like page views, unique visitors, and their demographics. All these analytics enable you to track the success of your campaigns and your overall performance, so that you can compare your LinkedIn marketing results against your investment to measure ROI. This information can mean the difference when it comes to making the adjustments and tweaks that make your campaign a success.

#282 GROW YOUR LINKEDIN CONNECTIONS INTO OFFLINE RELATIONSHIPS

Remember the core purpose of using LinkedIn for your B2B marketing; to boost your branding, boost lead generation, and, ultimately, to boost sales. Going the extra mile and nurturing your LinkedIn connections into real-life contacts is bound to support your goals because it boosts each of these things.

Turning LinkedIn contacts into customers, brand advocates, partners, and even employees begins with an initial exchange with your target contacts. Conduct thorough research to get this exchange right. Cultivate a good understanding of their priorities, needs, and pain points. This will put you in an ideal position to extend an offer that's mutually exclusive. Later, you can suggest meeting up at a conference or industry event, or perhaps invite them to stop by your office the next time they're in town. Make it personal and meaningful, but make that initial contact on LinkedIn.

CHAPTER 28

GOING THE EXTRA MILE WITH YOUR MARKETING

B2B marketers are always on the lookout for new opportunities to expand their marketing opportunities and apply new innovations. Content marketing has proven to be one of the most effective methods available for this. Content marketing remains highly significant today because it can easily adapt to new trends and tactics. It's no wonder that 73 percent of B2B marketers say they're actively including it in their marketing strategies.

We've covered some of the most common inbound and content marketing techniques like blogging (both in-house and guest blogging), premium content creation, and social media promotion. Other powerful techniques include email marketing—one of the top ways to nurture leads—and influencer marketing, which allows you to harness industry expertise to grow your brand and reach new customers.

Investing in the most popular and proven marketing methods is crucial, but there are also additional approaches you might not have considered. Behavioral targeting, sales enablement, and relationship marketing are just a few of these additional tools at a modern marketer's disposal.

I'd like to close by sharing the top ten often overlooked best practices to use alongside your marketing strategy. These are key to building your brand and helping your B2B company win over new prospects.

#283 MASTER SALES ENABLEMENT MARKETING

Sales enablement marketing is an elusive concept that even seasoned B2B marketers still struggle to define. In fact, many activities that you're probably already doing fall into the "sales enablement" category such as coaching your sales team members or providing them with quality content. Making the most out of sales enablement is just a matter of consolidating and streamlining these efforts.

Sales enablement entails effective communication between different areas of your company. You need to devise quality onboarding and training programs for new and existing sales personnel to guarantee they'll be on the same page as your marketing team. The purpose of sales enablement is to boost sales productivity by providing your representatives with the training, marketing assets, and metrics they need to do their job well. When properly executed, sales enablement can have a significant impact on your sales forces.

#284 TAKE A SHOT AT BEHAVIORAL TARGETING

Retargeting ads serves as a more sophisticated alternative to traditional forms of online advertising. Also known as behavioral targeting, this approach involves displaying relevant advertising messages to prospects who have *already* interacted with your brand.

The two most common types of retargeting are pixel-based and list-based.

In pixel-based retargeting, ad platforms show your ads to people who have visited your website.

In list-based retargeting, you upload the emails of existing prospects to platforms like Twitter or Facebook, which then display your messages to these specific individuals.

Retargeting gives you a greater level of control over who sees your ads, and when. Using this tactic can also allow you to segment lists and display various messages to different visitors. Finally, if you do choose to adopt this technique, be sure to track click-through and view-through conversions to measure success.

#285 OPTIMIZE FOR LOCAL SEARCH MARKETING

Local search marketing means tailoring your online presence for local directories and search engines. This type of marketing can help you differentiate your company based on physical proximity, which can factor into buying decisions for local customers.

Through focusing on local searches, anyone in the area looking for the services you offer will be more likely to discover your business. Also, don't forget local PPC advertising. It allows you to test out geo-targeted campaigns for specific areas or cities. Remember, the higher level of relevance in local ads makes for better performance than campaigns with a larger reach.

#286 GET ON BOARD WITH PERSONALIZATION

"Personalization" has become a B2C marketing buzzword. True, making things personal increases customer retention and satisfaction and can potentially boost a company's revenue. But personalization isn't only reserved for B2C. Data shows that B2B decision-makers also expect personalization in their interactions with brands.

You can use a combination of marketing automation software and content management to offer increasingly personalized recommendations (or other targeted content) to potential buyers. This increases brand awareness and can help you forge relationships with prospects even before they consider a purchase, which can reinforce lead generation.

You can personalize your communications with account-based marketing (targeting groups rather than individuals), customized messaging within product trials, and segmented emails. Keep in mind that business buyers are driven by similar motivations to those that drive consumers.

#287 BRING YOUR BRAND TO LIFE WITH INTERACTIVE CONTENT

You can effectively demonstrate relevance to an audience through interactive content. This has already been tested in B2C and is now slowly entering the B2B world as well. With engaging interactive content, you can break through the content overload your prospects are experiencing and differentiate your company.

Interactive content can include a wide range of assets that can engage online visitors and enhance their experience with your brand; games, quizzes, assessments, interactive visuals, and videos are just a few examples. These content types are more dynamic than traditional forms. They can better hold viewers' attention by putting them in the driver's seat, and they can also offer the opportunity for two-way communication with your content.

While bringing your brand to life, interactive content also gives you deeper insight into your customers' preferences. You can use analytics at different stages of your users' interaction with this content to leverage data to inform personalization campaigns and other content initiatives.

#288 MEET THE NEW B2B TREND: VLOGGING

Video is on the rise in all avenues of marketing today. Vlogging (video blogging) is a natural outgrowth of this trend. More and more B2B marketers are experimenting with the immediacy a video blog provides. It can boost B2B brands' emotional resonance and visibility and give your communications a personal touch.

Vlogging entails creating regular video content, usually centered around a prominent person, a specific topic, or industry. As with any other kind of content, it can inform, educate, and entertain your audience. It can be just as informative as written content, but its bite-size format helps to engage today's digitally savvy customers.

Distribution is another benefit of vlogging, since videos get shared 12 times more than other content types. You should get to know your audience's preferences well before you launch your video campaigns in order to craft attention-grabbing vlogs just for them.

And while video can go viral more easily, note that not every video guarantees success. Be sure to balance information, humor, and problem-solving for the best results.

#289 START A WEBINAR SERIES

You can educate your audience while increasing brand awareness by creating a webinar. These online broadcasts are great for helping your B2B audience grasp new concepts and acquire new skills. The results can include both higher engagement and a shorter buying cycle, plus it positions your business giving the webinar as a team of experts knowledgeable in the field. Today, two-thirds of B2B marketers consider webinars an effective part of a marketing mix.

Before you launch a one-time event or webinar series, consider the topic, speakers and participants, timing, and registration. Preparation is crucial, especially for live webinars. Give yourself time to plan and rehearse, and schedule things far in advance. When brainstorming topics for your webinars, consider the relevance, and feature presentations that show your business has its finger on the pulse of recent developments. These are all keys to success.

Invite industry leaders and influencers to be guest speakers, since they bring their own audiences with them. Guest presenters not only increase your reach, but also position your brand as a thought leader in your industry.

After your webinar, try sharing the slides and repurposing the webinar content into different formats for further distribution. You can even post recorded webinars behind a gate.

#290 ATTRACT NEW AUDIENCES THROUGH PODCASTS

A less costly alternative to a webinar is doing a podcast. A podcast's purpose is similar; it also aims to educate and offer listeners new ideas and skills. Informative and engaging podcasts can improve your brand's position as an industry expert and pull in new traffic and attract new leads.

A podcast is like a prerecorded radio show that can be replayed at any time. As with other content marketing efforts, podcasts are most successful when they aim for relevance. Podcasts can cover a wide range of subjects and can also include input from guest experts and influencers. They shouldn't be viewed as a means to sell your products and services. Rather, they are a channel to demonstrate your knowledge base to your prospects. Still, always add calls to action in podcasts to create opportunities to lead your listeners down the funnel.

Once recorded, use your social media networks and email campaigns to distribute your podcasts. Podcasts are frequently listened to while commuting to work, and the average American commute of 26.4 minutes offers us an interesting guideline for episode length. Highly valuable or engaging podcasts will be reshared. If you've interviewed influencers, their audiences will also be exposed to your content (as with webinars). Thus, podcasts are also great for SEO purposes, but make sure to invest time and resources in adequate distribution.

#291 ENRICH YOUR CONTENT WITH VISUAL STORYTELLING

Visual storytelling isn't a marketing method, but it is an approach that's worth applying to your overall content strategy. Visual storytelling may require employing the services of a graphic designer or artist on a regular basis. Visuals are powerful for B2C and B2B alike, since visual information is much more easily digested, and often has a stronger emotional impact.

The forms that your visual storytelling can take are limitless, from infographics, visual narratives and employee-generated content, to simply adding images to your social media updates. As with any other venture, you'll want to take a moment to formulate a strategy. You can create a series of infographics over time that each cover different problems your prospects are likely to be experiencing. Or you can start simply by placing images within your blog posts or other content assets that you promote regularly.

Don't be afraid to take risks and try new things. Why not execute a fully visual campaign for your next product launch? Or create an illustrated story for your lead nurturing emails instead of regular text?

Don't let any misconceptions about B2B buyers' tastes stop you; imagery is easier to consume and relatable for everyone. Used properly, it can strengthen your marketing impact every time it's used.

#292 BUILD UPON RELATIONSHIP MARKETING

Last but not least, relationship marketing is a great foundation for B2B marketing. This is a holistic approach that allows you to build stronger, longer-lasting relationships with your customers. It's the opposite of arbitrary display ads and empty sales messages.

The basis of relationship marketing is using evidence-based data to adapt your strategy to customer behavior and expectations. For this, you'll need extensive research and constant testing. Examine your sales funnel carefully to see where people are falling off. That's how you'll learn where to focus on relationship building.

Consider also your customer's preferred channels of communication. Open up interactions with people where they already like to get their information, and in a way that they'd feel comfortable with.

Once you've made contacts, following up is important as well, as it's the key to making your brand memorable.

EXPLORE NEW METHODS FOR YOUR B2B MARKETING

Many of these ten practices have already been successfully deployed in B2C marketing as reliable ways to raise brand awareness and generate new leads. But there is still huge potential and "green space" for B2B marketers to test out traditionally B2C techniques in order to stand out from the crowd.

No matter what direction you decide to take, remember these two takeaways: remain relevant, and don't be afraid to experiment.

FINAL THOUGHTS

We're living in exciting times when it comes to B2B marketing. We have more tools at our disposal than we've ever had before, and incredibly powerful ways to get our messages across. Yet at the same time, the marketplace is crowded. Our competition also has these powerful new tools, and it's easier than ever for our messages to get lost in a sea of noise. On top of that, our potential customers have more distractions making an appeal for their attention than ever before.

But I hope I've made clear in this book that with the right tactics, it's possible for B2B marketers to reach through this noise and make powerful connections with customers. In order to be effective marketers in this new environment, we need to avail ourselves of all the best practices that can give us an edge. In this book, I've tried to lay out the best practices that have helped me to succeed personally, and that I believe can translate to anyone working anywhere in the B2B content marketing spectrum. It's my hope that you can take these approaches, find the ones that work best for you, and make them your own. Because if you can do that, nothing's going to stop you.

Happy marketing!

REFERENCES

Chapter 1

32 Stats & Facts That Prove Infographics Aren't Dead. (n.d.). *Marq Blog*. Retrieved June 30, 2023, from https://www.marq.com/blog/32-infographic-stats-facts

Adamson, B. & Toman, N. (2020, August 04). 5 Ways the Future of B2B Buying Will Rewrite the Rules of Effective Selling. *Gartner*. Retrieved June 30, 2023, from https://www.gartner.com/en/sales/insights/b2b-buying-journey

Berezhetskaya, V. (2023, March 06). Inbound vs Outbound B2B Marketing. *Involve.me Blog*. Retrieved June 30, 2023, from https://www.involve.me/blog/inbound-vs-outbound-b2b-marketing

Bretous, M. (2022, April 12). 7 B2C Marketing Examples to Learn From. *Hubspot Blog*. Retrieved June 30, 2023, from https://blog.hubspot.com/agency/b2c-campaigns-b2b-marketers-learn

Campbell, K. (2023, June 08). 2023 Online Reputation Management Statistics. *Reputation X Blog*. Retrieved June 30, 2023, from https://blog.reputationx.com/online-reputation-management-statistics

Kusinitz, S. (2022, May 6). The Definition of a Buyer Persona [in Under 100 Words]. *Hubspot Blog*. Retrieved June 30, 2023, from http://blog.hubspot.com/marketing/buyer-persona-definition-under-100-sr

Lead Nurturing. (2022, July 22). Lead Nurturing. *Adobe Experience Cloud Blog*. Retrieved June 30, 2023, from https://business.adobe.com/blog/basics/lead-nurturing

Mawhinney, J. (2022, September 27). 50 Visual Content Marketing Statistics You Should Know in 2022. *Hubspot Blog*. Retrieved June 30, 2023, from http://blog.hubspot.com/marketing/visual-content-marketing-strategy

McGinley, C. (2023, January 20). 20 of the Best Marketing Tips, According to HubSpot Blog Data and Experts. *Hubspot Insiders*. Retrieved June 30, 2023, from https://blog.hubspot.com/insiders/inbound-marketing-tips

Nelson, A. (2016, July 22). 50 Awesome Content Marketing Stats. *Marketing Cloud Blog*. Retrieved December 22, 2016, from https://www.marketingcloud.com/blog/50-content-marketing-stats/

Pitre, A. (2022, August 10). 39 Simple Ways to Grow Your Email List. *Hubspot Blog*. Retrieved June 30, 2023, from http://blog.hubspot

.com/blog/tabid/6307/bid/32028/25-Clever-Ways-to-Grow-Your-Email-Marketing-List.aspx

Scherer, J. (2016, December 05). The Complete Guide to Gating your Content. *Wishpond Blog.* Retrieved December 22, 2016, from http://blog.wishpond.com/post/115675436300/gated-content

Schneider, D. (2022, September 03). How to Invite Influencers to Guest Post on your Blog. *Neal Schaffer Blog.* Retrieved June 30, 2023, from https://nealschaffer.com/invite-influencers-guest-post-blog/

Stahl, S. (2022, October 19). 7 Things B2B Content Marketers Need in 2023. *Content Marketing Institute Blog.* Retrieved June 30, 2023, from https://contentmarketinginstitute.com/articles/b2b-content-marketing-research-trends-statistics

Trimble, C. (2015, July 30). Why online video is the future of content marketing. *The Guardian.* Retrieved December 22, 2016, from http://www.theguardian.com/small-business-network/2014/jan/14/video-content-marketing-media-online

Wainwright, C. (2017, August 29). 38 Fantastic Inbound Marketing Blogs You Ought to Be Reading. *Hubspot Blog.* Retrieved June 30, 2023, from http://blog.hubspot.com/blog/tabid/6307/bid/34133/39-Fantastic-Inbound-Marketing-Blogs-You-Ought-to-Be-Reading.aspx

Walter, E. (2013, March 3). B2B Marketing Doesn't Have to Be Boring: 3 Companies That Effectively Add Humor to Their Marketing Mix. *Forbes.* Retrieved December 22, 2016, from http://www.forbes.com/sites/ekaterinawalter/2013/12/03/b2b-marketing-doesnt-have-to-be-boring-3-companies-that-effectively-add-humor-to-their-marketing-mix/#4e19d97739ab

Chapter 2

Berger, B. (2022, December 30). People Are Talking about Your Brand—Here's How to Engage. *Mention.* Retrieved July 03, 2023, from https://mention.com/en/blog/engage-with-brand-audience/

Best Social Media Monitoring Software. (n.d.). *G2Crowd.* Retrieved December 22, 2016, from https://www.g2crowd.com/categories/social-media-monitoring?order=survey_responses_count

Brandwatch. (n.d.). *Brandwatch.* Retrieved July 03, 2023, from https://www.brandwatch.com/

Insights. (n.d.). *Hootsuite.* Retrieved July 03, 2023, from https://www.hootsuite.com/products/insights

Karr, D. (2015, September 25). There's a Ton of Value for B2B in Social Media. *Marketing Tech Blog.* Retrieved July 03, 2023, from https://martech.zone/theres-a-ton-of-value-for-b2b-in-social-media/

Monitoring and Social Media Management. (n.d.). *Mention.* Retrieved July 03, 2023, from https://mention.com/en/

Social Listening & Market Intelligence Platform. (n.d.). *Digimind*. Retrieved July 03, 2023, from http://www.digimind.com/

Social media listening guide. (2022, September 05). *Talkwalker Blog*. Retrieved July 03, 2023, from https://www.talkwalker.com/blog/social-media-listening-guide

Chapter 3

Anderson, M. K. (2021, May 25). The Best of B2B Marketing Content: 10 Examples. *Hubspot Blog*. Retrieved July 03, 2023, from https://blog.hubspot.com/marketing/b2b-content-marketing-examples

Content Idea Generator - Portent. (n.d.). *Portent*. Retrieved December 22, 2016, from https://www.portent.com/tools/title-maker

Cox, L. K. (2021, October 29). 15 Testimonial Page Examples You'll Want to Copy. *Hubspot Blog*. Retrieved July 03, 2023, from https://blog.hubspot.com/service/testimonial-page-examples

De Mers, J. (2016, February 15). 7 Ways to use Your Competitors to Your Advantage for SEO. *Forbes*. Retrieved December 22, 2016, from http://www.forbes.com/sites/jaysondemers/2016/02/15/7-ways-to-use-your-competitors-to-your-advantage-for-seo/#75b6925c6b19

Enge, E. (2015, May 26). Using Partnerships to Accelerate Content Marketing & Link Building. *Search Engine Land Blog*. Retrieved December 22, 2016, from http://searchengineland.com/using-partnerships-accelerate-content-marketing-221208

Grimm, J. (2015, December 10). The Best Branded Content Partnerships of 2015. *Adage Blog*. Retrieved December 22, 2016, from http://adage.com/article/digitalnext/brand-content-partnerships-2015/301683/

McCormack, L. (n.d.). Content Marketing 101. *Buildfire Blog*. Retrieved July 03, 2023, from https://buildfire.com/content-marketing-101-primer-part/

Miller, N. (2016, April 04). Twitter Chats 101: A Step-by-Step Guide to Hosting or Joining a Twitter Chat. *BufferApp Blog*. Retrieved December 22, 2016, from https://blog.bufferapp.com/twitter-chat-101

Patel, N. (2016, January 21). 38 Content Marketing Stats that Every Marketer Needs to Know. *Neil Patel Blog*. Retrieved December 22, 2016, from http://neilpatel.com/2016/01/21/38-content-marketing-stats-that-every-marketer-needs-to-know/

The State of Content Marketing: 2023 Global Report. (n.d.). *Semrush GoodContent*. Retrieved July 03, 2023, from https://www.semrush.com/goodcontent/state-of-content-marketing/

Chapter 4

100m Articles Analyzed: What You Need To Write The Best Headlines [2021]. (2021, August 17). *BuzzSumo Blog*. Retrieved July 03, 2023, from https://buzzsumo.com/blog/most-shared-headlines-study/

Aagaard, M. (2013, July 24). 5 Landing Page Headline Formulas Tested. *Unbounce Blog*. Retrieved July 03, 2023, from https://unbounce.com /landing-pages/5-landing-page-headline-formulas-tested/

Bauer, E. (2021, March 23). 7 Formulas for Landing Page Headlines that Practically Write Themselves (With Examples). *Unbounce Blog*. Retrieved July 03, 2023, from https://unbounce.com/landing-page-examples /formulas-for-landing-page-headlines-with-examples/

Bennett, A. (2016, September 25). Headlines: When the Best Brings the Worst and the Worst Brings the Best. *Outbrain Blog*. Retrieved December 22, 2016, from http://www.outbrain.com/blog/2013/07/headlines-when -the-best-brings-the-worst-and-the-worst-brings-the-best.html

Betteridge's law of headlines. (n.d.). *Wikipedia*. Retrieved July 03, 2023, from https://en.wikipedia.org/wiki/Betteridge's_law_of_headlines

Cavagnetto, S. (2023, January 16). How to Create Blog Posts that Get Results in 2023. *Koozai Blog*. Retrieved July 03, 2023, from https://www.koo-zai.com/blog/content-marketing-seo/anatomy-perfect-blog-post/

Clark, B. (2022, June 02). How to Write Headlines that Work. *Copyblogger Blog*. Retrieved June 03, 2023, from https://copyblogger.com/how-to -write-headlines-that-work/

Dopson, E. (2021, September 08). How to Increase Blog Traffic in 9 Proven Steps. *CoSchedule Blog*. Retrieved July 03, 2023, from https://cosched ule.com/blog/how-to-increase-blog-traffic

Headline Analyzer. (n.d.). *Advanced Marketing Institute*. Retrieved July 03, 2023, from http://www.aminstitute.com/headline/

Headline Analyzer. (n.d.). *CoSchedule*. Retrieved July 03, 2023, from http://coschedule.com/headline-analyzer

Leaning, B. (2017, February 01). A Data-Driven Guide to Writing Better Headlines [Free Ebook]. *Hubspot Blog*. Retrieved July 03, 2023, from https://blog.hubspot.com/marketing/write-effective-headlines

Molyneux, L. & Coddington, M. (2020). Aggregation, Clickbait and Their Effect on Perceptions of Journalistic Credibility and Quality. *Journalism Practice*, 14:4, 429-446. Retrieved July 03, 2023, from https://www.tandfonline.com/doi/abs/10.1080/17512786.2019.1628658 ?journalCode=rjop20

Morris, J. (2014, January 27). Could This Headline Technique Double Your Click-Throughs Too? *Copyblogger Blog*. Retrieved July 03, 2023, from http://www.copyblogger.com/question-headlines/

Patel, N. (n.d.). The Definitive Guide to Writing a Headline that Doesn't Suck (Tips, Tactics & Tools Included). *Neil Patel Blog*. Retrieved July 03, 2023, from https://neilpatel.com/blog/write-better-headlines/

Patel, N. (2022, December 23). Headlines that Convert: 5 Key Characteristics. *CXL Blog*. Retrieved July 03, 2023, from https://cxl.com/blog/5-characteristics-high-converting-headlines/

Perricone, C. (n.d.). Everything You Need to Know About Ecommerce Marketing. *Hubspot Blog*. Retrieved July 03, 2023, from https://blog.hubspot.com/marketing/ecommerce-marketing

Reeves, K. (2011, June 03). 5 Tips to improve Your Headline Click-Through Rate. *Content Marketing Institute Blog*. Retrieved July 03, 2023, from https://contentmarketinginstitute.com/articles/headline-click-through-rate/

Shoor, I. (2013, June 06). The Dark Science Of Naming Your Post: Based On Studying 100 Blogs. *Oribi Blog*. Retrieved July 03, 2023, from http://blog.oribi.io/the-dark-science-of-naming-your-post-based-on-studying-100-blogs/

Stop Writing Boring Headlines: 11 Types of Headlines That Pique Reader Interest. (2015, December 02). *QuickSprout Blog*. Retrieved July 03, 2023, from https://www.quicksprout.com/headline-examples/

Widrich, L. (2013, June 18). A Scientific Guide to Writing Great Headlines on Twitter, Facebook, and Your Blog. *Buffer Blog*. Retrieved July 03, 2023, from https://buffer.com/resources/a-scientific-guide-to-writing-great-headlines-on-twitter-facebook-and-your-blog/

Wishart, M. (2022, October 18). Top 10 Tips for Marketers When Writing Listicles. *KNB Communications Blog*. Retrieved July 03, 2023, from https://www.knbcomm.com/blog/top-10-tips-for-marketers-when-writing-listicles

Chapter 6

Consumer Email Tracker 2021. (2021, March 29). *Validity Blog*. Retrieved July 03, 2023, from https://www.validity.com/resource-center/consumer-email-tracker/

An Introduction to Lead Generation. (n.d.). *HubSpot Blog*. Retrieved July 03, 2023, from https://offers.hubspot.com/lead-generation-introduction.

Mester, M. (2020, July 04). Top MarTech Blog: What Are the Key Challenges for Marketing Automation Experts? *MarTech Series*. Retrieved July 03, 2023, from https://martechseries.com/mts-insights/guest-authors/what-are-the-key-challenges-of-marketing-automation-experts/

Chapter 7

B2B Buyers Rely on Vendor Websites for Content. (2020, April 8). *Marketing Charts*. Retrieved July 03, 2023, from https://www.marketingcharts.com/industries/business-to-business-112579

The Beginner's Guide to Email Marketing. (n.d.). *Hubspot.* Retrieved July 03, 2023, from https://offers.hubspot.com/an-introduction-to-email-marketing

Bernat, K. (2023, June 8). Top B2B Marketing Trends 2023: Profitability, AI, and Customer Experience. *WPromote Blog.* Retrieved July 03, 2023

Bernazzani, S. (2021, June 09). 30 Ways to Slice Your Email Database for Better Email List Segmentation. *Hubspot Blog.* Retrieved July 04, 2023, from https://blog.hubspot.com/marketing/email-list-segmentation

Bunskoek, K. (n.d.). 4 Strategies to Optimize Your Email Segmentation Campaigns. *Wishpond Blog.* Retrieved July 04, 2023, from http://blog.wishpond.com/post/68789242665/4-strategies-to-optimize-your-email-segmentation

Capland, A. (2017, February 01). What Content Should You Use in Your Lead Nurturing Emails? *Hubspot Blog.* Retrieved July 04, 2023, from http://blog.hubspot.com/customers/bid/185316/What-Content-Should-You-Use-in-Your-Lead-Nurturing-Emails

The Complete Guide to B2B Email Marketing. (n.d.). *Salesforce.* Retrieved July 04, 2023, from https://www.salesforce.com/form/marketing/the-complete-guide-to-b2b-email-marketing/

Cox, L. K. (2022, October 07). 14 of the Best Examples of Beautiful Email Design. *Hubspot Blog.* Retrieved July 04, 2023, from https://blog.hubspot.com/marketing/email-design-templates-and-inspiration

Cox, L. K. (2023, June 23). How to Write a Marketing Email: 10 Tips for Writing Strong Email Copy. *Hubspot Blog.* Retrieved July 04, 2023, from https://blog.hubspot.com/blog/tabid/6307/bid/32606/The-9-Must-Have-Components-of-Compelling-Email-Copy.aspx

Email Course 101: 5 Things to Know When Creating an Automated Email Series. (2019, May 29). *Campaign Monitor.* Retrieved July 04, 2023, from https://www.campaignmonitor.com/blog/email-marketing/2016/05/email-course-101-5-things-know-when-creating-automated-email-series/

Email Marketing Statistics & Benchmarks. (n.d.). *Mailchimp Blog.* Retrieved July 04, 2023, from https://mailchimp.com/resources/email-marketing-benchmarks/

Hongcharu, B. (2019, February). Effects of Message Variation and Communication Tools Choices on Consumer Response. *Global Business Review,* 20:1, 42-56. Retrieved July 04, 2023, from https://journals.sagepub.com/doi/10.1177/0972150918803528

How to Create a Curated Email Newsletter That Drives Results for Your Business. (2019, June 25). *Campaign Monitor.* Retrieved July 04, 2023, from https://www.campaignmonitor.com/blog/email-marketing/curated-email-newsletters/

Kirsch, K. (2023, May 12). The Ultimate List of Email Marketing Stats for 2023. *Hubspot Blog.* Retrieved July 03, 2023, from https://blog.hubspot.com/marketing/email-marketing-stats

Leszczynski, M. (n.d.). 2023 Email Marketing Benchmarks by GetResponse. *GetResponse Blog.* Retrieved July 04, 2023, from https://www.getresponse.com/resources/reports/email-marketing-benchmarks

Máté, Z. (2023, June 09). Single opt-in vs double opt-in – the definitive answer to the age-old question. *GetResponse Blog.* Retrieved July 04, 2023, from https://www.getresponse.com/blog/single-opt-in-vs-double-opt-in

Rimmer, A. (2023, January 18). What is Marketing Automation? A Beginner's Guide. *Hubspot Insiders.* Retrieved July 04, 2023, from https://blog.hubspot.com/insiders/what-is-marketing-automation-a-beginners-guide

Rumberger, J. (2023, March 10). 14 Real-Life Examples of CTA Copy YOU Should Copy. *Hubspot Blog.* Retrieved July 04, 2023, from http://blog.hubspot.com/blog/tabid/6307/bid/33401/14-Real-Life-Examples-of-CTA-Copy-YOU-Should-Copy.aspx#sm.oooei1cw614gyeccz2611a ehjq87w

What's Email Authentication? How Does It Apply to Me? (2023, February 15). *AWeber.* Retrieved July 04, 2023, from https://help.aweber.com/hc/en-us/articles/204026716-What-s-Email-Authentication-How-Does-It-Apply-To-Me-

Chapter 8

18 Proven Email Marketing Best Practices. (n.d.). *Adobe Resource Center.* Retrieved July 05, 2023, from https://business.adobe.com/resources/articles/email-marketing-best-practices.html

About Spam Filters. (n.d.). *Mailchimp.* Retrieved July 05, 2023, from https://mailchimp.com/en/help/about-spam-filters/

B2B Email marketing best practices. (2013, November 20). *Smart Insights.* Retrieved July 05, 2023, from http://www.smartinsights.com/email-marketing/email-creative-and-copywriting/b2b-email-marketing-best-practices/

Best Practices for Email Subject Lines. (n.d.). *Mailchimp.* Retrieved July 05, 2023, from https://mailchimp.com/help/best-practices-for-email-subject-lines/

Bonderud, D. (2023, April 18). 20 Statistics About Sales Email Subject Lines You Need to Know for 2023. *Hubspot Blog.* Retrieved July 05, 2023, from https://blog.hubspot.com/sales/subject-line-stats-open-rates-slideshare

Borden, T. (2018, March 9). Proof That B2B Executives Are Using Mobile to Make Purchase Decisions. *Weidert Blog.* Retrieved July 05, 2023, from https://www.weidert.com/blog/proof-that-b2b-executives-are-using-mobile-to-make-purchase-decisions

The Complete Guide to B2B Email Marketing. (n.d.). *Salesforce*. Retrieved July 05, 2023, from https://www.salesforce.com/form/marketing/the -complete-guide-to-b2b-email-marketing/

Email Client Market Share. (2023, May). *Litmus*. Retrieved July 05, 2023, from https://www.litmus.com/email-client-market-share

Email Deliverability Cheat Sheet. (n.d.). *Adobe Resource Center*. Retrieved July 05, 2023, from https://business.adobe.com/resources/articles/email -deliverability.html

Kirsch, K. (2023, May 12). The Ultimate List of Email Marketing Stats for 2023. *Hubspot Blog*. Retrieved July 05, 2023, from https://blog .hubspot.com/marketing/email-marketing-stats

The New Rules of Email Marketing. (n.d.). *Campaign Monitor*. Retrieved July 05, 2023, from https://www.campaignmonitor.com/resources/guides /email-marketing-new-rules/

Patel, N. (n.d.). 7 Marketing Lessons from Eye-Tracking Studies. *Neil Patel Blog*. Retrieved July 05, 2023, from https://neilpatel.com/blog /eye-tracking-studies/

The path to email engagement. (n.d.). *Mailjet Blog*. Retrieved July 05, 2023, from https://www.mailjet.com/resources/research/email-engagement-2021/

Shiryan, Y. (2021, May 23). It Only Takes 6 Seconds to Decide Whether or Not to Open an Email. *QuantifyNinja Blog*. Retrieved July 05, 2023, from https://quantifyninja.com/a/blog/it-only-takes-6 -seconds-to-decide-whether-or-not-to-open-an-email

Vocell, J. (2022, July 17). The Difference Between Marketing Email and Transactional Email. *Hubspot Blog*. Retrieved July 05, 2023, from http://blog.hubspot.com/customers/difference-between-transactional -and-marketing-email

Chapter 9

12 Second Rule: How Can You Plan Your Emails Accordingly? (n.d.). *Upland Blog*. Retrieved July 05, 2023, from https://uplandsoftware.com /adestra/resources/blog/12-second-rule/

Carpenter, C. (2012, December 13). A Meta-Analysis of the Effectiveness of the "But You Are Free" Compliance-Gaining Technique. Retrieved July 05, 2023, from http://www.tandfonline.com/doi/abs/10.1080 /10510974.2012.727941

Griffel, M. (n.d.). How to Get a Busy Person to Respond to Your Email. *Huffington Post*. Retrieved July 05, 2023, from http://www.huffing tonpost.com/mattan-griffel/email-etiquette_b_4849649.html

Hayden, B. (2016, April 05). Your Step-by-Step Email Marketing Strategy Guide [Free Checklist]. *Copyblogger Blog*. Retrieved July 05, 2023, from https://copyblogger.com/email-marketing-checklist/

Huang, K. (2022, February 28). Tips for Writing Compelling Email Call-To-Action (CTA) Copy. *Litmus Blog*. Retrieved July 05, 2023, from https://www.litmus.com/blog/email-cta-copy-tips

Kirsch, K. (2023, May 12). The Ultimate List of Email Marketing Stats for 2023. *Hubspot Blog*. Retrieved July 05, 2023, from https://blog.hubspot.com/marketing/email-marketing-stats

Paul, A. M. (2012, March 17). Your Brain on Fiction. *New York Times*. Retrieved July 05, 2023, from http://www.nytimes.com/2012/03/18/opinion/sunday/the-neuroscience-of-your-brain-on-fiction.html

Seeling, T. (2010, January 06). Harnessing the Thrill of Surprise. *Psychology Today*. Retrieved July 05, 2023, from https://www.psychologytoday.com/blog/creativityrulz/201001/harnessing-the-thrill-surprise

Shiryan, Y. (2021, May 23). It Only Takes 6 Seconds to Decide Whether or Not to Open an Email. *QuantifyNinja Blog*. Retrieved July 05, 2023, from https://quantifyninja.com/a/blog/it-only-takes-6-seconds-to-decide-whether-or-not-to-open-an-email

Chapter 10

Bramley, E. (2016, January 13). How to Conduct a Complete PPC Audit. *SEMRush*. Retrieved July 05, 2023, from https://www.semrush.com/blog/how-to-conduct-a-complete-ppc-audit/

Chaffey, D. (2021, July 16). Landing page examples and 12 tips. The Perfect Landing Page. *Smart Insights*. Retrieved December 22, 2016, from http://www.smartinsights.com/lead-generation/lead-generation-strategy/perfect-landing-page/

Cosley, J. (2015, April 01). Bing Ads Power Tools: Ad Insights. *Search Engine Land*. Retrieved July 05, 2023, from http://searchengineland.com/bing-ads-power-tools-ad-insights-217118

Dane, J. (2016, April 20). Three PPC Landing Page Tips Hardly Anyone Takes Advantage Of. *Marketing Profs*. Retrieved July 05, 2023, from http://www.marketingprofs.com/articles/2016/29769/three-ppc-landing-page-tips-hardly-anyone-takes-advantage-of

Irvine, M. (2021, November 22). 7 Ways Bing Ads Beats Google AdWords. *WordStream*. Retrieved July 05, 2023, from http://www.wordstream.com/blog/ws/2015/02/25/bings-ads-vs-google-adwords

Jones, H. (2014, June 25). 13 Reasons Branded PPC Campaigns Are Beneficial for B2B Brands. *Search Engine Land*. Retrieved July 05, 2023, from http://searchengineland.com/13-reasons-branded-ppc-campaigns-beneficial-b2b-brands-193786

Kerschbaum, J. (2015, January 21). Taking a Closer Look at Google In-Market vs. Affinity Audiences. *Search Engine Watch*. Retrieved July 05, 2023, from https://searchenginewatch.com/sew/how-to/2391214/taking-a-closer-look-at-google-in-market-vs-affinity-audiences

Marvin, G. (2016, July 28). Google AdWords to break up tablet & desktop and enable a mobile base bid. *Search Engine Land*. Retrieved July 05, 2023, from http://searchengineland.com/google-adwords-break-tablet-desktop-enable-mobile-base-bid-250214

Mohsin, M. (2023, January 13). 10 Google Search Statistics You Need to Know in 2023 [Infographic]. *Oberlo Blog*. Retrieved July 05, 2023, https://www.oberlo.com/blog/google-search-statistics

O'Brien, C. (2023, February 16). How to do a PPC Competitive Analysis. *Digital Marketing Institute Blog*. Retrieved July 05, 2023, from https://digitalmarketinginstitute.com/blog/how-to-do-a-ppc-competitive-analysis

Patel, N. (n.d.). PPC Tools to Improve Your Ad Campaigns. *Neil Patel Blog*. Retrieved July 05, 2023, from https://neilpatel.com/blog/ppc-automation/

Perricone, C. (n.d.). The Ultimate Guide to PPC Marketing. *Hubspot Blog*. Retrieved July 05, 2023, from https://blog.hubspot.com/marketing/ppc#sm.0000e1dueky7ze9ntpx18ueqfirv7

Soames, C. (2012, September 19). Mini Guide to Adwords Remarketing. *Smart Insights*. Retrieved July 05, 2023, from http://www.smartinsights.com/internet-advertising/behavioural-ad-targeting/mini-guide-to-adwords-remarketing/

The State of PPC 2019-2020. (n.d.). *Brainlabs*. Retrieved July 05, 2023, from https://www.brainlabsdigital.com/marketing-library/state-of-ppc-2019-2020/

The State of PPC: Global Report 2022. (n.d.). *PPC Survey*. Retrieved July 05, 2023, from https://www.ppcsurvey.com/

Working with Dynamic Text Replacement. (2022, October 19). *Unbounce*. Retrieved July 05, 2023, from http://documentation.unbounce.com/hc/en-us/articles/203661004-Using-Dynamic-Text-Replacement-pro

Chapter 11

Davis, S. (2023, July 05). Programmatic Advertising Trends, Stats, & News. *ROI Revolution Blog*. Retrieved July 05, 2023, from https://roirevolution.com/blog/programmatic-advertising-trends-stats-news/

Hughes, D. (2021, October 12). The Beginner's Guide to Programmatic Advertising. *Digital Marketing Institute Blog*. Retrieved July 05, 2023, from https://digitalmarketinginstitute.com/blog/the-beginners-guide-to-programmatic-advertising

Kesler, A. (n.d.). Programmatic Media Buying for B2B. *INFUSEmedia Insights*. Retrieved July 05, 2023, from https://infusemedia.com/insight/programmatic-media-buying-for-b2b/

Liu, A. (2022, July 06). Powerful Programmatic Advertising Strategies for Clients. *AgencyAnalitics Blog*. Retrieved July 05, 2023, from https://agencyanalytics.com/blog/programmatic-campaign-best-practices

Chapter 12

Bilton, R. (2014, July 09). Why interactivity is taking over publishers' native ads. *Digiday*. Retrieved July 06, 2023, from http://digiday.com/publishers/publishers-bring-interativity-to-native-ads/

Chaffey, D. (2023, February 14). 2023 average ad click through rates (CTRs) for paid search, display and social media. *Smart Insights*. Retrieved July 06, 2023, from https://www.smartinsights.com/internet-advertising/internet-advertising-analytics/display-advertising-clickthrough-rates/

Digital Industry Insider. (n.d.). *Business Insider*. Retrieved July 06, 2023, from http://www.businessinsider.com/digital-industry-insider

Ginns, D. (2023, January 26). Study shows native ads are most effective channel for brand favorability. Taboola. *The Drum's Open Mic*. Retrieved July 05, 2023, from https://www.thedrum.com/profile/taboola/news/study-shows-native-ads-are-most-effective-channel-for-brand-favorability

Ha, A. (2013, June 23). BuzzFeed Says New 'Flight Mode' Campaign Shows 'The Consumerization of B2B Marketing.' *TechCrunch*. Retrieved July 06, 2023, from https://techcrunch.com/2013/06/23/buzzfeed-flight-mode/

In Full Disclosure: Why We Love Transparency in Native Advertising. (n.d.). *Giant Media*. Retrieved July 06, 2023, from http://www.giantmedia.com/in-full-disclosure-why-we-love-transparency-in-native-advertising/

Kloot, L. (2022, May 12). Top Native Advertising Statistics for 2022. *Outbrain Blog*. Retrieved July 05, 2023, from https://www.outbrain.com/blog/native-advertising-statistics/

Martin, M. (2023, March 13). 29 Twitter Stats That Matter to Marketers in 2023. *Hootsuite Blog*. Retrieved July 06, 2023, from https://blog.hootsuite.com/twitter-statistics/

Native Ads in B2B Advertising and Marketing; A Few Best Practices. (2022, March 04). *Martech Series Insights*. Retrieved July 06, 2023, from https://martechseries.com/mts-insights/staff-writers/native-ads-in-b2b-advertising-and-marketing-a-few-best-practices/

Native Advertising from B2B Brands: a June 2021 Update. (n.d.). *MediaRadar Blog*. Retrieved July 05, 2023, from https://mediaradar.com/blog/native-advertising-b2b-brands-june-update/

Native Advertising—It's organic. It's fresh. It's handcrafted. (n.d.). *Visually*. Retrieved July 06, 2023, from http://visual.ly/native-advertising-its-organic-its-fresh-its-handcrafted

Newberry, C. (2022, September 12). Twitter Ads for Beginners: The 2023 Guide. *Hootsuite Blog*. Retrieved July 06, 2023, from https://blog.hootsuite.com/twitter-ads/

Patel, N. (n.d.). LinkedIn Ad Best Practices: Comprehensive Guide. *Neil Patel Blog.* Retrieved July 06, 2023, from https://neilpatel.com/blog/guide-to-linkedin-ads1/

Peterson, T. (2015, September 29). YouTube's Most Native Ad Yet Puts Shoppable Cards into Organic Videos. *Adage.* Retrieved July 06, 2023, from http://adage.com/article/digital/youtube-shopping-ads-akin-google-search-ads-pre-rolls/300635/

Sibley, A. (2021, June 11). How to Use LinkedIn's 'Sponsored Updates,' a New Type of Ad for Company Pages. *Hubspot Blog.* Retrieved July 06, 2023, from http://blog.hubspot.com/marketing/linkedin-launches-sponsored-updates-nj#sm.oooei1cw614gyeccz2611aehjq87w

The Ultimate Guide to Advertorials. (2023, February 20). *Native Advertising Institute Blog.* Retrieved July 06, 2023, from https://www.nativeadvertisinginstitute.com/blog/the-ultimate-guide-to-advertorials

Umbriac, M. (2023, July 04). How Native Advertising Is on the Rise for SaaS B2B Marketing. *LinkedIn Pulse.* Retrieved July 06, 2023, from https://www.linkedin.com/pulse/how-native-advertising-rise-saas-b2b-marketing-matt-umbriac/?trk=public_post

Why Mobile Apps Have Higher Conversion Rates Than Websites. (2021, October 28). *Eventya Blog.* Retrieved July 06, 2023, from https://www.eventya.net/eventya-platform-news/why-mobile-apps-have-higher-conversion-rates-than-websites/

Young, B. (2016, May 27). The Best Native Advertising Examples. *Nudge.* Retrieved July 06, 2023, from http://giveitanudge.com/best-native-advertising-examples/

Chapter 13

12th Annual B2B Content Marketing Benchmarks, Budgets, and Trends. (2022). *Content Marketing Institute.* Retrieved July 06, 2023, from https://contentmarketinginstitute.com/wp-content/uploads/2021/10/B2B_2022_Research.pdf

The 2016 B2B Buyer's Survey Report. (n.d.). *Demand Gen Report.* Retrieved July 06, 2023, from https://www.demandgenreport.com/resources/research/2016-b2b-buyer-s-survey-report

Abdalslam, A. (2023, January 29). Lead Scoring Statistics, Trends and Facts 2023. *Abdalslam Blog.* Retrieved March 31, 2023, from https://abdalslam.com/lead-scoring-statistics

Best Social Media Platforms for B2B Marketers in 2023. (n.d.). *Khoros Blog.* Retrieved July 06, 2023, from https://khoros.com/blog/top-social-media-platforms-b2b-marketers

Chaffey, D., Jones, R., & Leszczynski, M. (n.d.). Email Marketing and Marketing Automation Excellence 2018. *GetResponse.* Retrieved

July 06, 2023, from https://www.getresponse.com/resources/reports /email-marketing-and-marketing-automation-excellence-2018

Davidson, S. (2022, October 10). Where Do Marketers Get Leads? [Data]. *Hubspot Blog.* Retrieved July 06, 2023, from https://blog.hubspot.com /marketing/where-do-marketers-get-leads-data

Dean, B. (2023, March 27). 30 Crucial B2B Marketing Statistics (2023). *Backlinko Blog.* Retrieved July 06, 2023, from https://backlinko.com /b2b-marketing-stats

Fontanella, C. (2020, December 14). 25 Stats That Make the Case for Infographics in Your Marketing. *Hubspot Blog.* Retrieved July 06, 2023, from https://blog.hubspot.com/marketing/infographic-stats

Gartner Sales Survey Finds 83% of B2B Buyers Prefer Ordering or Paying Through Digital Commerce. (2022, June 22). *Gartner.* Retrieved July 06, 2023, from https://www.gartner.com/en/newsroom/press -releases/2022-06-22-gartner-sales-survey-finbds-b2b-buyers -prefer-ordering-paying-through--digital-commerce

Gynn, A. (2023, January 12). Why You Struggle to Prove Content ROI— and How to Settle Up (or Down). *Content Marketing Institute Blog.* Retrieved July 06, 2023, from https://contentmarketinginstitute.com /articles/content-roi-struggle

Heltzman, A. (2023, March 15). Organic vs. Paid Search: (84 Astonishing) Statistics for 2023. *Highervisibility Insite Blog.* Retrieved July 06, 2023, from https://www.highervisibility.com/seo/learn/organic-vs-paid-search -statistics/

How to Match Content to Buyer's Journey Stage. (2017, February 16). *Ironpaper B2B Articles.* Retrieved July 06, 2023, from https://www.ironpaper .com/webintel/articles/how-to-match-content-to-buyers-journey-stage

The Impact of Reviews on B2B Buyers and Sellers. (n.d.). *G2.* Retrieved July 06, 2023, from https://learn.g2.com/hubfs/Sell%20Microsite%20 Files/The%20Impact%20of%20Reviews%20on%20B2B%20-%20 Report.pdf

Kenny, J. (2023, January 05). How to Nail Sales and Marketing Alignment in 2023. *Sopro Blog.* Retrieved July 06, 2023, from https://sopro.io /resources/blog/complete-guide-sales-marketing-alignment/

McCue, I. (2022, December 14). 13 Omnichannel Challenges and How to Avoid Them. *Oracle NetSuite Blog.* Retrieved July 06, 2023, from https://www.netsuite.com/portal/resource/articles/ecommerce/omnichannel -challenges.shtml

Raichshtain, G. (2014, November 20). B2B Sales Benchmark Research Finds Some Pipeline Surprises (Infographic). *Salesforce's The 360 Blog.* Retrieved July 06, 2023, from https://www.salesforce.com/blog/b2b -sales-benchmark-research-finds-some-pipeline-surprises-infographic/

Sirohi, A. (2023, June 05). What Is the Average Email Marketing ROI? *Constant Contact Blog*. Retrieved July 06, 2023, from https://www.constantcontact.com/blog/what-is-the-roi-of-email-marketing/

Stenitzer, G. (2023) Top 100 Content Marketing Question: What are the top 3 most popular types of content marketing? Which are most effective? *Crystal Clear Comms Blog*. Retrieved July 06, 2023, from https://crystalclearcomms.com/most-popular-types-of-content-marketing/

Thakkar, D. (n.d.). 25+ Lead Nurturing Statistics to Drive More Revenue. *Salesmate Blog*. Retrieved July 06, 2023, from https://www.salesmate.io/blog/lead-nurturing-statistics/

Witt, T. (2023, February 28). LinkedIn Statistics for Marketers in 2023. *SproutSocial Insights*. Retrieved July 06, 2023, from https://sproutsocial.com/insights/linkedin-statistics/

Chapter 14

Korolov, M. (2022, October 26). 4 Data Quality Challenges That Hinder Data Operations. *TechTarget*. Retrieved July 06, 2023, from https://www.techtarget.com/searchdatamanagement/tip/Data-quality-challenges-that-hinder-data-operations

Zarrella, D. (2021, June 11). Which Types of Form Fields Lower Landing Page Conversions? *Hubspot Blog*. Retrieved July 06, 2023, from https://blog.hubspot.com/blog/tabid/6307/bid/6746/Which-Types-of-Form-Fields-Lower-Landing-Page-Conversions.aspx

Chapter 15

2020 Predictions From Leading B2B Marketing Practitioners. (n.d.). *PathFactory Blog*. Retrieved July 06, 2023, from https://www.pathfactory.com/blog/2020-predictions-from-leading-b2b-marketing-practitioners/

Baruffati, A. (2023, May 19). Account-Based Marketing Statistics 2023: How Effective Is This Strategy? *Gitnux Blog*. Retrieved July 06, 2023, from https://blog.gitnux.com/account-based-marketing-statistics/

Chapter 16

Awasthi, A. (n.d.). B2B Customers Want Great Experiences Too and Here Are 4 Ways to Meet Their Expectations. *Adweek*. Retrieved July 06, 2023, from https://www.adweek.com/partner-articles/b2b-customers-want-great-experiences-too-and-here-are-4-ways-to-meet-their-expectations/

The B2B Buying Journey. (n.d.). *Gartner*. Retrieved July 06, 2023, from https://www.gartner.com/en/sales/insights/b2b-buying-journey

The Definitive Guide to Lead Generation. (n.d.). *Adobe Experience Cloud*. Retrieved July 06, 2023, from https://business.adobe.com/resources/guides/lead-generation/

Russell, A. (2022, September 27). Display Advertising—The Ultimate Guide to Remarketing. *Grapeseed Media Blog*. Retrieved July 06, 2023, from https://grapeseedmedia.com/blog/display-advertising-the-ultimate-guide-to-remarketing/

Chapter 17

B2B Influencer Marketing Report. (2022, July 07). *TopRank Marketing Blog*. Retrieved July 06, 2023, from https://www.toprankmarketing.com/guide/b2b-influencer-marketing-research-report/

Baruffati, A. (2023, June 13). The Most Important B2B Marketing Statistics & Trends 2023. *Gitnux Blog*. Retrieved July 06, 2023, from https://blog.gitnux.com/b2b-marketing-statistics/

Edwards, S. (2015, April 28). 9 Valuable Tips for Conducting PR Outreach. *Inc*. Retrieved July 06, 2023, from http://www.inc.com/samuel-edwards/9-valuable-tips-for-conducting-pr-outreach.html

Fletcher, K. (2022, May 14). 5 Ways PR Wins at Generating B2B Sales. *Entrepreneur*. Retrieved July 06, 2023, from https://www.entrepreneur.com/growing-a-business/5-ways-pr-wins-at-generating-b2b-sales/424576

Greesonbach, S. (n.d.). Is There a Difference Between Digital PR and Inbound Marketing? *Whittington Consulting Blog*. Retrieved July 06, 2023, from https://www.rickwhittington.com/blog/difference-between-digital-pr-inbound-marketing/

Joyner, R. (2017, July 28). 7 Important PR Lessons Every Content Marketer Needs to Learn. *Hubspot Blog*. Retrieved July 06, 2023, from http://blog.hubspot.com/marketing/important-pr-lessons

Patel, N. (n.d.). The Definitive Guide to Online Reputation Management. *Neil Patel Blog*. Retrieved July 06, 2023, from https://neilpatel.com/blog/guide-to-reputation-management/

Pinkowska, M. (2023, February 19). How to Measure the Results of a PR Campaign? *Brand24 Blog*. Retrieved July 06, 2023, from https://brand24.com/blog/measure-pr-campaign/

Schwartz, B. (2022, July 28). Google Search Quality Raters Guidelines Updated Today. *Search Engine Land*. Retrieved July 06, 2023, from https://searchengineland.com/google-search-quality-guidelines-updated-today-386798

Sweezey, M. (n.d.). 80 Percent of B2B Buyers Expect Real-Time Interaction. *Convince & Convert Blog*. Retrieved July 06, 2023, from https://www.convinceandconvert.com/customer-experience/buyers-expect-real-time-interaction/

Weerarathna, T. (2022, January 22). The Role of Storytelling in PR. *LinkedIn Pulse*. Retrieved July 06, 2023, from https://www.linkedin.com/pulse/role-storytelling-pr-thilani-weerarathna/

Wittersheim, A. (2023, January 17). The Top 8 Most Important B2B Social Media Marketing Trends in 2023. *Stefanini Group Insights*. Retrieved July 06, 2023, from https://stefanini.com/en/insights/articles /the-top-8-most-important-b2b-social-media-marketing-trends-in-2023

Chapter 18

Arruda, N. (2013, October 8). Three Steps For Transforming Employees Into Brand Ambassadors. *Forbes*. Retrieved July 07, 2023, from http: //www.forbes.com/sites/williamarruda/2013/10/08/three-steps-for -transforming-employees-into-brand-ambassadors/#784687c53a53

Brand Advocates Share More Info. (2011, May 09). *Marketing Charts*. Retrieved July 07, 2023, from http://www.marketingcharts.com/online /brand-advocates-share-more-info-17369/

Cass, J. (2015, February 18). Start Building Social Media Brand Advocates —Here's How. *Just Creative*. Retrieved July 07, 2023, from http: //justcreative.com/2015/01/27/social-media-advocates/

Essential Loyalty Marketing Statistics for 2019. (n.d.). *Saasquatch Blog*. Retrieved July 07, 2023, from https://www.saasquatch.com/blog/essential -customer-loyalty-statistics-for-2019/

Hoffman, A. (2023, January 11). What Is Customer Advocacy? *Influitive Blog*. Retrieved July 07, 2023, from https://influitive.com/blog/what-is -customer-advocacy/

Ongino, S. (n.d.). Boosting B2B Sales with Customer Loyalty + Advocate Marketing Software. *Annex Cloud Blog*. Retrieved July 07, 2023, from https://www.annexcloud.com/blog/b2b-loyalty-advocate-marketing -software/

Richards, R. (2020, August 10). What Is Customer Advocacy and 11 Reasons Why It's the Bedrock of Your Business. *Jitbit Blog*. Retrieved July 07, 2023, from https://www.jitbit.com/news/customer-advocacy/

Stoller, K. (2021, May 20). Employees Are More Vital to a Company's Success Than Shareholders, New Survey Finds. *Forbes*. Retrieved July 07, 2023, from https://www.forbes.com/sites/kristinstoller/2021/05/20 /employees-are-more-vital-to-a-companys-success-than-shareholders -new-survey-finds/

Witt, T. (2023, April 04). The Power of Brand Advocacy and Its Uses. *SproutSocial Insights*. Retrieved July 07, 2023, from https://sproutsocial .com/insights/brand-advocacy/

Chapter 19

As Consumer Trust Thins, Marketers Must Pivot to Earned Media. (n.d.). *Cision Blog*. Retrieved July 07, 2023, from https://www.cision.com /resources/articles/as-consumer-trust-thins--marketers-must-pivot-to -earned-media/

Baer, J. (n.d.). 11 Things You Must Know About B2B Influencer Marketing. *Convince & Convert Blog*. Retrieved July 07, 2023, from https://www .convinceandconvert.com/digital-marketing/11-things-you-must-know -about-b2b-influencer-marketing/

Budzienski, J. (2015, April 23). 3 Ways to Be Constantly Recruiting Star Talent Through Social Media. *Entrepreneur*. Retrieved July 07, 2023, from http://www.entrepreneur.com/article/245295

A Guide to Building Relationships Through Blogging: Connecting with Your Audience and Collaborating. (2023, May 11). *AIContentfy Blog*. Retrieved July 07, 2023, from https://aicontentfy.com/en/blog/guide -to-building-relationships-through-blogging-connecting-with-audience -and-collaborating

Hoos, B. (2019, August 22). The Psychology of Influencer Marketing. *Forbes*. Retrieved July 07, 2023, from https://www.forbes.com/sites/forbesagency council/2019/08/22/the-psychology-of-influencer-marketing/?sh =6360566ae1be

How to Build a B2B Influencer Relations Program. (n.d.). *PAN Communications*. Retrieved July 07, 2023, from https://www.pan communications.com/insights/how-to-build-a-b2b-influencer-relations -program/

Influencer Marketing: Social Media Influencer Market Stats and Research for 2022. (2022, March 15). *Insider Intelligence*. Retrieved July 07, 2023, from https://www.insiderintelligence.com/insights /influencer-marketing-report/

Influencer Marketing Strategy in 5 Steps. (n.d.). *Traackr*. Retrieved July 07, 2023, from http://traackr.com/influencer-marketing-framework/

Patel, N. (n.d.). What Is Guest Posting & 5 Ways to Guest Post. *Neil Patel Blog*. Retrieved July 07, 2023, from https://neilpatel.com/blog/guide-to -guest-blogging/

Roy, L. G. (2021, May 30). Definitive Guide: How to Influence the Decision Making of B2B Buyers. *LinkedIn Pulse*. Retrieved July 07, 2023, from https://www.linkedin.com/pulse/definitive-guide-how-influence-decision -making-b2b-buyers-guha-roy/

Srivastava, S. (2023, April 17). The Need to Leverage Influencer Marketing in B2B. *Forbes*. Retrieved July 07, 2023, from https://www.forbes .com/sites/forbestechcouncil/2023/04/17/the-need-to-leverage -influencer-marketing-in-b2b/?sh=7f93f30a40f8

Chapter 20

Bogdashin, S. (2022, December 20). How Many Landing Pages Should My Website Have? *Comrade Digital Marketing Blog*. Retrieved July 07, 2023, from https://comradeweb.com/blog/should-my-website-have -multiple-landing-pages/

Digital Experience Insights, User Testing & Product Analytics. (n.d.). *Trymata*. Retrieved July 07, 2023, from https://trymata.com/

[GA4] URL Builders: Collect Campaign Data with Custom URLs. (n.d.). *Google*. Retrieved July 07, 2023, from https://support.google.com/analytics /answer/10917952?hl=en&sjid=13030682146930535746-SA#zippy =%2Cin-this-article

Understand what it's like to be your customer. (n.d.). *User Testing*. Retrieved July 07, 2023, from https://www.usertesting.com/

Chapter 21

Alfred, L. (2022, May 23). 50 Video Marketing Statistics to Inform Your 2022 Strategy [New Data]. *Hubspot Blog*. Retrieved July 07, 2023, from https://blog.hubspot.com/marketing/video-marketing-statistics

Bowman, M. (2017, February 03). Video Marketing: The Future of Content Marketing. *Forbes*. Retrieved July 07, 2023, from https: //www.forbes.com/sites/forbesagencycouncil/2017/02/03/video-marketing -the-future-of-content-marketing/?sh=42e7c6276b53

Consumer Privacy Survey: The Growing Imperative of Getting Data Privacy Right. (2019, November 20). *Cisco Blogs*. Retrieved July 07, 2023, from https://www.cisco.com/c/dam/global/en_uk/products/collateral /security/cybersecurity-series-2019-cps.pdf

Dobrilova, T. (2023, May 20). The Most Relevant Mobile Marketing Statistics in 2023. *Review42*. Retrieved July 07, 2023, from https: //review42.com/resources/mobile-marketing-statistics/

Kirgin, T. (2023, January 18). Why SMS Marketing for B2B is Just as Effective as Email. *Hubspot Blog*. Retrieved July 07, 2023, from http: //blog.hubspot.com/insiders/sms-marketing-for-b2b

Kirsch, K. (2023, May 12). The Ultimate List of Email Marketing Stats for 2023. *Hubspot Blog*. Retrieved July 07, 2023, from https://blog.hubspot .com/marketing/email-marketing-stats#mobile

Komack, A. (2022, July). 200 Negative Keywords to Consider for B2B PPC. *KoMarketing*. Retrieved July 07, 2023, from http://www .komarketingassociates.com/blog/200-plus-negative-keywords-to -consider-for-b2b-ppc/

Kunst, A. (2023, June 07). Most Used Social Media Platforms by Type in the U.S. as of March 2023. *Statista*. Retrieved July 07, 2023, from https://www.statista.com/forecasts/997190/most-used-social-media -platforms-by-type-in-the-us

Merlin, N. (2021, October 25). Creating a Simple Responsive HTML Email. *Tuts Plus*. Retrieved July 07, 2023, from http://webdesign.tutsplus .com/articles/creating-a-simple-responsive-html-email—webdesign -12978

Mobile-Friendly Test. (n.d.). *Google*. Retrieved July 07, 2023, from https://www.google.com/webmasters/tools/mobile-friendly/

PageSpeed Insights. (n.d.). *Google*. Retrieved July 07, 2023, from https://developers.google.com/speed/pagespeed/insights/

Paid Search for B2B: Mistakes to Avoid When Implementing and Strategies to Utilize for Successful Campaigns. (2022, January 26). *Launch Marketing Blog*. Retrieved July 07, 2023, from https://www.launch-marketing.com/paid-search-b2b-mistakes-to-avoid/

Reinhart, P. (2017, December 11). Mobilegeddon: A Complete Guide to Google's Mobile-Friendly Update. *Search Engine Journal*. Retrieved July 07, 2023, from https://www.searchenginejournal.com/google-algorithm-history/mobile-friendly-update/#close

Schultz, M., Croston, B., & Flaherty, M. (n.d.). Top Performance in Sales Prospecting: Research on What Works and What Doesn't for Buyers and Sellers. *RAIN Group Research Report*. Retrieved July 07, 2023, from https://www.rainsalestraining.com/sales-research/sales-prospecting-research/report

Sterling, G. (2020, February 14). B2B Buyers Consume an Average of 13 Content Pieces Before Deciding on a Vendor. *MarTech Blog*. Retrieved July 07, 2023, from https://martech.org/b2b-buyers-consume-an-average-of-13-content-pieces-before-deciding-on-a-vendor/

Welch, C. (2014, December 31). FTC finalizes privacy settlement with Snapchat over "deceived" users. *The Verge*. Retrieved July 07, 2023, from http://www.theverge.com/2014/12/31/7476157/ftc-approves-final-snapchat-privacy-order

Williams, R. (2019, October 28). Mobile Snags 70% of All Paid Search Impressions in Q3, Study Finds. *Marketing Dive Brief*. Retrieved July 07, 2023, from https://www.marketingdive.com/news/mobile-snags-70-of-all-paid-search-impressions-in-q3-study-finds/565924/

Wilson, J. (2021, August 18). 5 Reasons Why B2B Mobile Commerce Is Going the B2C Way. *NYC Design*. Retrieved July 07, 2023, from https://medium.com/nyc-design/5-reasons-why-b2b-mobile-commerce-is-going-the-b2c-way-5d1530f30d10

Zakrzewski, C. (2015, October 08). Mobile Searches Surpass Desktop Searches At Google For The First Time. *TechCrunch*. Retrieved July 07, 2023, from https://techcrunch.com/2015/10/08/mobile-searches-surpass-desktop-searches-at-google-for-the-first-time/

Chapter 22

Baruffati, A. (2023, June 13). The Most Important B2B Marketing Statistics & Trends 2023. *Gitnux Blog*. Retrieved July 07, 2023, from https://blog.gitnux.com/b2b-marketing-statistics/

Eaton, K. (2012, July 30). How One Second Could Cost Amazon $1.6 Billion in Sales. *Fast Company*. Retrieved July 07, 2023, from http://www.fastcompany.com/1825005/how-one-second-could-cost-amazon-16-billion-sales

Edmond, D. (2020, January 07). How B2B Demand Generation Marketers Perform Keyword Research in Today's Search Engine Results Landscape. *KoMarketing Blog*. Retrieved July 07, 2023, from https://komarketing.com/blog/b2b-keyword-research-for-demand-generation-marketers/

The Most Surprising Website Load Time Statistics And Trends in 2023. (2023, June 13). *Gitnux Blog*. Retrieved July 07, 2023, from https://blog.gitnux.com/website-load-time-statistics/

Page Speed SEO. (n.d.). *Oncrawl Blog*. Retrieved July 07, 2023, from https://www.oncrawl.com/tag/page-speed/

Picard, M. (2022). What Is the Length of a Sales Cycle? *Anyleads Blog*. Retrieved July 07, 2023, from https://anyleads.com/what-is-the-length-of-a-sales-cycle

Taylor, G. (2017, May 01). Milliseconds Matter: A 0.1 Second Delay Can Hurt Conversions 7%. Retail *TouchPoints Blog*. Retrieved July 07, 2023, from https://www.retailtouchpoints.com/topics/digital-commerce/milliseconds-matter-a-0-1-second-delay-can-hurt-conversions-7

Today's B2B Buyer is Different Than Yesterday's. How Well Do You Know Your Buyers? (2022, June 06). *Steel Croissant Blog*. Retrieved July 07, 2023, from https://www.steelcroissant.com/blog/todays-b2b-buyer-is-different-than-yesterdays-how-well-do-you-know-your-buyers

Chapter 23

Albee, A. (2015, November 09). Get Your Fans to Share Their Love: What Every Brand Can Learn from GoPro. *Content Marketing Institute*. Retrieved July 07, 2023, from http://contentmarketinginstitute.com/2015/09/brand-learn-from-gopro/

Alfred, L. (2022, May 23). 50 Video Marketing Statistics to Inform Your 2022 Strategy [New Data]. *Hubspot Blog*. Retrieved July 07, 2023, from https://blog.hubspot.com/marketing/video-marketing-statistics

Bochicchio, M. (2021, April 28). 7 Video Distribution Channels for B2B Brands. *Wistia Blog*. Retrieved July 07, 2023, from https://wistia.com/learn/marketing/video-distribution-channels

Bump, P. (2023, April 03). How Video Consumption is Changing in 2023 [New Research]. *Hubspot Blog*. Retrieved July 07, 2023, from https://blog.hubspot.com/marketing/how-video-consumption-is-changing

Jackson, I. (2021, April 02). 5 Reasons Why Video Marketing Needs to be Consistent. *Volta Media Blog*. Retrieved July 07, 2023, from https://voltamediahouse.com/blog/5-reasons-why-video-marketing-needs-to-be-consistent/

Parsons, N. (2018, June 14). Do Visuals Really Trump Text? *LivePlan Blog*. Retrieved July 07, 2023, from https://www.liveplan.com/blog /scientific-reasons-why-you-should-present-your-data-visually/

Ryan, B. (2021, June 24). Humor in B2B Marketing: 8 Myth-Busting Examples that Will Make You Glad You Went There. *Pointed Copywriting Blog*. Retrieved July 07, 2023, from https://pointedcopy writing.com/blog/humor-in-b2b-marketing/

Sahni, H. (2023, April 14). 9 Types of Branding Videos to Inspire Your Next Campaign. *Piktochart Blog*. Retrieved July 07, 2023, from https: //piktochart.com/blog/branding-videos/

Shrivastava, S. (2023, May 26). The Power of Visual Content in Your Content Marketing Strategy. *Rankwatch*. Retrieved July 07, 2023, from http://rankwatch.com/blog/the-power-of-visual-content-in-your -content-marketing-strategy/

Unlocking the Power of B2B Video Marketing: A Look at the Latest Statistics. (2023, June 13). *Gitnux Blog*. Retrieved July 07, 2023, from https://blog.gitnux.com/b2b-video-marketing-statistics/

Video SEO Best Practices. (2023, May 23). *Google Search Central*. Retrieved July 07, 2023, from https://developers.google.com/search/docs /appearance/video

Walker, M. (2013, May 09). Execute Your Video Content Strategy in 8 Steps. *Content Marketing Institute*. Retrieved July 07, 2023, from http: //contentmarketinginstitute.com/2013/05/execute-video-content -strategy/

Walker, M. (2015, November 09). How to Use Video Content to Drive Awareness, Leads, and Sales: A Guide. *Content Marketing Institute*. Retrieved July 07, 2023, from http://contentmarketinginstitute.com /2013/04/video-content-b2b-content-marketing/

Walters, K. (2019, October 27). How to Use Video Storytelling to Drive Connection Through Narrative. *Vidyard Blog*. Retrieved July 07, 2023, from https://www.vidyard.com/blog/video-storytelling/

Wegert, A. T. (2015, November 12). Welcome to the new era of B2B video. *Clickz*. Retrieved July 07, 2023, from https://www.clickz.com/clickz /column/2434214/welcome-to-the-new-era-of-b2b-video

Yohn, D. (2014, July 03). Stop selling products and start making emotional connections. *Sales and Marketing*. Retrieved July 07, 2023, from https://salesandmarketing.com/content/stop-selling-products-and-start -making-emotional-connections

Chapter 24

B2B Marketing Channels: What Are the Best B2B Marketing Channels? (n.d.). *WebFX Blog*. Retrieved July 07, 2023, from https://www.webfx .com/digital-marketing/b2b/best-marketing-channels/

Brenner, M. (2022, June 16). The Importance of B2B Storytelling. Marketing Insider Group. Retrieved July 07, 2023, from https://marketinginsidergroup.com/content-marketing/importance-b2b-storytelling/

Burchill, A. (2023, March 16). Video Marketing Statistics for Your 2023 Campaigns. Dash Blog. Retrieved July 07, 2023, from https://dash.app/blog/video-marketing-statistics

DesMarais, C. (2014, June 30). How to Build a Highly Engaged User Community: 9 Tips. *Inc.* Retrieved July 07, 2023, from http://www.inc.com/christina-desmarais/how-to-build-a-highly-engaged-user-community-9-tips.html

McCormick, K. (2022, October 15). The 19 Best B2B Marketing Strategies (Based on Data!). *WordStream Blog.* Retrieved July 07, 2023, from https://www.wordstream.com/blog/ws/2021/06/02/b2b-marketing-strategies

Nandan, A. (2021, October 15). Road to Product-Market Fit. *Products, Demystified.* Retrieved July 07, 2023, from https://medium.com/products-demystified/road-to-product-market-fit-b4d62fcabd9

Shewan, D. (2022, June 15). What Is Customer Profiling in Marketing? *The Pipeline.* Retrieved July 07, 2023, from https://pipeline.zoominfo.com/marketing/what-is-customer-profiling-in-marketing

Walker, M. (2013, April 26). How to Use Video Content to Drive Awareness, Leads, and Sales: A Guide. *Content Marketing Institute.* Retrieved July 07, 2023, from http://contentmarketinginstitute.com/2013/04/video-content-b2b-content-marketing/

Wittersheim, A. (2023, January 17). The Top 8 Most Important B2B Social Media Marketing Trends In 2023. *Stefanini Group Insights.* Retrieved July 07, 2023, from https://stefanini.com/en/insights/articles/the-top-8-most-important-b2b-social-media-marketing-trends-in-2023

Chapter 25

B2B Sales and Marketing: Alignment for the Win. (n.d.). *Adobe Experience Cloud.* Retrieved July 10, 2023, from https://business.adobe.com/resources/articles/b2b-sales-and-marketing-alignment-for-the-win.html

Boudinet, J. (2015, June 8). Maintaining Accountability to Sales & Marketing KPIs. *Ambition Blog.* Retrieved July 10, 2023, from https://ambition.com/blog/entry/2015-6-8-maintaining-accountability-to-sales-marketing-kpis/

Bump, P. (2023, June 08). 31 Stats That Prove the Power of Sales and Marketing Alignment. *Hubspot Blog.* Retrieved July 10, 2023, from https://blog.hubspot.com/sales/stats-that-prove-the-power-of-smarketing-slideshare

Davidoff, D. (2020, January 22). How to Create an Effective Sales and Marketing SLA. *Hubspot Blog.* Retrieved July 10, 2023, from http://blog.hubspot.com/marketing/how-to-align-create-an-effective-sla

The Definitive Guide to Lead Scoring. (n.d.). *Adobe Experience Cloud.* Retrieved July 10, 2023, from https://business.adobe.com/resources /guides/lead-scoring.html

Drenik, G. (2022, December 13). What Significant Shifts In B2B Buyer Behavior Means For 2023. *Forbes.* Retrieved July 10, 2023, from https://www.forbes.com/sites/garydrenik/2022/12/13/what-significant -shifts-in-b2b-buyer-behavior-means-for-2023/?sh=76dda2671c43

Mapping Lead Generation to Your Sales Funnel. (n.d.). *Adobe Experience Cloud.* Retrieved July 10, 2023, from https://business.adobe.com /resources/articles/mapping-lead-generation-to-your-sales-funnel.html

Miller, A.K. (2014, May 27). What Role Can C-Levels Play in Marketing and Sales Alignment? *Clickz.* Retrieved July 10, 2023, from https://www.clickz.com /what-role-can-c-levels-play-in-marketing-and-sales-alignment/31350/

O'Neill, S. (2023, June 05). Sales and Marketing Alignment: Stats and Trends for 2023. *LXA Hub Stories.* Retrieved July 10, 2023, from https://www.lxa-hub.com/stories/sales-and-marketing-alignment-stats-and-trends-2023

Patel, N. (n.d.). A Straight-Forward Guide to Funnel Optimization. *Neil Patel Blog.* Retrieved July 10, 2023, from https://neilpatel.com/blog /guide-to-optimizing-funnels/

Samsing, C. (2022, October 07). 10 Tried-and-True Tips for Sales and Marketing Alignment. *Hubspot Blog.* Retrieved July 10, 2023, from http://blog.hubspot.com/marketing/tried-and-true-sales-marketing-alignment

Stahl, S. (2022, October 19). 7 Things B2B Content Marketers Need in 2023 [New Research]. *Content Marketing Institute.* Retrieved July 10, 2023, from https://contentmarketinginstitute.com/articles/b2b-content -marketing-research-trends-statistics

Chapter 26

Akinsowon, V. (2023, January 23). 9 Event Trends You Should Know in 2023. *CVent Blog.* Retrieved July 10, 2023, from https://www.cvent.com /en/blog/events/event-trends

Bookout, T. (2019, October 29). Better Understand Your Event Attendees by Creating Personas. *Event Architecture Blog.* Retrieved July 10, 2023, from https://event-architecture.com/blog/2019/10/29/better-understand -your-event-attendees-by-creating-personas

Bose, I. (2023, January 24). A Comprehensive Guide to B2B Event Marketing. *Eventible Learning.* Retrieved July 10, 2023, from https://eventible.com/learning/b2b-event-marketing/

Curtiss, K. (2023, May 23). How to Create an Event Hashtag to Build Engagement at Your Next Event. *Constant Contact Blog.* Retrieved July 10, 2023, from https://www.constantcontact.com/blog/hashtag -event-engagement/

Dodge, B. (2015, October 28). Tradeshow Hero: How to Use Email and Marketing Automation for Live-Event Success. *Marketing Profs*. Retrieved July 10, 2023, from http://www.marketingprofs.com/articles /2015/28725/tradeshow-hero-how-to-use-email-and-marketing -automation-for-live-event-success

How to Measure the ROI from B2B Roadshow Tours. (n.d.). *ProMotion*. Retrieved July 10, 2023, from https://promotion1.com/how -to-measure-the-roi-from-a-b2b-roadshow-tour/

Joseph, E. (2022, June 28). Event Marketing Automation: How Can It Help Your Event Planning Process. *Eventtia Blog*. Retrieved July 10, 2023, from https://www.eventtia.com/en/blog/event-marketing-automation -how-can-it-help-your-event-planning-process

Lang, S. (2016, January 15). Five Tips for Creating and Using a Great Event Hashtag. *Marketing Profs*. Retrieved July 10, 2023, from http://www .marketingprofs.com/articles/2016/29156/five-tips-for-creating-and -using-a-great-event-hashtag

Murray, R. (2022, October 13). How Data-Driven Event Marketing Can Multiply ROI for Your Next Event. *Walls.io Blog*. Retrieved July 10, 2023, from https://blog.walls.io/events/data-driven-event-marketing/

Norris, J. (2021, June 09). How to Use SEO to Promote Your B2B Event. *93x Blog*. Retrieved July 10, 2023, from https://www.93x.agency/blog /b2b-marketing/how-to-use-seo-to-promote-your-b2b-event/

Scaling Your Event Strategy: The Ultimate Guide to Virtual and Hybrid Events. (n.d.). *Hubspot Blog*. Retrieved July 10, 2023, from https: //offers.hubspot.com/scaling-your-event-strategy

Stahl, S. (2021, October 13). B2B Content Marketing Insights for 2022: More Budget, More Work, More Empathy [Research]. *Content Marketing Institute*. Retrieved July 10, 2023, from https://contentmarketing institute.com/articles/b2b-power-content-marketing-research/

The Viral Impact of Events: Best Practices to Amplify Event Content. (n.d.). *Freeman*. Retrieved July 10, 2023, from https://www.eventmarketer .com/wp-content/uploads/2015/01/ViralImpactOfEvents.pdf

Chapter 27

Becker, J. (2023, June 22). LinkedIn Could Become Your Most Powerful Distribution Channel. *Impact Blog*. Retrieved July 10, 2023, from https://www.impactplus.com/blog/linkedin-distribution-channel

Best Social Media Platforms for B2B Marketers in 2023. (2018, May 15). *Khoros Blog*. Retrieved July 10, 2023, from https://khoros.com/blog /top-social-media-platforms-b2b-marketers

Bhagat, V. (2014, February 08). B2B Marketing: Why (and How) to Focus on Reviews, Not Case Studies. *Content Marketing Institute*. Retrieved July 10, 2023, from http://contentmarketinginstitute.com/2014/02/b2b -marketing-reviews-not-case-studies/

Bibbial, J. (2015, February 09). 12 Ways to Build Social Proof on LinkedIn. *LinkedIn Pulse*. Retrieved July 10, 2023, from https://www.linkedin.com/pulse/12-ways-build-social-proof-linkedin-nathanial-bibby/

Gallant, J. (2023, February 20). 50+ LinkedIn Statistics Marketers Need to Know in 2023. *Foundation Blog*. Retrieved July 10, 2023, from https://foundationinc.co/lab/b2b-marketing-linkedin-stats/

Gullo, F. (2012, August 31). 10 Tips for Building Strong Professional Relationships. *Business Insider*. Retrieved July 10, 2023, from http://www.businessinsider.com/10-tips-for-appreciating-your-network-contacts-2012-8

Haden, J. (2013, November 13). The Complete Guide to LinkedIn Sponsored Updates. *Inc*. Retrieved July 10, 2023, from http://www.inc.com/jeff-haden/the-complete-guide-to-linkedin-sponsored-updates.html

How to Use LinkedIn Sponsored InMail for Lead Generation. (2015, September 02). *Form Stack*. Retrieved July 10, 2023, from https://www.formstack.com/blog/2015/linkedin-sponsored-inmail-lead-generation/

Laferte, S. (2020, January 08). A Beginner's Guide to LinkedIn Showcase Pages. *Hubspot Blog*. Retrieved July 10, 2023, from http://blog.hubspot.com/marketing/linkedin-showcase-pages-beginners-guide-ht

LinkedIn Conversation Ads. (n.d.). *LinkedIn*. Retrieved July 10, 2023, from https://business.linkedin.com/marketing-solutions/conversation-ads

Native Advertising: Sponsored Content with LinkedIn. (n.d.). *LinkedIn*. Retrieved July 10, 2023, from https://business.linkedin.com/marketing-solutions/products/native-advertising

Patel, N. (n.d.). How to Use LinkedIn Insights in an Actionable Way. *Neil Patel Blog*. Retrieved July 10, 2023, from https://neilpatel.com/blog/linkedin-insights/

Patel, N. (n.d.). LinkedIn Pulse: A Complete Guide (+ Examples). *Neil Patel Blog*. Retrieved July 10, 2023, from https://neilpatel.com/blog/linkedin-pulse/

Stahl, S. (2022, October 19). 7 Things B2B Content Marketers Need in 2023 [New Research]. *Content Marketing Institute*. Retrieved July 10, 2023, from https://contentmarketinginstitute.com/articles/b2b-content-marketing-research-trends-statistics

Talbot, P. (2019, January 29). Best Practices For B2B Marketers On LinkedIn. *Forbes*. Retrieved July 10, 2023, from https://www.forbes.com/sites/paultalbot/2019/01/29/best-practices-for-b2b-marketers-on-linkedin/

Understanding the Importance of Visual Content in Social Media Marketing. (2021, September 06). *Rockcontent Blog*. Retrieved July 10, 2023, from https://rockcontent.com/blog/importance-of-visual-content-in-social-media/

Walgrove, A. (n.d.). 5 B2B Brands That Rock LinkedIn. *The Content Strategist*. Retrieved July 10, 2023, from https://contently.com/strategist/2015/02/24/5-b2b-brands-that-rock-linkedin/

Chapter 28

18 Expert Tips For Creating A Successful B2B Podcast. (2023, April 18). *Forbes*. Retrieved July 10, 2023, from https://www.forbes.com /sites/forbesagencycouncil/2023/04/18/18-expert-tips-for-creating- a-successful-b2b-podcast/?sh=e3e055f5b057

7 Insightful Tips for Super-Effective Local PPC. (2021, December 02). *WordStream Blog*. Retrieved July 10, 2023, from https://www.word stream.com/blog/ws/2015/06/11/local-ppc-tips

Bashir, W. (n.d.). How to Use Webinar Automation for B2B Lead Generation. *Apexure Blog*. Retrieved July 10, 2023, from https://www.apexure .com/blog/how-to-use-webinar-automation-for-b2b-lead-generation

Carmicheal, K. (2021, August 05). What Is Retargeting? How To Set Up an Ad Retargeting Campaign. *Hubspot Blog*. Retrieved July 10, 2023, from https://blog.hubspot.com/marketing/retargeting-campaigns-beginner -guide

Crowe, A. (2021, March 25). Webinars That Work: 5 Strategies for Building a Successful B2B Webinar [Webinar Recap]. *Leadfeeder Blog*. Retrieved July 10, 2023, from https://www.leadfeeder.com/blog /b2b-webinar-strategies/

Deeb, G. (2021, August 02). The Rise of Account Based Marketing. *Forbes*. Retrieved July 10, 2023, from https://www.forbes.com/sites /georgedeeb/2021/08/02/the-rise-of-account-based-marketing/

Doughty, D. (2021, February 04). Now is the Time for B2B Vlogging: A 7-Step How-to Guide. *Marsden Marketing Blog*. Retrieved July 10, 2023, from https://www.marsdenmarketing.com/blog/now-is-the-time -for-b2b-vlogging-a-7-step-how-to-guide

Do Webinars Work for B2B? (2021, October 14). *Ironpaper Blog*. Retrieved July 10, 2023, from https://www.ironpaper.com/webintel /do-webinars-work-for-b2b

Gocklin, B. (2023, February 28). How to Use Podcasts as Part of Your Content Marketing Strategy. *Contently's The Content Strategy*. Retrieved July 10, 2023, from https://contently.com/2023/02/28 /content-marketing-podcast-strategy/

Hewitt, C. (2023, May 07). 35 Podcast Statistics You Must Know to Grow Your Show. *Castos Blog*. Retrieved July 10, 2023, from https://castos .com/podcast-statistics/

Jackson, E. (2023, June 16). The Power of Social Video Strategy: Tips to Boost Video Reach on Each Platform. *Digital Joy Blog*. Retrieved July 10, 2023, from https://www.digitaljoy.media/the-power-of-social -video-strategy/

Kapur, D. (2023, April 24). Retargeting: How to Win Back Visitors with PPC Ads. *LinkedIn Pulse*. Retrieved July 10, 2023, from https://www.linkedin .com/pulse/retargeting-how-win-back-visitors-ppc-ads-devika-kapur/

Lahey, C. (2020, September 17). 8 Types of Interactive Content and Engaging Examples. *Semrush Blog.* Retrieved July 10, 2023, from https://www.semrush.com/blog/interactive-content/

O'Kelley, L. (n.d.). Blogs, Vlogs, Newsletters and Podcasts: B2B Marketing Pros and Cons. *MLT Creative.* Retrieved July 10, 2023, from https://www.mltcreative.com/blog/blogs-vlogs-newsletters-podcasts-b2b-marketing/

Olenski, S. (2013, April 01). B2B and B2C Marketers Agree Relationships Marketing Is Where It's At. *Forbes.* Retrieved July 10, 2023, from http://www.forbes.com/sites/marketshare/2013/04/01/b2b-and-b2c-marketers-agree-relationship-marketing-is-where-its-at/#2f341257567f

Patel, N. (n.d.). Behind the Scenes of Behavioral Advertising. *Neil Patel Blog.* Retrieved July 10, 2023, from https://neilpatel.com/blog/behavioral-advertising/

Peterson, A. (2020, March 27). Understanding Personalized B2B Marketing. *Technology Advice.* Retrieved July 10, 2023, from http://technologyadvice.com/blog/marketing/3-killer-examples-personalized-b2b-marketing/

Pinney, S. (2022, January 07). 7 Best Practices for Lead Nurturing Emails. *Hubspot Blog.* Retrieved July 10, 2023, from https://blog.hubspot.com/blog/tabid/6307/bid/5917/5-best-practices-for-lead-nurturing-emails.aspx

Rahal, A. (2020, November 20). Four Steps for Creating Infographics That Convert. *Forbes.* Retrieved July 10, 2023, from https://www.forbes.com/sites/theyec/2020/11/20/four-steps-for-creating-infographics-that-convert/?sh=129ac14c21d9

Riddall, J. (2023, January 06). 30 Content Marketing Statistics You Should Know. *Search Engine Journal.* Retrieved July 10, 2023, from https://www.searchenginejournal.com/content-marketing-statistics/475206/

Riddall, J. (2022, April 27). Local B2B SEO: The Complete Guide for Local Businesses. *Search Engine Journal.* Retrieved July 10, 2023, from https://www.searchenginejournal.com/local-b2b-seo/446339/

Sales Enablement Benchmark Report. (n.d.). *Demand Metric.* Retrieved July 10, 2023, from http://www.demandmetric.com/content/sales-enablement-benchmark-report

Stahl, S. (2022, October 19). 7 Things B2B Content Marketers Need in 2023 [New Research]. *Content Marketing Institute.* Retrieved July 10, 2023, from https://contentmarketinginstitute.com/articles/b2b-content-marketing-research-trends-statistics

What is Content Marketing? (n.d.). *Content Marketing Institute.* Retrieved July 10, 2023, from http://contentmarketinginstitute.com/what-is-content-marketing/

What Is Sales Enablement? (n.d.). *Hubspot.* Retrieved July 10, 2023, from https://www.hubspot.com/sales-enablement

INDEX

A

ABM. *See* account-based marketing (ABM)

"above the fold" area, 176

A/B testing, 175–176, 185

account-based marketing (ABM)

content syndication and, 133–134

data in, 132

defined, 129–130

effectiveness of, 130–131

efficiency of, 131

inbound marketing *vs.*, 129–130

multichannel lead nurturing in, 134

return on investment with, 131

sales and, 131

scaling, 132

social media in, 132–133

traditional marketing *vs.*, 130

virtual conferences in, 135

webinars in, 135

advertorials, 88

advocate marketing

beyond customer references, 158–159

business objectives and, 156

customer rewards program and, 159

effectiveness of, 155–156

employees in, 159–160

personas in, 156–157

relationships in, 161

results measurement in, 160–161

software in, 160

team in, 157–158

analytics. *See* data; web analytics

asset library, 16–22

auction, open, 81

audience

content and, 34

event management and, 230

inbound marketing and, 4

in intent-driven marketing, 139–140

lead generation and, 97–98

native advertising and, 90

podcast, 250

in public relations, 150–151

in web analytics, 196–197

authentication, in email marketing, 54

automation, marketing, 41–48, 54–55, 143, 217–218, 227, 231

automation engine, 41–42

B

BDRs. *See* business development representatives (BDRs)

"before and after" approach, 65–66

behavioral targeting, 246–247

Bing, 75

blogging, 5–6, 18–19, 167

BOFU. *See* bottom of the funnel (BOFU)

bottom of the funnel (BOFU), 77

brand advocacy. *See* advocate marketing

branded campaigns, 74–75

brevity, in email marketing, 69–70

business development representatives (BDRs), 113–114

buyer journey, 51–52

buyer personas, 4, 9, 10, 11

buys, media, 79–86

buzz content, 233–234

C

calendar, content, 32–34
call to action (CTA), 6, 52–53, 61, 104, 178–179, 206–207
cohort analysis, 197
community, team training and, 218
company page, 238–239
competition
  asset library and, 19–20
  public relations and, 151
  researching, 75–76
  social media monitoring and, 13–14
complements, in email marketing, 70
conferences, virtual, 135
content
  for asset library, 16–22
  audience and, 34
  bad, 34–35
  in blogging, 5–6
  buzz, 233–234
  calendar, 32–34
  from customers, 19
  in email marketing, 56
  event management and, 233–234
  existing, 16–17
  focus in, 30–31
  gated, 102
  guest, 167–168
  informative, 233
  interactive, 91, 248
  key performance indicators and, 31–32
  in lead generation, 99–102
  lead generation vendors and, 118
  loading speed, 189
  in marketing automation, 46–47
  marketing plan, 239–240
  mobile optimization of, 152
  in native advertising, 88
  partnership topics, 20–21
  patience with, 38
  pay-per-click with, 36
  premium, 6–7

  promoting, 35–37
  in public relations, 149–150, 152
  redundancy, 49
  relevant, 50–51
  repurposing, 8
  reuse, 234
  sales alignment and, 223
  search engine optimization and, 35
  sequels to, 21
  series, 17–18
  simplicity with, 35
  sponsored, 88
  spotlight, 118
  stats measurement with, 37
  strategy, 30–38
  structure with, 30–31
  syndication, 36, 133–134
  tactics, 32, 33
  team know-how and, 17
  testing, 37
  topics, 31–32
  useful, 50–51, 149
conversational marketing, 44
conversion optimization
  "above the fold" area in, 176
  calls to action in, 178–179
  copy in, 176–178
  curiosity in, 185
  data-driven mentality in, 175–176
  distractions and, 181
  experience optimization in, 174
  false bottoms and, 184–185
  forms and, 180–181
  information gaps in, 185
  landing pages in, 179–180
  long-form sales pages in, 183–184
  messaging alignment in, 175
  origins in, 173
  painlessness in, 182–183
  personalization in, 174
  testing in, 175–176
  touchpoints in, 173–175
  trust and, 181–182

NOTES

NOTES

NOTES

NOTES

NOTES

NOTES

NOTES

NOTES

NOTES

NOTES

NOTES

NOTES